A Gate in the Wall

A Gate in the Wall
A Pacific War POW's Secret Diary and a Family's Path Toward Reconciliation

MELINDA BARNHARDT

Foreword by James L. Huffman

McFarland & Company, Inc., Publishers
Jefferson, North Carolina

Portions of this book previously appeared in a Japanese language book: E.W. Lindeijer, Sr., Kisses to Nel and the Children from a POW Camp in Japan, translated by Takamitsu Muraoka (Misuzu Shobo, Ltd., 2000)

LIBRARY OF CONGRESS CATALOGING-IN-PUBLICATION DATA

Names: Barnhardt, Melinda, 1943– author.
Title: A gate in the wall : a Pacific War POW's secret diary and a family's path toward reconciliation / Melinda Barnhardt ; foreword by James L. Huffman.
Other titles: Pacific War POW's secret diary and a family's path toward reconciliation
Description: Jefferson, North Carolina : McFarland & Company, Inc., Publishers, 2025. | Includes bibliographical references and index.
Identifiers: LCCN 2024055826 | ISBN 9781476696973 (paperback : acid free paper) | ISBN 9781476655031 (ebook) ∞
Subjects: LCSH: Lindeijer, Evert Willem, Sr., approximately 1919—-Diaries. | Prisoners of war—Netherlands. | Prisoners of war—Japan. | World War, 1939-1945—Prisoners and prisons, Japanese. | World War, 1939-1945—Indonesia—Java. | Lindeijer family. | Dutch—Indonesia—Biography. | Reconciliation. | Prisoner-of-war camps—Japan.
Classification: LCC D805.J3 B356 2025 | DDC 940.54/7252092 [B]—dc23/eng/20250114
LC record available at https://lccn.loc.gov/2024055826

ISBN (print) 978-1-4766-9697-3
ISBN (ebook) 978-1-4766-5503-1

© 2025 Melinda Barnhardt. All rights reserved

No part of this book may be reproduced or transmitted in any form or by any means, electronic or mechanical, including photocopying or recording, or by any information storage and retrieval system, without permission in writing from the publisher.

Front cover: (left photograph) Petronella J. Lindeijer-Verhulst ("Nel") and Evert Willem "Wim" Lindeijer Sr., Bandung, Java, 1937; (right photograph) Nel Lindeijer (middle) and the Lindeijer children—(left to right) Herman, Joke, Nel, Wim Jr., and Freddy (Frits), Bandung, Java, May 1942 (both photographs from the Lindeijer Family Archive); (background) the Lindeijer Diary cover (Brieven, "Letters"), with the first letter entry (May 15, 1942) showing. Front cover design by Ernst de Groot

Printed in the United States of America

McFarland & Company, Inc., Publishers
Box 611, Jefferson, North Carolina 28640
www.mcfarlandpub.com

For Hank

Acknowledgments

Of the remarkable people to whom I owe gratitude for help with this book, two truly exceptional individuals stand out: the late Wim Lindeijer Jr., who wanted his father's wartime story known, and his "second mother," the late Adrie Lindeijer-van der Baan. Without either of them the reconciliation efforts in Kamaishi could neither have happened nor have been told. I am forever humbled by their decision to entrust me with documenting their family's experience—and further humbled by the way in which Wim's wife, Ada, and his siblings born before and after the war immediately supported my project. Herman Lindeyer talked for the first time about his Mother Nel's death, then jumped into translating her letter and his father's diary into English (with consideration to Dame Elisabeth Foppen's translations); from there, moving on to Wim Gribnau's materials and additional family letters. Niels accompanied me on visits with Dutch historians (as did Ada); Joke and Frits sat for interviews; Hans supplied video expertise; and Dirk Jan made me think twice about my project's purpose (as did Joke). Wim's son Eloy has been unfailingly helpful in every way possible as the family's representative for the book—coordinating with the family regarding legalities, fact-checking his father's information, and even retracing and verifying his father's route in fleeing the camp guard at Muntilan.

Likewise, people in Japan with relation to Wim's story and the Lindeijer diary could not have been more welcoming and supportive during my research in their country. In Kamaishi, International Exchange Association Chair Naoko Kato described the impact of Wim's visits, and with her assistant, Takemi Wada, arranged for meetings with association members and for an interview with student play director Mr. Shinya Morimoto; city officials organized tours of the camp mine and museum. In Mizumaki, Fukuoka Prefecture, American city employee Ralph Shriock provided information on the Dutch visits to the monument, and Eburi School Principal Motoaki Aono on the visits to the city's schools; Hidetoshi Kurokawa, chair of the Cross Monument Committee, and his brother Kyoichi

Acknowledgments

provided a tour of the monument site; Shoji Kurokawa and his wife, Chiai, who maintained the site, furnished tapes of Shoji's interview with Wim; and school teacher Hiroko Uchida gave me photographs of the student artwork in the style of Escher. For access to Wim's letters from Mizumaki, I'm grateful to his wife, Ada, and for their translation, to Arthur Faber.

I'm indebted to Professor Takamitsu Muraoka—translator of the Lindeijer diary into Japanese, and subsequent founder, with Wim Jr., Adrie Lindeijer, and others, of the Dialogue Netherlands-Japan-Indonesia (NJI)—for his gracious release of publishing rights related to the diary, with the exception of his translation, and to Misuzu Shobo Publishers for release of publishing rights other than their rights in the Japanese publication. I'm further indebted to Professor Muraoka for his English translation of the Ohashi Camp Report, and grateful both to him and POW Research Network Japan founder Yoshiko Tamura, for their respective English translations of certain materials of the Japanese camp liaison Hiroe Iwashita. Professor Muraoka, through his translation of the pages of Iwashita's diary given to Wim Jr. by Iwashita's son, Fumio, and Yoshiko Tamura, through her translation of Iwashita's camp notebook, have contributed to a fuller portrait of this important figure—as has Yoshiko's co-founder, Taeko Sassamoto, who obtained permission for me to quote from the camp notebook from Fumio Iwashita. Additional thanks for translation from Japanese go to John Jasper, Tanya Maus, and Madoka Yamakawa Ermarth.

Prominent Dutch East Asian historians have helped during multiple visits: Leonard Blussé recommended that Nel's letter begin the book, alerted me to Louis de Jong's standard history of the Netherlands during World War II, and mentored nearly throughout. Petra Groen helped identify the Gumbel Pass and pointed me to the John Dower article I reference regarding the recognition by Japanese scientists (but not their military) of the impossibility of their country's developing wartime atomic capability. Willem Remmelink helped resolve a related detail via email. Jeroen Kemperman answered countless questions about the camps in Java and the overseas transports.

In the United States, I am indebted to East Asian scholar James L. Huffman for his gracious support, including contribution of the foreword to this volume, and opportunities to speak about my project in classes and colloquia at Wittenberg University. Additional people helped with research: Eric Van Slander, of the National Archives at College Park; Wes Injerd, of the Center for Research Allied Prisoners under the Japanese; and Satoko Kogure, *Newsweek Japan* writer, who provided access to former Dutch POWs' postwar letters to her grandfather, Lieutenant Inaki.

Acknowledgments

Former Ohashi camp POWs made time for in-person interviews, phone calls, email, or letters: Jack Feliz, William "Bill" Stewart, and Basil Bunyard, formerly of the USS *Houston*; Frank Planton and Kenneth Horne of the RAF; George MacDonnell of the Canadian Royal Rifles; and Keith Edmonds, of the RAAF, all generously told of their camp experience and remembered "Lindy."

So many remarkable contributors! Yet in the final analysis, a book such as this, spanning decades and continents, could not have been written without the help of steadfast friends and supporters. First and foremost among them was the late Charles Chatfield, former professor of history at Wittenberg University, and an authority on peace history who almost single-handedly established peace studies as an academic discipline. Charles' intensive involvement (and therefore, that of his wife, Mary) elevated my project considerably. Former President and CEO of New Directions Publishers, Peggy Fox, and her husband, biographer Ian S. MacNiven, for years read and critiqued my text and cheered me on. Historian Susan Bailey read multiple drafts. Tim Waltonen's eyes gleamed at the mere mention of an Escher print and a premonitory dream, helping me believe that Wim Jr.'s trauma belonged in my history writing; Cynthia Richards reinforced the idea. Judy Bunch, daughter of American POW Jerry Bunch, operator of the secret radio at the Ohashi Camp, made me aware of the records of former USS *Houston* and Texas National Guard personnel, and accompanied me on visits to her father's colleagues. Lindeijer family friend Fumi Hoshino accompanied my late husband, Henry Jud, and me as our guide during my research in Japan. Nano Scientist Hiroshige Mori and his wife, Hiroko, hosted Hank and me in Kyoto, recounting their experience with Wim. British friend Ann Henshaw accompanied us on a visit with former Ohashi POW Frank Planton in King's Lynn, Norfolk; Planton in turn referred me to Australian citizen David Peck, who shared access with me to Yoshiko Tamura's English translation of the camp notebook that Iwashita gave to his father, former Ohashi British POW Richard Peck. Former Dialogue NJI Chair, Yukari Tangena Suzuki, hosted Hank and me in the Netherlands, and kept me updated about dialogue conferences and projects she coordinated in Japan.

To all those above, and to Elizabeth Foxwell and the entire McFarland team, I cannot thank you enough!

Table of Contents

Acknowledgments — vi
Foreword by James L. Huffman — 1
Preface — 9
A Note on the Text — 13

Part I: The Trauma of War—"Whatever Is Torn Away" — 15

1. Ohashi, Japan, 1944—Revisiting the Collapse of a World — 19
2. Bandung, Java, 1942—A Sundering of Ties — 26
3. Transport Overseas, 1942—"The Most Horrible Thing" — 43
4. Ohashi, Japan, 1942—Between High Mountains, Snow — 58
5. Ohashi, Japan, 1943—"We Rise in the Wind's Eye" — 67
6. 1 March 1943—A Single Day's "Enormous Range of Thoughts" — 74
7. Spring and Summer, 1943—"It Lasts So Terribly Long" — 81
8. Kamaishi, Fall-Winter 1943-44—A Space Where There Was None — 98
9. Ohashi, 1944—"Quite Something Has Emerged" — 107
10. Ohashi, June 1944-April 1945—"*Amicitia Vitam Ornat*" — 122
11. Ohashi, April-August 1945—Edge of the Inferno — 136
12. Ohashi, August-September 1945—The Slow Return — 148

Part II: Traumatic Memory—Echoes from Past to Present — **161**

13. Delft, 1992–95—A Son's Memory Work — 167
14. Delft to Japan, 1995—A Gate in the Wall — 179
15. The Unexpected Importance of the Once-Secret Diary in the Twenty-First Century — 187

Chapter Notes — 195
Bibliography — 219
Index — 223

Foreword

BY JAMES L. HUFFMAN

The Japanese word *naruhodo* connotes an epiphany, a flash of light: "Aha! Now I see it!" The study of Japanese history, for me, has yielded many *naruhodo* moments, the most recent of which came as I read Melinda Barnhardt's presentation of the wartime letters of Wim (Lindy) Lindeijer, a Dutchman in the Netherlands-Indies, now Indonesia, who spent much of World War II in a Japanese prison. The letters, written in secret and hidden from his captors, include the usual wartime themes: harsh conditions, brutality, courage. But they do more than that; they reveal a level of human complexity that is not typical of war memoirs. Again and again, they made me say, "Aha! So, that is the way we ought to expect people in horrific situations to act if they have the will to do so." The experiences of Lindeijer and his family complicated, and yet clarified, wartime imprisonment for me as no other war memoir has done.

First, they brought home how lively the issue of war memory continues to be, at every level of Japanese society. The dominant motif since 1945 has been that the Japanese have been less rigorous than the Germans in examining their role in the war: their human experiments in China, the "rape of Nanjing," the forcing of "comfort women" by the thousands into sex slavery, the racist subjugation of colonial peoples in southeast Asia. As the historian Michael Bess puts it, most Japanese "have tended to view World War II through a distorting lens that deemphasizes the atrocities committed by their armies throughout Asia, and that highlights instead the suffering endured by the Japanese people as a result of the war."[1]

Few would disagree with the kernel of truth in that complaint, but as Barnhardt's account makes clear, Bess misses the vigor and variety of the country's war-memory debates. From the early postwar years, a vocal and influential element on the right has been ready always to defend (or wash away) Japan's wartime aggressions. John Dower, the preeminent

American student of Japan's immediate postwar years, describes conservative leaders who worked systematically after the surrender to rehabilitate the memories even of executed war criminals such as Prime Minister Tōjō Hideki by publishing their last thoughts in a 741-page tome titled *Testaments of the Century* (*Seiki no isho*): "a nationalistic plea to forgive the dishonored dead" and hide "the horrendous reality of Japanese war crimes and atrocities."[2] Ultra-nationalists and mainstream conservative politicians continue to this day to make official visits to the Yasukuni Shrine where the spirits of all dead soldiers (including convicted war criminals) are enshrined, and officials still refuse to take responsibility for the treatment of the "comfort women."[3]

None of this means, however, that the anti-military side has been silent. Japanese at all levels of society have engaged in heated discussions and debates over their country's wartime responsibilities, from 1945 to the present. The historian of war guilt Ian Buruma says it was "extraordinary how honestly Japanese novelists and filmmakers dealt with the horrors of militarism" in the first decades after the war[4]—and they were not alone. When Haruko and Theodore Cook interviewed former Japanese soldiers, many confessed openly to their sense of war guilt, echoing Tamura Yoshio, a soldier in China who admitted: "I have to say war is a dirty thing ... I am a war criminal because of the things I actually did. Not in theory."[5] One of the most persistent critics across the years was Ienaga Saburō, who wrote a widely read book, *Taiheiyō sensō* (The Pacific War), expressly "to stimulate reflection and self-criticism about the war."[6] Even government leaders spoke out repeatedly against Japan's wartime role well into the twenty-first century. In 1993, Prime Minister Hosokawa Morihiro publicly described the Pacific War as "a war of aggression and a mistake"; two years later, Prime Minister Murayama Tomiichi expressed his "deep remorse and ... heartfelt apology" for the suffering Japan imposed on Asia[7]; and Emperor Akihito called repeatedly on the Japanese people to reflect carefully on the war.[8] When Nagasaki Mayor Motoshima Hitoshi blamed the dying emperor in 1988 for his "responsibility for the war," a right-wing zealot attempted to assassinate him but thousands wrote letters thanking Motoshima for his honesty and courage. One said that when he saw Hirohito on television, "I shouted at the television screen: you idiot, who asked you to start a war, it was you bastards who started the fighting, feeding us that self-serving nonsense about a sacred war."[9]

The point of all this—a point that serves as the backdrop for *A Gate in the Wall*—is that private individuals and local groups long have been (and continue to be) deeply involved in discussions of what World War II means for their country. Those who think deeply about war in Japan include national opinion leaders, local teachers, members of ideological organizations, and participants in after-school clubs. And they speak in a cacophony, articulating opinions of every stripe.

If national war memory was the first issue in *A Gate in the Wall* that triggered a *naruhodo* moment for me, the effect of war on the people who engage in it was the second. Indeed, I found the changes it wrought in Wim's and his family's way of thinking, along with its power to bring out the worst and best in people, even more gripping. We see in Barnhardt's treatment the ironically serene toughness prison life gave Wim Sr., the letter writer; we see what it taught him about ways to survive as a decent person; we grapple along with him about what it required for people on both sides of the conflict to remain human; we are shown how simple acts of writing and teaching affected his view of both Japanese and Allies in the prison. This work is, in other words, rendered particularly powerful as the wartime story of a single man, his diary—and the impact both diary and man had on the world around them.

Several things make this focus on the individual differ from other war memoirs. There is, for example, the matter-of-fact tone of Wim's writing. There is his use of letters (hidden under a loose board on the floor of his barracks) as a substitute for diaries—letters his wife Nel, tragically, never would see. There is the scribe-like attention to detail that one might expect from a scientist. And there is Lindy's eschewal of stereotyping and sensationalism; never does he engage in the emotional victimization we find in "comfort woman" memoirs or the demonization that marks popular wartime accounts such as *Unbroken* and *Railway Man*.[10] Cruelty is there, but it is not exaggerated. Nobility is there too; so is courage. But they appear in the everyday way that marks most lives, even outside of prison.

One of the surprising revelations of the letters is the cloudy, yet somehow clear, understanding prisoners had of the war's chronology. The conflict's early nature was easy for Lindy to understand, since he was directly involved in it. Japan's successes as its army marched almost unchallenged down the southeast Asian peninsula in the first half of 1942 resulted in his conscription—and then his capture. But even after the capture, he and his fellows were able to construct a fairly accurate picture of what was happening. When "what we have feared for so long" happened and he "was to be carried far away" in October,[11] the dreadful shipboard conditions hinted that Japan's resources were thin and that Japan had begun to encounter losses. By the time he and ninety other Dutchmen reached the prison camp at Ohashi in northern Japan on November 30, thirty of his compatriots had died from inadequate food and rampaging sickness. For the next two and a half years, the prisoners were able to trace the outlines of Japan's increasingly dire situation through scraps of mail from family members (Lindeijer himself never received any), guards' comments, and, most ingeniously, a jerry-rigged hidden radio. They thus knew with surprising speed about the Allied island-hopping in the Pacific from 1943 onward, about D-day in Europe in the spring of 1944, and about Douglas MacArthur's return to the Philippines in October 1944. The signs of Allied progress were not always welcomed, especially after the Allies started bombing Japan itself. On Christmas Day in 1944, Lindeijer reported that the science books a Japanese official had promised to get him were no longer available because the bookstores of Tokyo had been destroyed by Allied planes. And in mid-July and early August 1945, Allied battleships shelled the nearby town of Kamaishi, killing Allied prisoners along with Japanese.

For me, the most complicated "aha moment" connected with the war's chronology was the way Lindy and his fellow captives experienced its ending. Although they heard almost immediately about Hirohito's surrender speech on August 15, more than a week would pass before American planes came and prompted his note, "Oh, what a joy! Freedom at last, Nel!"[12] and more than a month before ships even began to take men home. Not until the following January, after Nel had died, was Wim himself reunited with his family. Ending wars, we learn in Wim's understated style, can be nearly as fraught as starting and fighting them.

The most striking characteristic of Lindeijer's style surely is its matter-of-factness. He writes as a husband and father conveying his daily happenings to loved ones, focusing on the exigencies of daily life rather than on the dramatic. Not only does that approach give the work authenticity; it enables us to see with unusual clarity the ins and outs of daily prison life in the frigid winters and steamy summers of northern Japan: the personal interactions, the passing of exhausting day after wearisome day, the poignancy of separation, the joys, the good moments, and those filled with pain.

There is cruelty and hardship aplenty. He described the trip to Japan in the late fall of 1942 as excruciating, with men stashed together like sardines, denied medicine, beaten, starved, allowed to vomit on each other, and left often to die. Once in Japan, Lindy wrote frequently about sick men forced to work in freezing rain, about the constant struggle against fleas, about shivering in threadbare shirts when winter winds screamed through gaps in walls. ("Oh, that this might really be the last winter here!"[13]) And guards were sometimes lazy, sometimes stupid, and often cruel, stealing packages sent by the Red Cross and "lashing out at the slightest opportunity."[14] No theme appears more frequently than loneliness—on birthdays, on holidays, during stretches when it seemed that prison and separation might never end. Deprivation and cruelty were part of prison life, and Lindeijer wrote about them regularly.

The distinctive thing about these descriptions is that they are written without special drama, as part of a larger whole. Many days were good, some guards were compassionate, many fellow prisoners were kind and loving, others were greedy or bigoted. More than half a century ago, the theologian Langdon Gilkey wrote that one of the lessons he learned in another Japanese war camp, this one in China, was that, as human beings, people were the same, whether they were Japanese or European. "The universal problem of selfishness," he said, existed among both prisoners and captors.[15] Lindeijer described the same kind of ordinariness, day in day out.

The thing that gave him this insight was, more than anything else, his ability to adhere to ordinary life patterns even as a prisoner. Once he recovered from the horrors of the voyage to Japan, he took up lifelong practices that accorded to his skills and gave shape to his days. He nurtured friendships, sometimes among the Japanese. He practiced his highly rational faith. He wrote the letters that form the backbone of *A Gate in the Wall*. He found ingenious, sometimes secret ways to secure life's necessities. Like the protagonist in Abe Kōbō's classic novel *Woman in the Dunes*, he found tasks that gave life meaning and reduced his need to escape.[16]

Most of all, he taught and he learned. Not long after being taken captive, he began studying Japanese. Almost as soon as he arrived at the prison camp, he reported to Nel that he was going to use a small bedroom to teach a course on electrochemistry and that more than a hundred inmates had signed up for it, though "we have no blackboard or chalk."[17] Once the prison routine became established, he used the hours before and after work each day to study differential calculus, trigonometry, and advanced calculus. He wrote a high school chemistry textbook, then translated it into English. And he finagled to get his hands on books, even selling his cigarette allotments (he was not a smoker) to get money to reimburse friendly Japanese willing to buy him books in the city. The fact that he managed to get away with all this says something about the lenient side of prison life.

A Gate in the Wall also tells a tale of reconciliation—across generations and across continents. It is not unusual for prison memoirists to talk about reconciliation. We read often about Allied veterans who meet with Japanese counterparts, exchange war memories, and express forgiveness (usually, for what was done *to* them). *Unbroken* and *Railway Man* even use words such as "redemption" and "forgiveness" in their titles. But Lindeijer's story gives reconciliation a wholly different meaning.

For one thing, his nationality would give attempts at reconciliation a special meaning, in part because the people of the Netherlands experienced World War II differently from the way most countries did. Their heavy-handed occupation by the Germans, for example, gave war a bitter taste that made reconnection with former enemies unthinkable for many of Wim's fellow citizens. A lengthy study of war memories in the postwar Netherlands contains not a single reference to ideas of reconciliation.[18] As late as 1989, lingering war resentments resulted in such a furor when Queen Beatrix decided to attend Hirohito's funeral that the government changed course and had her stay home.

And relationship issues were even more complicated for men like Wim, who had been colonials in Indonesia (then, the Dutch East Indies), living in comfort atop a centuries-old imperialist system in which the Dutch and a few local elites profited from a modern economy while nearly all of the "indigenous population remained trapped" in a subsistence world, "impoverished and locked out from modernity."[19] Most of the Lindeijers' Dutch peers lived in their own privileged communities, prompting one Japanese official, Nogi Harumichi, to note, "We didn't take anything from the Indonesians, only from the Dutch"[20]—because the Indonesians had nothing worth taking. And once the war was over, the gap between the Dutch and the Indonesians grew both wider and more violent.

Shocked by the humiliating way in which their Dutch masters submitted to the Japanese and emboldened by Japan's pan–Asianist rhetoric, which promised liberation from colonialism, the Indonesians announced their own independence, with Sukarno as leader, just two days after Hirohito's surrender speech. When the Dutch, loath to lose their colony just after defeating Germany, refused to give up their hold on the country, a brutal, half-decade war broke out, with wanton atrocities committed by both sides—but especially by the Dutch, who made torture and killings an "integral component" of their policy. One episode, the Rawagede massacre of hundreds of Java villagers in 1947, has been dubbed by historians as the "Dutch My Lai."[21] Only in 1949 did the war end, with Indonesia's declaration of independence.

The challenges inherent in this need to grapple with two imperialisms become obvious in the last chapters of the Barnhardt account, as Wim Jr. struggles with his need, both psychologically and as a matter of moral principle, to confront both the Dutch oppression of the Indonesians and the Japanese imprisonment of his father. For decades, his compatriots had suffered from amnesia about the cruelties they imposed as colonial masters and civil war enemies, because reality ran counter to myths of Dutch superiority and goodness. By the 1990s, however, that amnesia had started to lift, with a visit at last by Queen Beatrix to Indonesia in 1995 and a Dutch recognition a decade later of the "political and moral" importance of August 17, Indonesia's Independence Day. A decade after that, the prominent historian Remy Limpach's publication of *De brandende campongs van Generaal Spoor* (The burning villages of General Spoor), which demonstrated that "extreme violence" was endemic during the Indonesian independence struggle, prompted the government to launch a full-scale inquiry into its own war crimes.[22]

Being Dutch thus made the Lindeijers' movement toward reconciliation not only more complicated but more remarkable. That movement began, of course, with Wim Sr.'s own behavior in prison, which he described as a place "full of the enormous range of thoughts and deeds which we, as God's creatures, display."[23] He may have depicted nasty behavior but he avoided the broad labeling of enemy tendencies that readers found in *Unbroken*—and in Ernest Gordon's best-selling *Through the Valley of the Kwai*, which told an inspiring story of survival in Japan's infamous Thai prison camp but indicted all Japanese as practitioners of a stereotyped samurai culture. As he put it, "If they didn't care a tinker's damn for their own, why should they care for us?" Cruelty was part of the national soul.[24]

In Wim Sr.'s view, by contrast, people act the way they do because of circumstances and personality, not culture. No relationship illustrated his approach more vividly than the interaction with Iwashita Hiroe, "a small Japanese man" who appeared in a March 1, 1943, letter as a man "dressed in black, with a little white kerchief tucked into his belt in back," a man who wrote novels, knew "some English and French," and gave potatoes, pepper, salt, and cigarettes to some of the captives. As Barnhardt's narration makes clear, Lindeijer knew that Iwashita was loyal to his own country, but he also knew that he respected him as an individual trapped by circumstance. Iwashita occasionally brought a Victrola to the prisoners' quarters; he sometimes shared quiet news about the war, and he accepted chocolates from captives. At the end of the war, he wrote his name in English in Lindeijer's diary. And he was just one among many in the Lindy letters who made it possible for the prisoners to see the Japanese as complex human beings responding to circumstances not of their own choosing.

Thankfully, reconciliation stopped neither with Wim, nor with the completion of his diary. In perhaps the most extraordinary part of Barnhardt's work, forgiveness and understanding continued into the twenty-first century to drive the Lindeijer family, their Dutch communities, and the people of Kamaishi. After being warned by his dying mother, Nel, that hatred for the Japanese would lead only to more wars, Wim Jr. gave much of his life to the reconciliation processes.

The account of his struggles with nightmares and memories of his mother's death, his willingness to use therapy as he regained mental health, and his repeated returns to Japan to engage in interchanges with his family's captors is remarkable, as is his search for forgiveness for the hatred he found himself harboring toward the Japanese. So is the story of reconciliation in Japan, particularly among the people of Kamaishi. When Wim Jr. first visited the city of 40,000, he found people relatively ignorant of the Ohashi prison camp, not unlike the residents of Weimar in Germany who professed to have known nothing about the concentration camp outside town. But his visit lit a spark in Japan, resulting in extensive press coverage, followed by a Japanese translation of his father's letters, and then a dramatic reenactment in Kamaishi's middle school of his story, concluding with the deathbed encounter where Nel tells Wim Jr., "As long as you've hate in your heart, you won't be able to love anybody."

War memory remains an issue in both Japan and the West, including the Netherlands. Within Japan, powerful conservative elements strive to induce amnesia, or even pride, regarding Japan's role in World War II, while the government increases its military budgets almost yearly. When Wim Jr. visited Kamaishi in 2001, he met well-meaning teachers who argued that children should be shielded from teachings about war. In the west, particularly in America, the most popular narratives still ignore Allied atrocities and attribute Japanese cruelty to "national traits." *A Gate in the Wall* treads a different path. It eschews nationalist ideologies, recounting quotidian prison life and accounting for evil and good not as products of culture but as consequences of people being placed in situations over which they had little, if any, control. Doing that, it shows how the Lindeijers laid the ground for new connections and spiritual renewal among the captors and the captured. And it makes it clear that honest, serious reflection on war remains a vital part of Japan's intellectual scene.

James Huffman is H. Orth Hirt Professor of History Emeritus at Wittenberg University, where he taught East Asian history for thirty years. Having published nine books on Japanese history, including Japan and Imperialism *and* Japan in World History, *he resides in Chicago, where he serves on the board of Chicago Area Peace Action. Half of his family reside in Tokyo, half in Chicago.*

Preface

My Dutch friend's quiet remark that he had been held in a Japanese prison camp as a child gave me chills. This first contact with the story of a World War II Dutch East Indies family, the Lindeijers, took place decades ago in Cincinnati, when during a conversation about the concentration camps in Europe, my Dutch friend whom I knew at the time as "Bill," and only later as "Wim," said simply that he had been in a camp in Java with his mother and siblings as a child; while they were in the camp his mother had died. Like the other Americans present, I had no sense of the war's circumstances in Indonesia, or what his family would have been doing there. I recall learning that his parents had come to Java from Holland in 1935 because his father, Wim Sr., found a teaching position there during a worldwide depression; that his father had been taken off to prison in Japan after that country invaded; and that the senior Lindeijer kept a prohibited prison diary in the form of letters to his family that he was never able to mail. But Americans tend to know more about the war in Europe, so the discussion quickly turned back to that.

Yet something in Wim's voice that night stayed with me. Visiting him and his family in the Netherlands later, I asked about the diary and was able to read it in rough English translation, fascinated by its gripping first-hand account: of what it was like to be a medic in the midst of gunfire and bombing, without air support during the 1942 Dutch defense of Java; what it was like to attempt to minister to the sick and dying in the lowest hold of a ship during a month's long journey from Java to Japan; and what it was like to survive three hard years in an iron mining camp in the mountains of northeast Honshu. This was the record of a remarkable individual who despite extreme worry about his family, kept his calm, consistently helped others, and without glossing over ill-treatment expressed no hatred or animosity toward his captors.

I was amazed to learn of the diary's publication in Japanese (only) by a leading Japanese publisher, Misuzu Shobo, in 2000. I knew that Wim's travels to Japan and talks there in the mid–1990s had stimulated interest.

But why the emergence of this particular POW diary, in Japan in the twenty-first century? Why the numerous reviews, accompanied by the photograph of the mother who died and her children? Neither Wim nor the diary itself could fully answer my questions; a prohibited diary necessarily leaves a good deal out. I had the sense that there was much more to the story that not only the Japanese, but westerners needed to know.

Events during the next two years expanded my view. In 2004, students in Kamaishi, near the former prison, read the diary and responded with an empathetic dramatic and choral presentation, sent on video to Wim and others in the Netherlands. In 2005, they sent a complete reenactment, a balanced view that included the United States' twice shelling their city. I was struck by the recognition of a distinction between the family, as victims, and myself, as an American. Identifying with the Lindeijer family's suffering had come at a cost to my objectivity. Though I knew better than to generalize, I had begun thinking of "the Japanese," during the wartime, at least, as uniformly hostile.

I had been thinking about the importance of stories, since this is the form that our historical memory usually takes. Yet I was coming to realize stories' limits in a situation like war, where there are winners and losers, and the winners' stories dominate. Until fairly recently, there had been one dominant narrative of World War II in the Pacific, with Japan as the evil aggressor—and for Americans, an accompanying myth, that this was our "good war," a conflict between Good and Evil, in which we were essentially "pure." The "good war" was embedded in my culture and had affected my view. I had the sudden realization that the narrative unfolding around me was not only the story of Wim and his family, but also the story of townspeople in Kamaishi; that understanding and documenting it more fully could be of great benefit not only to me, but to others, too.

Immersing myself in the records of the Allied nationalities at Lindeijer's camp—Americans, British, Australians, Canadians, and Dutch—I found stories that contradicted stereotypes on either side. There was severe mistreatment of prisoners, of course, the result of a harsh military authority and individual cruelty. Yet the POW stories show instances of people on both sides helping people, revealing that things were more complicated than the dominant narrative showed. During the course of the war, the prisoners were changing, at times recognizing other stories besides those of their own suffering.

I, myself, was changing, aware of my previous failure to understand the war's broader impact on all participants, as well as my own implication in the events I had decided to document. In Wim's case, rereading his father's diary and his mother's farewell letter from the camp helped him view his traumatic childhood events from a fuller, more accurate perspective. I have endeavored to do something similar in this book: complementing the necessarily cryptic diary entries with commentary based on the records of Wim Sr.'s POW colleagues, interviews with camp survivors, and the notebook of a Japanese camp liaison, to bring the camp's complex wartime relationships more fully to life.[1]

What follows is neither an overview of POW experience during the Pacific War, nor an assessment of the Japanese camps. It is rather the record of a family, who in coming to terms with their wartime trauma, reached out to their former captors—who had their own trauma, yet took the family's lead, in working to gain an accurate historical understanding and overcome ghosts of their past. May it help similarly traumatized families and communities now and in the future.

A Note on the Text

Dr. Evert Willem "Wim" Lindeijer Sr. (pronounced "Villem," or "Vim," "Lindeyer") began his secret wartime diary in a Japanese prison camp in his home city of Bandung, Java, in the Dutch East Indies (now Indonesia), on 15 May 1942. He ended it on an Allied hospital ship in Yokohama on 17 September 1945. The manuscript consists of 113 pages, handwritten in pencil in Dutch, on both sides of notebook-sized looseleaf sheets (each side numbered), without paragraphing and with little or no margins. Paper was scarce, and concealment dictated small size. Stored with it and integral to its story were two reports written in English at the unusual request of camp authorities in northeast Japan; and even more integral, a well-traveled photograph of the wife and four children left behind, to whom every letter-entry of the diary is addressed. To provide context for the experience he relates, I have added narrative commentary based on interviews with camp survivors, the records of fellow prisoners, and notably, those of a Japanese camp liaison. The regular font of the letter entries alternates with the italicized text of the commentary. Diary annotations supplement the commentary, identifying sources and clarifying the means by which I've pieced together a more complete camp picture. In the annotations, Lindeijer Sr. is referred to as "E.W."

For the diary's English translation, I have consulted the unpublished British- and Australian-influenced versions of Dame Elisabeth Foppen and naturalized Australian citizen Herman Lindeyer, respectively, to produce a Mid-Atlantic version. In my transcription of the diary, I designated paragraph units based on the scientist Lindeijer's organized thought. I removed some repetitions, indicating these edits with ellipses. On occasion I inserted text between square brackets to clarify content—for instance, to point out that when Lindeijer mentions "Silver Cross certification" he means to suggest Red Cross equivalency. I have not included strikethroughs, which for Lindeijer amount to corrections made at the time to entries necessarily written in haste. Likewise, I've considered insertions above or below the line of an entry to be integral to it and unworthy of comment unless otherwise indicated (e.g., a later insertion in ink, unavailable at the camp). Any underscores or lines across the bottom of an entry are Lindeijer's. I've spelled out otherwise cryptic Dutch abbreviations and translated foreign words and phrases, though where the foreign phrasing matters—in an organization title, for instance—I've included it along with the translation. To eliminate repetition and trim the size of the diary I've omitted sections of text (in a few cases, whole entries) and inserted ellipses. Finally, in the case of two instances where Lindeijer removed several lines of an entry, and also in the more critical matter of the diary's four missing pages (59–62), I've drawn attention with ellipses and clarifying text.

A word about names and dates: Japanese surnames precede given names; however, the prisoners favored western name order (Hiroe Iwashita, over Iwashita Hiroe). I've followed suit. Place names that in the colonial era in Java were either Dutch or native names with Dutch-influenced spelling were changed to native names after Indonesian independence. Examples from the diary include Batavia (today Jakarta) and Tjihapit (today Cihapit). I've indicated both names as needed. For date notation, I've used the convention appropriate to the referenced document (typically, DD.MM.YYYY for documents of European and British-influenced nationalities, as well as Japanese; MM.DD.YYYY for American, and some Canadian).

Structure-wise, Part I consists of the diary's entries, which fall naturally into chronological chapters recording the POW experience—with the exception that Lindeijer's two reports, on the defense of Java, and on his overseas transport, necessarily become Chapters 1 and 3, despite not having been written until January 1944. Part II consists of the postwar diary story, beginning in the 1990s, and told primarily in three chapters via family letters, interviews in Japan, and a Japanese student script. Critical to this structure, however, and a requisite frame for both parts, is the farewell letter of the wife left behind, dictated in a camp in Java, two days before she died, in July 1945. Positioned prior to the Part I diary ("A Letter of Farewell"), it functions as subtle undercurrent to the letter-entries; reappearing in the forefront in Part II ("Letters of Loss and Renewal"), it assists a son's work on traumatic memory and the diary's resulting emergence in Japan in the twenty-first century.

PART I

The Trauma of War—
"Whatever Is Torn Away"

*Muntilan, Java, 1945—
A Letter of Farewell*

Three weeks prior to the end of hostilities in Southeast Asia, thirty-eight-year-old Nel Lindeijer lay critically ill with amoebic dysentery in a Japanese internment camp near Muntilan, Central Java. She and her four children, ages four through nine, had arrived here in a transport from a camp in Solo (Surakarta)—and prior to that, from a camp in their home city of Bandung—on the 26th of May. The high elevation of the Muntilan camp, swept by Indian Ocean winds, was preferable to the humidity they had experienced in Surakarta. Yet the improved location, here on a lower, western slope of the Merapi volcano, was negated by the camp's unhealthy conditions. The Japanese military had consolidated its internees further inland out of concern over a potential Allied invasion. Four thousand predominantly women and children civilian internees now found themselves crowded inside the walls of Muntilan's former Roman Catholic monastery, Nel and her children among them. Added to this, camp workers had allowed cans of meat to sit open in the sun for hours before giving them to the unsuspecting internees, sickening many people. Already ill when she arrived, Nel had succumbed rapidly.

Whether she might have recovered without such carelessness Nel couldn't know. Staring at the high ceiling of the tropical building, she would have held the thought for no more than a moment before letting it go. She had come to terms with her imminent passing, placing the harrowing experience of internment behind her. Her thoughts were now focused exclusively on her young family; her surroundings, including this hospital protruding beyond the camp wall, no longer relevant, with the single exception of a veranda overlooking the main gate, where her children slept in the care of Mrs. Marijnen and her daughter, Tieneke.[1]

Nel had instilled in the children the belief that at the war's end their father would return and the family would reunite. Recognition that the reunion would take place without her had been poignant, but with acceptance had come the insight that a last act still open to her—the composition of a letter—could smooth her family's way in the future.

Memories that might otherwise be lost to them raced through her mind like the images of the black-and-white movies they had taken before the war: the house on the Dago Road, Wimmie and Herman in sailor suits, her husband bicycling home from a day's teaching at the Lyceum, tea with friends on the veranda[2]... The letter addressed to her husband and dictated a day earlier would enable them to reclaim this past but also move forward, freed to an extent from the effects of the war. A friend of the last few weeks, Christien Slotemaker-de Bruine, had taken it all down.[3]

The photographs taken at the conflict's start would help them further in coming to terms with her loss; notably, the one from the garden behind their house. Thoughts of the photo-taking afternoon more than three years prior might have prompted a weak smile even now. Two attempts to have them taken at professional shops had ended in disaster.[4] The children had been shell-shocked during the Japanese invasion. At the sight of a black-cloaked photographer lunging toward them with his camera, they began shrieking in terror. Freddy, who was three at the time, would start, but this was all it took to get Herman, aged four and a half, and their little sister, Joke,[5] barely a year, to join in. Wimmie, at six, was calmer. The snapshot at home in the garden was a last resort. Fortunately, Adrie, the young schoolteacher who frequently visited, was with them and able to take it. Adrie with her sister Riek had helped with the children during their internment, until November 1944. Then Nel and the children had been transported to Solo, and Adrie and Riek, elsewhere.

From the photographs Nel's thoughts would have turned as a matter of course to her husband. Her confidence in him, as much as her recent change in perspective, had allowed the words of her letter to come with such clarity. Mrs. Marijnen would deliver it along with the children as soon as the war in Southeast Asia was over.

Dear Wim,

Now that in all likelihood I am going to die, I just want to take leave of you, and tell you how happy I've been with you all these years. Perhaps I have at times caused you sorrow, and for that I ask your forgiveness. But my dearest thoughts have always been about you.

You will understand what a struggle it has been for me to acquiesce—to accept God's decision. But I can now surrender all in peace. You'll also know that during these years of separation I've fully done my duty toward the children. They have such generous young hearts, and Wimmie, especially, has a firm belief. In Bandung, Riek van der Baan helped me with the children for about a year. She was like a mother to them, full of care and devotion. For this I've loved her dearly.

Wim, you should not continue to grieve for me. We have had our life together. Start a new life, with another wife. Only one thing, I beseech you: look for a good mother for the children. It would fulfill my deepest wish if it might be one of the Van der Baan girls; but, of course, I cannot look into your heart. Riek has such a rich inner life, but you know how I love Adrie too.

I hope that God will guide you in the choice of your new life.

Would you be a comfort for my parents? It will be a terrible blow for them when they learn that I'm no longer there. Please let them enjoy the children. Mrs. Marijnen has taken over their care, and with so much love and devotion that I can't be sufficiently thankful.

So far, the children have been none the worse for all of this, and I hope God grants that in the final stage—when I am gone—they will also manage to come through undamaged.

Now I'll bid you goodbye. God keep you and grant you an abundant life, full of faith. Live in the knowledge that you have always been embraced by my thoughts. God will strengthen you to overcome this loss.

A deeply felt kiss from your Nel

P.S. Wim try to get in touch with Miss Christien Slotemaker-de Bruine.

Petronella J. Lindeijer-Verhulst ("Nel") and Evert Willem "Wim" Lindeijer, Sr., Bandung, 1937 (Lindeijer Family Archive).

During the last few weeks she has been one of my dearest friends and has strengthened me immensely. From the bottom of my heart I hope you will get to know her. Please do all you can. My heartfelt greetings to Riek and Adrie. Thank them again for all they did for me and the children. My best wishes also for your whole family, brothers and sisters. Tell them how I regret that I will not see them again.

What else had there been? Only the locations of their most valued possessions, added to the reverse side of the letter.

Three chests of books at the Technical University

Weiss Family—opposite the Residency Office (father of Roosje Weiss): Piano and three or four cabin trunks or chests.

Cibadak Way #104: the bookcases from the study

Kouw from the Bible Society: one chest containing the principal study books and our wedding Bible.

Riek has taken care of the disposition of the remainder of our personal belongings.

Her husband would negotiate the family's future. Her eyes closed for the last time on 25 July 1945, three weeks prior to Japan's surrender, and ten years to the day after her arrival in Java as a young bride.[6]

But who was this man in whom she trusted so implicitly—and who at the same time had been writing letters to her that she never received? We can best know by letting him speak to us in his own words.

1

Ohashi, Japan, 1944— Revisiting the Collapse of a World

Evert Willem Lindeijer, the "Wim" to whom Nel wrote, was a twenty-six-year-old with a freshly minted doctorate in chemistry from Leiden University, when in 1935 he arrived in Bandung, Java, with her as his new wife. His teaching position at Bandung's highly regarded gymnasium level Lyceum provided the means for starting a family and also allowed him to meet a requirement to serve for a minimum of four years in the Dutch East Indies in return for a government study grant. During those years the experience of life in Java worked its spell; and in any case, by his completion of the requirement in 1939, a depression and high unemployment in the Netherlands made returning there unattractive. He and Nel decided to stay.

Ironically, no more than a year later, in May 1940, the fall of the Netherlands to Germany made the position of the Dutch in the Indies uncertain. Yet in practical terms, they were removed from the war in Europe, Lindeijer and his compatriots thought, and safe. True, Japanese demands for quantities of their bauxite and oil had created months of unease. But an American warning against interference in their affairs, and the success of the colonial government in refusing to meet the demands or to join a "Co-Prosperity Sphere," seemed to stabilize things.

Then Japan's aggression in French Indochina had raised the stakes. The Americans and the British imposed an embargo—to which the Japanese responded with the attack on Pearl Harbor. When, on the eighth of December 1941, the Government of the Netherlands in exile in London declared war on Japan, the East Indies was caught in a vise: by default it had declared war also. Even then, Dutch Indies residents, Lindeijer included, felt confident of Allied support. Drafted as a private and given basic training, he'd posed for lighthearted photographs with a gas mask, never seriously believing that the sky would fall in.

Until February, that is, when the Allies lost Singapore. By the first of March much of the Dutch East Indies was in Japanese hands and the disaster during the Battle of the Java Sea had already taken place. Java effectively stood alone when the Dutch government in exile counseled no surrender. Assigned to the Fifteenth Battalion Medical Corps of the Dutch East Indies Army (Koninklijk Nederlands-Indisch Leger, or KNIL), Lindeijer took part in the ill-fated week-long defense, and by 9 March had become a prisoner of war.

Only much later, in 1944, at camp in Northeast Japan, was he to reconstruct the events of that week that had led to his separation by half a world from all he knew—in English, at the request of the Japanese.

My Experiences During the Japanese Invasion of Java

When the Japanese landed on Java, on the first of March '42 [Sunday],[1] I was attached to the Medical Corps of the 15th [Infantry] Battalion [of the Royal Army of the Dutch East Indies—the KNIL],[2] which at this time was stationed at Buitenzorg [Bogor].[3]

Many [conflicting] commands came to us from our headquarters [General Headquarters at Bandung], which was very confusing; no one seemed to know what they were doing. We packed our baggage, horses, kitchen, etc., 5 times in two days, only to unpack them again. We were rather tired when at last we were to leave Buitenzorg for Cimahi [the first leg of the journey to attempt to retake the airfield near the north coast at Kalijati].[4]

Tired, hungry and exhausted, we reached our destination [Cimahi[5]] on Monday night. There was no room in the barracks or anywhere else, so we slept alongside the road, on porches and most anywhere we could lie down. I was very fortunate. I slept on the porch of the chemist's shop attached to the Cimahi hospital.

Tuesday morning [March 3], we went to the Remonte Depot near Padalarang.[6] From here we could see how badly Bandung had been bombed. We were forced to carry our luggage [baggage] from one barracks to another, and after a scanty meal in the afternoon our officers told us to get as much rest as possible tonight because we were to move out the next morning.

Bandung! The terrible realization had finally come. His city, called the Paris of Java,[7] an oasis of climate and culture, with Art Deco buildings and European-style cafés along its major avenues, was to be the scene of war. On an ordinary day he would have focused on identifying scenic locations in the distance from the overlook by the depot: the Dago tea house[8] and the trail to the remarkable waterfall below, or the Maribaya falls and tea plantations near Lembang, farther off. That morning, however, high to the northwest ring of mountains surrounding the Bandung plateau, his interest was more likely on how soon the invasion would reach his home—number 121 on the road north from the city to the mountain village of Dago.

It was a great disappointment when, after half an hour of sleep, they woke us up again in order to start at once. We received ammunition. At 11:00 o'clock [p.m.] a big convoy of several hundred cars and trucks went toward Purwakarta.[9] After passing this point we got onto the wrong road. After an hour and a half we [the convoy] got turned around, leaving only a few cars and trucks [behind]. I saw a heavy six-wheeled truck trying to turn. Only because of his great skillfulness the driver succeeded in that. If he had not, all the vehicles which were originally in front of his truck would have had to be left behind.

The morale of the soldiers, which had improved at the announcement of the [impending] attack [on Kalijati], sagged again. The mistake was soon followed by another half an hour later. We stopped once more, only to turn around a second time. We lost much time because our native drivers were not experienced at driving in convoy. We were forced to stop and pull trucks which had gotten stuck in the mud out of our way.

It was of course the intention of our commander, Colonel Toorop,[10] to reach the point from which the infantry was to start its attack, before daylight. Never in my live [sic] did I feel so much anxiety in seeing the sun rise above the horizon. I was constantly looking for Japanese bombers, which could demolish the entire convoy in no more than 15 minutes. We had good luck, however. Not a single Jap.[11] plane was seen the whole morning.

At last we reached the point identified for the infantry attack. It had taken us 8 hours to cover a distance of about 100 km. The cars [all the vehicles] were driven into a rubber plantage [plantation], where the administrator's house was our headquarters. We were still about 15 kilometers from the airfield. It appeared afterward that the distance to the enemy was about the same. We should have drove [sic] further ... Not knowing the enemy's position, however, this would have been very dangerous.

Without breakfast the men started the attack on the airfield. Two companies were in the field on both sides of the road, with [the result that] our Medical Corps went down the road accompanied by 150 men. I learned later that our tanks had been destroyed by the guns left by the British at the airfield.

I was in the rear Eschalawn [sic], which was to set up our First Aid station about 2 or 3 km from the front. A Jap. observation plane came over trying to find our position. We took cover, but some fool fired his rifle at it. Of course, it turned around, bombed and machine-gunned the men, and set two trucks loaded with ammunition on fire. We were unable to put out the fire because of the continual explosions. The thick smoke soon directed several Japanese bombers to the scene. Until nightfall we and our infantry were heavily bombed and machine-gunned. Wounded were taken to our first aid station. Not a single allied [sic] fighter plane was seen the whole day. Incidently [sic], during the entire campaign I never saw one allied plane in the sky. In fact, we had lost already our best fighters and bombers over Malakka [Malacca].[12]

We felt hungry and miserable because no food supply [had] reached us.

After sunset the bombers went away and our soldiers came flying back down the road; Everything seemed to be disorganised [sic]. We went back to the house used as headquarters and found it badly dammaged [sic] by bombs. About 100 trucks and cars were burned out and much equipment was lost, including my own.

The hastily planned attempt to retake the airfield had failed. In retrospect, it had been doomed from the start—not least because of earlier losses by the air force of the Dutch East Indies during its participation in the defense of Singapore. Even before that their aircraft and tanks had been inadequate because of the priority placed on manufacturing orders for Europe. Just before Singapore's collapse, British troops fleeing the Malay Peninsula had arrived in Java in a chaotic rush, along with a handful of Australians; many without their equipment, communications, or supplies. It had been impossible to coordinate them into a well-organized force prior to the next phase.[13] The men of his own battalion (one could suppose it was true for others) had little to rely on other than their own sense of duty and character.

Our chief doctor now proved to be a good officer. He gave orders and regulated the retreat under very difficult conditions. He put me in charge of 5 passenger buses with orders to drive as far as possible toward the enemy, picking up our soldiers. As soon as a bus was full it could turn around and go back. I had driven about 10 km., when I found the commander of our batalion [sic] standing near a stone bridge over a deep canyon. Three of my buses had already left, packed with soldiers. In the next one there were about 20 men, but the commander told me not to go any further as the Japanese were already on the other side of the river. The commander gathered the officers present in order to deliberate the next move. They resolved to defend the bridge at all cost. The 20 boys from my bus were taken as a reinforcement. One officer was put in charge and was told in front of the soldiers to shoot any man who attempted to desert.

1. Ohashi, Japan, 1944

I had to go back to headquarters with one of the buses and make my report to the doctor. He told me to join my ambulance, which had already tried [sic] to leave for Bandung.

Many trucks, loaded with soldiers, were waiting alongside the road, but nobody knew why they could not move. It was quite dark and I walked to the head of the convoy, where I found that a heavy bomb had blown up the road over its whole breadth. [By working hard], at last we succeeded in creating a small passage on one side of the crater.

I continued my journey on the pillion of a motorcycle to a point where the driver had to rejoin his unit. There I climbed on a truck crowded with soldiers which reached Bandung at about 3:00 o'clock [a.m.]. I felt completely exhausted and staggered with my baggage the last 4 km. up the Dago Road[14] until I reached my house at 4 o'clock [a.m.].

The next morning, Thursday [March 5], having had a few hours' rest and a good breakfast, I went into town to arrange my money affairs and to buy toothpaste, razorbox [a box of razor blades], etc. The town looked dismal. Everyone realized that the defense of Java was collapsing.

At 11:00 o'clock [a.m.] I reported to headquarters. As soon as enough soldiers were gathered an officer took us to the cavalry barracks where we received new equipment. Here someone stole my steel helmet, and it was impossible to get a new one. So I was forced to steal someone else's. The captain in command authorized me to go home until next morning. I spent a happy day with my family. My nephew [and namesake, Evert-Wim Lindeijer], was there and had dinner with us. The next day [March 6] he was killed near Lembang.

This last was enough to give pause. The nephew who was his namesake had been in the Fifth KNIL Battalion positioned at the Ciater Pass north of Bandung, with directions to halt the Japanese advance south. After being strafed by enemy aircraft and overwhelmed by infantry, its members had engaged in desperate man-to-man combat until only an estimated seventy to eighty remained alive to be taken prisoner. Word had gone round afterward that in a bizarre display of compassion each had been given a cigarette before being tied up in groups of three and machine-gunned. Only two or three had managed to survive.[15]

Lindeijer's including his nephew's name was of personal importance—and at the same time insisted on the meaningful identity of one who might stand for the entire group of those massacred after being taken prisoners of war.

Friday morning [March 6], I returned to the cavalry barracks, where a small part of the 15th Battalion were [sic] gathered. We waited till noon before riding in trucks to Cimahi, where we (the Red Cross soldiers), got a place and a meal in the hospital. We assembled afterward at the office of the area commander. A rumor told [*sic*] of the landing of 80,000 Americans at Indramayu.[16]

That evening, the remains of the 4th, 10th, and 15th battalions were rearranged into a single new battalion. In the dark, several convoys were formed up and after a very scanty meal, we started for Lembang, where we had to take positions alongside the road to Bandung. We slept only the last part of that night.

Despite the rumor, what had seemed clear was that they would stand alone in defense of their homes and the city that had become their capital after the government of the Dutch East Indies had been moved inland from Batavia [Jakarta]. Just days before, the U.S. president had spoken over the wireless about Americans fighting in the Dutch East Indies, giving the impression of large numbers, with more on the way.[17] *That evening near Lembang, one had to question whether the words had been genuine. There had been only a single report of American help, from an artillery group that had supported some Australians in an attempt to stop the Japanese advance northwest of Bandung, at Leuwiliang.*[18] *The effort had been brilliant but had failed. Other than this, help had scarcely been in evidence, and any en route, certainly too late.*

Saturday morning [March 7], we camouflaged our trucks carefully and went into the field with stretchers, etc. At daylight, the Japanese bombed us, and this lasted until evening. At about noon one of our medical soldiers, a sergeant, became shell-shocked. I brought him down the road in search of our doctor and the First Aid station. At last, I found the doctor with about 10 orderlies hiding in a cavern. He promised to take care of the patient.

The entire day we again received no food at all. In a house we found a bottle of lemonade and a packet of custard powder. We cooked a pie and also some potatoes which we found in the field. In the meantime, all my equipment was stolen.

Just after nightfall an automobile came up the road carrying two big white flags. It was then we realized that we had capitulated.[19] Our captain ordered us to climb into our trucks, and at about 10 o'clock [p.m.] I was back home again.

The next morning, Sunday [March 8], the capitulation was announced over the wireless. Monday morning [March 9], I had to go to my battalion as a prisoner.[20] We were told, however, that we would be set free the same day—or, at least a few days later, exactly as the Germans freed prisoners after the capitulation of Holland.

Not until after he made contact with POWs from the 131st Field Artillery, Texas National Guard, who had been at Leuwiliang, and who were ultimately held with him at a camp in northeast Japan, had he realized just how little American—or any Allied—help there had been. The second battalion of the 131st had been the only American ground combat unit in Java during the invasion. Its members initially served as ground crew to a U.S. Army Air Corps bombardment group stationed at the eastern end of the island. When the bombardment group was evacuated to Australia on the second of March 1942,[21] nearly all of the men of the 131st had been intentionally left behind; in a word, sacrificed.

In effect, the same had been true for every Allied prisoner captured in Java. Every one of them—Americans, British, and Australians, in addition to Dutch—had been sacrificed to buy time and delay the Japanese.[22]

2

Bandung, Java, 1942—
A Sundering of Ties

Lindeijer found himself held prisoner in his own battalion's quarters. The large Fifteenth Battalion encampment, in the Cikudapateuh area of central Bandung, was bordered by city streets now swarming with refugees and Japanese troops. When it was initially taken over by the Japanese, disorderliness reigned in the camp itself. Discipline was lax, relatives visited, and even going home for the night was tolerated so long as one returned in time for morning roll call.[1] *The twenty-first of April marked an abrupt change, however. Three men who ignored a new policy against departing and attempted to leave as they had previously were taken into custody as "escapees."*[2] *By noon the next day, the three—Dutch seaman H. Karssen and KNIL gunners A. Hielkema and J.W. Mercus—were bound to the barbed wire enclosure and blindfolded. The camp's senior Dutch officer, Lieutenant Colonel H. Poulus, and his subordinates were ordered to attend their execution by a squad armed with bayonets.*[3]

As an orderly in the camp hospital, Lindeijer was not required to watch, but struggled afterward with what had taken place like everyone else. A fellow conscript, Van West de Veer, might well have spoken for all the Dutch who did observe: "We could not believe what we had seen," he later declared. "We were all in shock."[4] *Prisoners authorized to go out of the camp under guard to "forage"—that is, to purchase supplies—picked up word of identical executions at other camps in Java.*[5] *The message was clear. Their imprisonment was not to end soon and could be characterized by unpredictable cruelty. Unauthorized behavior, including unauthorized outside contact, was highly risky.*

An underlying trauma lingered, even after an interval of weeks. It was in this context that Lindeijer commenced communication with his family in writing—determinedly positive, as he focused on the memory of Nel, with all four of their children, at the front gate that day.

2. Bandung, Java, 1942

XV Bat.
Friday, 15 May '42

Dear Nel,

What a splendid day, today! How happy I am to have seen you in good health on Helmer's Road, and how well the children looked, too. Great that you brought so much; many thanks! Lucky that the boys were allowed to pass the packages through. Later, we received all kinds of delicacies—fruit especially—from various ladies, but nothing that surpassed that delicious *djeroeksap* [homemade orange juice] of yours! Above all, it was such a great relief to me to know that you can hold out financially for the time being. You know, just the previous afternoon, I had felt so depressed. And out of the blue, I had the opportunity to come along [to the camp gate], and with such a terrific result. The small tin [of food] is delicious too, you know! I almost regretted accepting it, because you will need such things badly yourself. Well, bye for now; the lights will be going out in the barracks; until next time!

Gas School Hospital
Thurs. 21 May '42

It's around midnight. I'm sitting in the ward among some 30 sleeping patients. My team has night duty. Doesn't this remind you of your own time in hospital? Last Sunday, I received the <u>two snapshots of you + youngsters</u> from Daan [Daan Barends, a colleague from the Lyceum]. Priceless, aren't they! That Joke has become such a fine child. I like the least focused one best of all. You and Joke and Freddy, in particular, show up so well. And the boys are so smart in their white shirts. I have the photos in front of me right now and can look at them at my leisure.

Barends had brought back the photos from forage duty, with the story of how they had been taken. They would need to be put safely away with his unpassed note of the fifteenth of May, but not out of mind. The intent faces would remain with him, along with his concern about Nel's health. Four pregnancies in the tropical heat had taken their toll, to the extent that she was treated for anemia. What was worse was the problem of her teeth: out of concern over lack of dental care during the occupation, she had made the decision to have them all pulled.[6]

How did it go with the new denture? All the best with it, dear! A vitamin deficiency causes teeth to loosen, doesn't it? I forgot to ask about the dentist who is treating you, and whether Wesenhagen [their general practitioner] is still at large, and accessible.

The hospital here is equipped miserably. We have only two urinals, two bed pans, and one thermometer for approx. 30 patients, 10 of whom have bacterial dysentery. The other ward (I'm always in Ward 2 of the Gas School Hospital)[7] has another 30 or so dysentery patients. I work with Elion and others, and we've knocked together some furniture for ourselves. The food is significantly better than in the XVth Bat. [non-hospital quarters], and there are glorious water heaters in the bathrooms. The work is therefore not too bad.

The hospital work would attract her interest. As a young pharmaceutical graduate, she had worked in the hospital laboratory in Leiden. On the heels of that came their shared history: courtship and marriage in a Leiden suburb; the two-day honeymoon in Genoa; voyage by freighter to Java; and subsequent family life, now interrupted.

He turned to description of his efforts with Poulus and others to set up an educational program. This would help restore prisoner morale in the wake of the executions, and renew the discipline lost after the confiscation of the Allied officers' badges of rank in early May.[8]

We work in 3 [hospital] shifts, so I can still teach my 4 chemistry [refresher course] periods per week. There is a 5th year HBS [Dutch secondary school] formed, which is to operate under supervision of a civil servant of the Ministry of Education and Religion. The idea is to give final exams, which may be officially valid later on. Great, isn't it? I'll teach Chemistry there.

Lecturers have also been assigned for preliminary Medicine, Agriculture, Pharmacy, and Botany. I'll teach Inorganic and Physical Chemistry. Altman teaches Organic Chemistry and Van der Tijl, Botany. They are also busy establishing a faculty for Literature. This Tuesday, I give the 1st of a series of three lectures on "Forces between Small Particles."

The books you spoke of have not arrived yet. I still stop in at the XVth Bat. frequently, and begin to apply pressure from this side also, although that seems hopeless. You understand that it would make things a lot easier for me if it could work ...

The literary faculty he mentioned was introduced to an enthusiastic reception. Some wit had the inspiration to dress up as a beadle—the sort of officer who ushered and kept order in a church, but who in this case promoted order through the cultivation of humor. Entering with long strides, to the tinkling of bells, he made pronouncements in Latin, while being followed by a line of professors wearing paper hats.[9] *The resulting hilarity nonplussed their captors. For the program's organizers, it demonstrated that the routine they were creating was restoring a degree of everyday life. And not only this, but something additional heartened the prisoners. Their lieutenant colonel had persuaded the camp's commandant, Captain Kawakatsu, to allow a prisoner-run police force. Its members saved lives by putting a stop to escapes. Each acted with full awareness of its hidden purpose: "to serve as a storm troop in the event of the Allied Forces' arrival ..."*[10]

Tuesday, 26 May '42

Dear Nel,

What a delightful day today. I just met that [Indonesian "over the fence"] boy who has been with Vogel [a fellow prisoner, and colleague from the

2. Bandung, Java, 1942

Lyceum], and who has told me that you are all well. Oh, how I would like to see Joke walking; but I'm also grateful that I don't have to worry about you and the little ones! Nice to hear that Herman is now also off to that little school. He'll surely enjoy it. Is your mouth still bothering you much now that you've had your upper teeth pulled as well? It's a difficult transition period, isn't it? Calls for eating porridge only, I suppose …

Every evening we have a quarter of an hour's evening service. Very nice, Nel, to have some time for contemplation, to think. I trust that you have also been able to find real support in our belief; otherwise, you would not come through this time so bravely.

To my delight, I also heard via that boy [who carries messages for Vogel] that Mr. Ferning was working in the backyard. Very sensible of you to begin using it as a fruit and vegetable garden.

The church services represented another dimension of the still-fragile order they were creating. As important to him personally, however, was the barest family news. Joke was walking. The European schools were closed,[11] but now Herman was going along with Wim to the clandestine classes taught by their neighbor. If only he were to hear that Freddy had recovered from shellshock …[12]

1 June '42

Dear Nel and children,

Once again it's been a long time since I've written to you. Time passes quickly here in the hospital, possibly due to the regular change of shifts. At times it really is hard, but I believe I can manage it, thanks primarily to the better [hospital] food …

Rations outside the hospital were decidedly less palatable. A talented artist-orderly, Charles Burki,[13] captured the men's sentiment in a drawing: a sheepish prisoner chef stood alongside a daily menu that read "Monday, Rice with soup; Tuesday, Soup with rice; Wednesday, Ricesoup; Thursday, Souprice" … and so on through the week. In an earlier work almost photographic in its realism, Burki had recorded the scene of the executed prisoners still bound to the barbed wire. Viewed surreptitiously in the hospital, his renderings were as critical as the education program to the reconstruction of community.[14]

I gave my first lecture [for preliminary examinations] today, and am quite satisfied. I really hope, though, that my books arrive. Until now nothing received, but effort is being made. I need most of all: Mellor, Modern Inorganic Chemistry; Kruyt, Colloids; and Van Arkel & De Boer, Chemical Bonding as Electrostatic Phenomenon. But beyond these, I can really use almost anything of the kind. I'm so glad that I studied more contemporary chemistry.

The 5th form also started today and I taught ± 15 pupils for an hour. I'm spending 3 hours a week there, 2 hours on an academic level, and 4 hours a week on a refresher chemistry course. If it becomes too much for me, I'll drop the latter. There are also plans for a 4th form high school, combined with a fifth form A.M.S. [intermediate] school …

Well, bye for now! Tomorrow, I have to give my second lecture at the XVth Bat. on "The Structure of Atoms." The first went quite well.

Kisses for you and the toddlers,
Your loving <u>Wim</u>.

P.S. Mother's birthday was on 5 June.

By the time he thought to commemorate it, his mother's birthday was already past. He was losing the points of reference that made up his personal compass. But he was hardly alone. In March, Dutch society in Java had lost contact with the outside world, when the Japanese had all radios known to them "castrated."[15] As of mid-June the Japanese had eliminated Dutch newspapers and only allowed postcards to be composed in Japanese or Indonesian.[16] In the absence of hard facts, for the Dutch hearsay and rumor held sway, gratifying emotional needs.

Burki skewered the phenomenon in a series of related caricatures: one prisoner passed word to another ("Fire in Soerabaia!")[17]; that prisoner to yet another; and so on, in consecutive frames. By the third, wishful thinking took over: Soerabaia [Surabaya] had been bombarded, and the Americans had landed. By the fifth, America had taken all of East Java; shortly thereafter, Middle Java, Semarang, Lembang, and Purwakarta. By the fifteenth frame, the war was over; thus, also the rumor, since this was a statement that no one could possibly believe.

12 June '42

Dear Nel and children,

It is not so easy to take a letter out any more: strict control and "punishments." Well, time will tell! What's more, two people made me happy yesterday, with news of you. First, Vogel, who had long been looking for me, and whom I am hoping to visit tonight, because we didn't have much opportunity to talk. Also, when I returned to my little post in the hospital, an unknown someone had left the information that you were all managing very well. You understand how happy I am with that message!

The "punishments" were often collective. Every POW could be mistreated for a small note tossed over the fence.[18] Sadly, the more he minimized danger to Vogel and the young Indonesian, the more tenuous his relation with the family. His collection of unpassed letters grew. Only the ability to carry on with the lectures helped sustain him.

My lectures on Colloid Chemistry are going well, especially now that I have been able to borrow the little book on the subject by Kruyt. I still have not heard anything about that chest of books. An interpreter tried to inquire at Japanese headquarters, but without result. See if you can get that chest back, Nel!

I would have given the third and last of the series of lectures yesterday, but because of my illness [bacillary dysentery] it was postponed till next week. The fifth form high school is running regularly and well. Altogether, good training in public speaking for me.

Of course, I often think of you all, especially Joke, whom I would so like to see. Yet, I'm so glad to know that you're battling your way through this, Nel, and that under all circumstances you will remain faithful to the interests of our children.

No more than a day later, the very sources of stability he mentioned— the classes and his relationship with the family—seemed threatened with dissolution.

Sat. 13 June '42

Today, it is rumored that we (all prisoners of war) will be moved somewhere else. It will be a road full of difficulty and worries that will separate us until the end of the war. But whatever is torn away we will always rebuild, as well as we can, again and again. And we will do that trusting in God's help and guidance. Surely there will be more than we now know to be grateful for. Don't forget that folded hands make us free: a truly free person is one who can fold his hands, because he has only one Master, whom he follows by his own free choice.

It is now evening and the news has developed as follows: all Indo Europeans [Indonesian Dutch] must go to Cimahi (or close thereby) on foot early tomorrow morning. The Europeans, thus, also Elion, remain here.

The prisoners of mixed parentage were being separated from the Europeans, regardless of their status as Dutch citizens.[19] The indigenous troops, with the exception of the primarily Christian Ambonese and Manadonese, were already removed from the rest, having been released. Much was taken away, but so far not his family—and hopefully, not his teaching.

The owner of the small textbook by Kruyt has taken it back, but Dr. van der Hoeven happened to get another copy, which I can borrow. Whether the lectures and such things will continue, I don't know.

Zonnenberg, who until now had remained outside the camp doing service (with bridges and the like),[20] turned up here yesterday. As I'm stationed in the hospital, I only see him sporadically.

You don't have to worry about me, Nel! You'll be happy to know that Elion and I have become good friends, as have Bakker and I, for that matter. Bakker, however, goes to Cimahi, tomorrow. Pity!

Dear Nel and little ones,   Monday, 15 June '42

Tonight Daan Barends surprised me with the news that he had spoken with Ritie [his wife], and that you and the children were doing fine. Again, you must know how happy I was! Especially Herman is doing well, Daan said. I have a feeling you passed this on in answer to my letter in which I wrote about that dream in which I saw Herman so intensely sad before me …

Yesterday was the sad exodus of the Indo Europeans. There were good friends among them, like Bakker, Vermeer, and Miero Altmann. Nonetheless I prepared myself for the lecture on Colloid Chemistry for Monday and when I arrived in the "lecture hall" this morning, the class could indeed proceed, although the number of students had diminished to about one-third. Only one of the lecturers is gone (Altmann, Organic Chemistry). I can't replace him without a book on Organic Chemistry …

Kisses for our darlings and for you! Your loving Wim.

Gradually, more news emerged. A small group of prisoners with technical backgrounds would join the Indonesian Dutch in Cimahi. The majority would be transferred to Cilacap in Central Java; sadly, with them their valued Lieutenant Colonel Poulus.[21]

Dear Nel, Wim, Herman, Freddy, and Joke!   Thursday, 18 June '42

Moves are in full swing, but we are doing well at not being too alarmed by this. The Depot Battalion and the Air Defense unit were moved this morning, but to where we don't know.[22] When I came to lecture, there were only three students present out of the original sixty. For the time being this and all other instruction has been discontinued.

The large-scale movement of prisoners seemed not to apply to the hospital staff. Nel might not need hover on the street to detect his departure, as so many women did now. Reportedly, at least one wife who tried to thrust money toward her husband as he passed was severely whipped. The man had no choice but to walk on "because resistance would have meant execution."[23]

We've just heard that the XVth Battalion will leave tomorrow. I saw Vogel and Jurriëns nonetheless. The latter asked me, if possible, to pass the message on to his wife that he was doing all right. Until now, the street complex [part of the camp] (where Toon,[24] Tijl, and Barends live) has still not received orders to depart, and neither have we. There is even a rumor that this hospital and its staff will remain here. That would be great! Only, the lectures and such would be over for me, while they might be resumed at Cimahi or elsewhere. But we are fine here and the chance to see you all is somewhat greater …

Bye for now! Kisses from
husband and father!

2. Bandung, Java, 1942

Dear Nel and children,   Monday, 22 June '42

The nearly unbelievable has happened! Only the hospital has remained, so that I now belong to the few Hollanders [European Dutch prisoners of war] left in Bandung. At the last moment, Toon was transferred to the hospital staff, thanks to his work as a masseur. Great, isn't it! The food is quite decent here. We're in the Depot Battalion barracks. My little room overlooks Van Oldenbarneveldt Street, while the doctors and Toon live in a private house on Sociëteit Street.

The finest thing is that now and then we have to pick up milk at the BMC [Bandung Milk Center].[25] I was there yesterday, but couldn't let you know in time. This Wednesday I'm going again and hope to be able to see you and speak to you, possibly with one of the children. That would be great!

The possibility of proximity to his family in the BMC's familiar surroundings was better luck than he could have hoped for. He might see for himself how they were doing, up close.

Many English and Australians are coming into the 15th Battalion quarters. In addition, we're receiving Ambonese and Manadonese patients.[26] Very busy at times, but also much leisure time. Today, many additional Englishmen arrived, so that we were suddenly faced with another 17 dysentery and malaria patients.

Well, bye now, kisses from Wim.
Until Wednesday!

Two days later, his hopes of a reunion of sorts were realized. And while he had been prevented from saying much in the presence of the Japanese guards, amazingly, limited contact had been allowed!

Dear Nel and youngsters, Wednesday, 24 June '42

How lovely it was this morning to see you all back again. Oh Nel, it has done me so much good to see you and the little ones standing there healthy and well. What a perfect darling Joke was, the way she perched there, crowing for joy on your arm! And how wonderfully well the boys looked, especially Herman. Those eating difficulties really are over now? Fantastic, you hear! I'll be so curious to hear about it all from you later, in detail.

It also struck me how Freddy had become taller! I'm certain he'll grow into a fine boy. In any case, they are all so natural and nice. I enjoyed seeing them so much at the BMC. In fact, I couldn't swallow any of the delicacies, myself, but I did give the youngsters an ice cream, for want of something better. Joke has been really sweet. She was only a little afraid of me in the beginning. Later, she wet on the BMC's chair: something they'll have to accept for our patronage! You also looked well, Nel. I'm sure that your mouth causes you some trouble. It was an unfamiliar sight but only in the beginning. Seeing my bald head [cropped, in the same manner as the other prisoners,' and concealed under a required cap] would surprise you too.[27] I do hope that you won't have to wait much longer…

Dear Nel and children, Bandung,   30 June '42
Depot Battalion,

Last week, the writing didn't go well, perhaps because in the back of my mind I had hoped to see you fairly regularly and talk. Unfortunately, there was a hitch somewhere, and we [I] may just have to be glad to be staying here in Bandung. I had so hoped to see you on Freddy's birthday! We will again have to "make the best of it"! I've picked up quite a mouthful of English from the Australians here, haven't I?

Great that I received Prins' booklet on Physics from you, Nel. I'm working through it systematically: plenty of reading matter, and work too. It's a pity that the really productive work of giving lectures has stopped. I did that with all my heart and soul! I may continue putting these lectures together, regardless of whether I give them or not. But as a matter of fact, the mental excitement is gone …

Goodbye for now! Now that I have seen you again I can better visualize how things are going in our big living room. Many kisses and God bless, your <u>Wim</u>.

The news as of the twenty-ninth of June hardly renewed his hopes. All Dutch males "with the exception of those who … demonstrated their loyalty and obedience to the Japanese authorities" were to be interned. Perhaps more ominous, "no measures of any kind [would] be taken against women and children and, indeed … consideration [was] being given to providing protection for them."[28] Clearly, the displacement of large segments of Dutch Indies society was far from over. Everyone had family members they were worried about. With the rest of the hospital staff, he tried to focus on "normal life." This morning's water fight between two fellow orderlies was a positive sign. In their own words (and to the consternation of the guards), Gribnau and Boon were "like naughty boys" who "soaked each other and had a romp."[29]

Dear Nel and little ones,   1 July '42

Today is our wedding day. Seven years already, Nel. We've known sad and very happy days. These days put us seriously to the test. The separation makes me very sad but it will also cause us to recover happiness in a purer form. My great fear is only that our family will not be spared poverty.

Toon and our little group of six living together here congratulated me. I treated them to a packet of cigarettes and oranges. Contact with the outside world has again been made more difficult. I happen to belong to the chosen ones allowed to go outside on regular daily duty, on the condition that I won't try to make the slightest "contact." So I will not be able to congratulate you on Freddy's third birthday. Pity. Yet, I will celebrate it here, of course. Again and again, I remember how the five of you were standing there at the BMC. That jubilant Joke, you know! And I could see that Herman was doing very well! Fine, Nel!

Dear Nel and youngsters,   4 July '42

Yesterday was Freddy's birthday. A pity we did not see each other, but I did remember it here. Among other things, I treated with sausages. I asked a man

2. Bandung, Java, 1942

on outside duty to order a cake, and heard that he succeeded. I hope that you feasted on it in good health and <u>with joy</u>. We also had something nice here, because Elion baked cookies. Really delicious!

This morning we were not allowed through the gate to set out for Bekude the butcher with Dr. Pruis' outside duty party. We'll try again in a few days. I'm working hard on the book by Prins and on learning Japanese.

Some among his compatriots associated study of their captors' language with fifth column activity. For Lindeijer the scientist, acquiring new knowledge that could assist with rational grasp of his surroundings only made sense. The blind, irrational authority associated with the camp administration doubtless resided with absent policy makers. Certain of the camp staff aligned themselves with its rule of fear, but a number were simply characterized by otherness that merited an effort to decipher: What was it, for instance, about the Dutch tendency to find humor in the severest of circumstances that so confounded the camp guards?[30] And how had it been possible for Poulus to negotiate even with Kawakatsu?

Dear Nel and little ones,   8 July '42

... Today I went to Bekude again, but contact is not really possible. No matter, so long as I know that you and our children are fine. About 900 Europeans [Dutch troops] from Yogya [Yogyakarta, in south central Java] arrived here this morning. Some of them were acquaintances of Toon. The hospital here is overflowing. Very busy!

                               Bye, kisses from husband
                               and father!

He chose not to write of the foraging difficulties on the fifteenth. One of their party suffered a beating over some silly matter concerning a note and a lady's purchasing cigarettes. Back inside the camp gate, each of them, Dr. Prius excepted, received a light bayonet stroke on the head. According to one of the men, "Only Boon bled."[31]

Dear Nel, Wim, Herman, Freddy, and Joke,   16 July '42

How are all of you? I trust that you are still on the best of terms with each other! The photo of Nel + array of children lies in front of me. How glad I am to have that, complemented by the memory of that morning at the BMC. How dearly I would love to cuddle Joke, if only once. Nice that everything continues to be fine! Here everything is fine too. I study regularly ... Now and then, we go on forage duty, but making "contact" is too risky. Toon is doing fine too.

He continued to buoy himself up when off-duty with technical studies; that is, until the series of deaths. The week prior to the twenty-third of July, two English youths, De Lange and Davies, and a Canadian, James, gave up the ghost. A fellow orderly exclaimed, "These boys have no resistance ...

*left; Davies was twenty years old!"*³² *Ominous in the background, Japanese bombers and fighters thundered over their heads.*

Dear Nel and toddlers,   Sunday, 26 July '42

    The day before yesterday I suddenly spotted you on Riouw street. Wonderful that you came. I don't know who tipped you off. Did you have to wait long? Great that you could signal that everything was going fine at home. It will become difficult because of the extra strain on you. Oh Nel, with all my heart, I wish you the strength to get through this time and to raise our little darlings. I trust that you and the children will always be able to find genuine joy and gratitude.

    All goes well [here]. But studying often goes by the wayside because of so many little jobs to be done. We sleep six men in a little room: with two bunk beds of three tiers each. A curious mix of individuals. In one of our sleep stacks there are, from bottom to top, a diamond dealer, a lithographer, and a lecturer; and in the other, an insurance agent, a law student, and an Institute of Technology graduate.

    We sell coffee in turns. This way we eat well and spend next to nothing. I've agreed with Dr. Pruis that I'll join the forage duty party once every four days, because once every other day is too often. It takes so much time, you see …

Dear Nel and children,   4 August '42

    Despite everything, it was still a day of celebration for me yesterday [on his birthday], particularly because of your caring! How wonderful, there in Riouw Street: all of you with beautiful clean suits on, and in a cheerful mood. You positioned everyone so strategically that I could enjoy seeing you for some time without attracting attention. What a sturdy boy little Wim has become. Because of such things I feel the absence of family togetherness painfully; but we both know and understand this sorrow, Nel!

    Herman searched the queue so hopefully and suddenly his little face lit up when he discovered me. Herman and Freddy look really well! And Joke, too, joins in for 100%, doesn't she? What a cheerful little slip of a girl! She waves so spontaneously with her little arm! And what an additional surprise to see you all again near the BMC. It's too bad you had to wait such a long time there. Through the side window I could still see Freddy frequently running back and forth, and could also continue to see you with Joke.

    Coming outside, I feared disaster, but luckily everything went well, and I still could see you all clearly. It was a good thing that you left from the butcher's shop, though, as a Chinese boy was beaten and handcuffed there by the Japanese guard for failure to have a vendor's license…

    I don't need anything here. For the time being, enough study books. Too many books increase the risk in case of a removal. Kisses for all of you from husband and father.

                                                     Until I see you again.
                                                     Your <u>Wim</u>!!

PS: Today is the birthday of Dr. Smits, our chief of staff. He received a nice drawing of himself in the lab, and we decorated the bedpans and urinals with flowers!

The artist, of course, was Burki, who outdid himself with the "nice drawing."[33] The good doctor stood amid bedpans and urinals, removing "something" from a bedpan with a pair of tongs. Merriment and hilarity ruled the day—even as the roundup of men and boys was underway outside.[34]

7 Aug. '42 We had a great walk this morning, didn't we! It was almost as though I was able to walk with you. That delightful darling, Joke! Such a very cute child, she is! And Wim, so sturdy on his scooter. It must have been repaired again recently. The guard indicated that I could speak with you, but Dr. Pruis had rather we didn't. It would seem that today of all days some fresh difficulties developed about the forage duties. Time will tell how serious it is. Bye for now. Kisses for all!

During off-hours, they continued their emphasis on "everyday" activities. A team of orderlies played soccer with a team of duty officers (0–0). In chess competitions between nationalities, Holland beat England, and both England and Holland beat Australia. At bridge, the Dutch shone again, as the orderly Gribnau played with one of the Yogyanese, "and won from the Australians with an eighty points' margin."[35]

Dear Nel and youngsters! Sunday evening,   9 August '42
For the first time, Pruis's forage duty did not go outside today. The necessities were brought in by the suppliers. It would be a great pity if the duty were not continued. It does seem, though, that just about anything is allowed to be brought in…
Many sirens today, weren't there?! Probably tests, just like those searchlights in the evening. For the first time, all lamps have to be shaded tonight. Let's keep our courage, Nel! Whatever may become of the world, we'll surely be able to have a modest little place to work and be happy! Bye! Kisses from Wim…

Tiring of competition, on the sixteenth of August, the Dutch hospital staff hosted what was billed as a "rapprochement meal" with the prisoners from Yogyakarta and a few from the other nationalities. Since "just about anything" could be brought in (so long as they paid for it out of their own pockets), the meal took the form of a rijsttafel—the celebratory Dutch banquet created from the multi-ethnic dishes of the Indonesian archipelago. Some seventy prisoners attended, each of whom contributed fifty cents. Five without money came by virtue of the charity of others. For the evening they were "at home again" in the Indies, feasting with undisguised pleasure on an array of spices and flavors.[36]

Koninginnedag 1943 (Queen's Day 1943), Charles Burki drawing (Collection Museon-Omniversum, The Hague).

That had been two weeks prior. Today, on the thirty-first, they marked the birthday of Wilhelmina, the Netherlands' queen in exile, with festivities that were necessarily covert. As early as April, expressions of patriotism had been forbidden. A radio announcer who played a recording of the Wilhelmus, the Dutch national anthem, had suffered beheading.[37] Thus, celebrating by stealth became an all the more marvelous achievement. At eight a.m. roll call, every Dutch prisoner appeared exceptionally well turned out. A festive mood pervaded the camp, including the laundry area (well-noted by Burki in a drawing).[38]

Patients in the hospital and regular prisoners received special foods by virtue of funds from a group kitty. "Especially the English and the Australians" were surprised, one of the Dutch reported, "about the way we celebrate our queen's birthday. They promised never to forget 31/8."[39] Not incidentally from Lindeijer's view, the thirty-first of August was Nel's birthday too.

Dear Nel, boys and Joke,   31 Aug. '42

How I would love to help make this day into a real celebration! One cannot prepare one's own birthday, that, of course, should be done by others. Yet, I imagine that the children will be dressed in their Sunday best, and I hope that you all will enjoy feasting on the fancy little cakes I ordered in a circuitous way some time ago. Whether such a thing comes off, one doesn't know for sure, of course! But in any case, Nel, in spirit an extra birthday kiss, with the heartfelt wish that in this new year of your life we may see the day on which we can resume the care of our family together. Perhaps in a few weeks I'll be joining a forage party again and we'll have a chance to see each other.

2. Bandung, Java, 1942

[Handwritten letter in Dutch, dated 31 Aug. '42]

Letter entry on 31 August '42, Nel's birthday and the Netherlands' Queen's Day (Lindeijer Family Archive).

In Holland they will be very anxious about our fate. I'm afraid that it will take some time before contact with Holland is possible. In any case, the post-war world is likely to look quite different. Even then, I trust that we'll be able to find a little place for our family, although the circumstances will surely become more difficult... From my heart, wishing you all the best and lots of love from your husband and father, Wim

Dear Nel and children, Sunday, 6 Sept. '42

A few days ago, I heard from Dr. Pruis that the cakes arrived in good order on 31 August. Now, that is nice. The youngsters can feel that their father is still thinking of them …

As you know, there are about 800 Europeans here from Yogya. At the request of some of them, I'll give 2 courses: one on Technical Chemistry and one on Modern Chemistry. Then the course on Colloid Chemistry is still pending. Thus, as you can see, there is work to be done.

This morning I went to church as usual, with De Koch and Van Leeuwen. Well, people, wishing you all the best and lots of love from your husband and father.

A kiss from <u>Wim</u>.

Reports of an incident that occurred while he was in "church" underscored the prisoners' coping via humor: the hospital's chief orderly had run into the so-called pharmacy, exclaiming "[Please] let someone give me some cigarette paper; the English [and the] Australians are now busy smoking their bibles." In the absence of such paper, the patients were making the most of what was available. The episode generated considerable amusement. Hearing the story later in the afternoon, the Australian Pastor Cameron pulled a small "bible" out of his pocket, proclaiming it also "very suitable to the purpose."[40]

My darling Nel and children, Wednesday, 30 Sept. '42

Though I did delay writing for a while, how often you've been in my thoughts! And now tomorrow is Herman's birthday. I'm so very sorry that I can't provide little cakes this time, because all contact is broken. But surely you'll arrange for something special, Nel! I managed, with a lot of trouble, to get a place on the forage party for tomorrow morning, but it would be quite coincidental if we should see each other.

It also seems that rules are sternly enforced these days. My little life here has become different—I no longer serve in the coffee stand [to earn pocket money], and therefore miss out on the tasty extra dishes in the evening. On the other hand, I have more time for my own plans now, outside of hospital working hours. As first priority, I'll try to learn English sufficiently well to fit right into an English-speaking country. Van der Velden, an English language teacher from Yogya, is teaching me; kind, isn't he!

I'm teaching Elementary Chemistry to Australian officers. In addition, the lessons in Technical and Theoretical chemistry (two hours a week each) have been going on for three weeks. The latter are for the Yogyanese, about 50 in all. I do this with pleasure, and those few small books I have are a great help to me.

Finally, I've started to learn Latin. I couldn't pass up the chance. Terbraak, the dean of the middle school in Yogya, offered to teach me and someone else. You know how I've wanted to learn Latin for a long time, and it's also great fun. The pace is very fast. We follow the normal Lyceum [high school] curriculum…

2. Bandung, Java, 1942

I forgot to tell you, I think, that the course for medical attendants (certification for the "Silver Cross" [with Red Cross equivalency]) has been in session for a few weeks. In total, I take 12 hours of instruction per week and give nine hours myself. Plenty of work, isn't there! Well darlings, best wishes and kisses from husband and father.

Your loving <u>Wim</u>.

His enjoyment of the activities he described was to be short-lived. At five-thirty the next morning, he and eight other medics were awakened abruptly and told to be ready to leave for Cimahi. Setting out on foot for the railway station with nearly three hundred of the group from Yogyakarta, they took no more than they could carry in one suitcase and a laundry bag.

From the station, they indeed embarked for Cimahi. Upon arrival they found this to be merely a stop for the addition of cars and seven hundred more prisoners from the camp there. Their journey continued in the direction of Batavia [Jakarta], and its harbor. The outcome he had hoped to avoid since spring—removal from Java—seemed unavoidable.[41]

News of the transport spread with lightning speed in spite of the hour. Dutch women "laid siege" at the crossings and stations, looking for loved ones.[42] *(Who was it who said that if only the Dutch women had been defending Java, the Japanese would have been defeated?)*[43] *The POWs shouted messages and cheers. Everyone knew something epochal was happening. Neither group might see the other again.*

Disembarking at Batavia in the afternoon, they first walked then climbed a number of slopes to reach a Chinese minority school taken over by the Japanese. Among the thousand or more prisoners already there, he and his group of eight found two additional Red Cross medics. Conditions were overcrowded and unhygienic: too many people, and too little water for washing. Recognizing a need, they set up a rudimentary sick bay, treating cases of dysentery with medicine they brought with them and Epsom salts scavenged from the school's chemistry classroom.[44]

[Tiong Hoa Hwe Koan
School Batavia]

My darling Nel and children, 1 October '42

In spirit, I congratulate my dear Herman on his fifth birthday. I hope that he may become a fine boy! One with a good character. How often I have that slight little fellow in mind! Nel, you will make it a day of celebration for him, won't you! Alas, I could not arrange anything, but what is worse: we left for Batavia [Jakarta] today, so an end to the shopping duty. We are sitting in a Chinese school, presumably not for long. On the way to Batavia, I saw Cathrientje Plas.

The encounter with his former student had been amazing good fortune. At one of the out-of-the-way stations where he and the others were being herded between trains, he caught sight of her searching the crowd for her fiancé. Passing her on the platform, he asked that she convey word to his wife: he believed that he was being taken to Japan. The message home might be his last for the rest of the war.[45]

How long will we remain separated, and how much sorrow remains in store for us? Despite that, let's keep courage and put our trust in God's guidance and care! Bye now! Kisses for all from husband and father and a special one for our Herman on his birthday!

Bye! Your <u>Wim</u>.

Dear People, 11 October '42

We've been in the "Tiong Hoa Hwe Koan" school for ten days already, and are busy packing for removal to—no one knows where. Bye! Kisses for all from father and <u>Wim</u>.

On the evening of the tenth, he and three others from his group of medics received an order to be ready to leave the following morning. By some obscure rationale, they were members of a group of five hundred selected for departure.[46] *The letters he had been unable to pass to his family were to become his diary. The scarcity of paper that caused him to use every line on both sides of a page proved a blessing in disguise: the entire package fit into the false double bottom of his field bag. Tucked securely between its sheets were the two photographs; the photograph of Nel and the children now more than ever his lodestar.*

3

Transport Overseas, 1942—"The Most Horrible Thing"

The five days since Lindeijer's 11 October departure from the Chinese school had been characterized by uncertainty and, frustratingly for him, the impossibility of writing. With the three others from his group of medics, he had walked early that morning, part of the five hundred being sent elsewhere, to Batavia's Bei Glodok Prison, where on arrival he'd narrowly escaped detection during an inspection for weapons that also included "papers with writing." Thereafter, he and the three colleagues had been held in confinement with eighty-some of the others in a nine-by-fifteen-meter cell; the only exceptions were periods when the entire five hundred were moved outside for further inspections, and what seemed endless counting of prisoners for reasons they feared related to likely transport overseas.

Their removal on the 16th with the rest of the five hundred by train to the city's harbor only served to confirm this—yet with an added revelation that conditions on the ship they had now boarded made undeniably clear: they were to be human cargo. Cargo, they could only hope, with a degree of value. Joined by an additional seventeen hundred prisoners at the dock, they lay virtually on top of one another in tiers of shelves in the ship's suffocating holds; the only air from a single center hatch of each hold up to the main deck.[1]

Dear wife and children   17 October '42

This time I'm writing on board an old Japanese troop transport ship [the *Tofuku Maru*].[2] What we have feared for so long has happened: we are to be carried far away, and it will be a sad separation for us until the bitter end of the war. What parental happiness will be lost to us! Yet I hardly dare think of the scene of our future reuniting. How will it be then? I do trust that you'll brave this, Nel. Perhaps it's fortunate that you have such excellent teaching qualifications. But what a heavy burden all this will be for you!

From that Chinese school, we were taken to Glodok Prison in Batavia, where some two thousand British were already held. Yesterday, after a rigorous inspection (owing to which I almost lost this letter), we had to pack and then go to Priok [Tandjong Priok] Harbor and embark: the fate we had feared most since 1 October. Luckily, I've found some good friends here. A great comfort: "Amicitia vitam ornat" ["Friendship adorns life"], my Latin lesson says. Bye for now! Kisses from <u>Father</u>.

He wrote with some difficulty in the hold's faint electric lighting. The act of writing provided distance from the circumstances he was writing about and placed him within the context of his family. Nel might find it possible to band together with friends in the same manner he had with Wim Gribnau and Jür Stenfert,[3] fellow Red Cross medics from his Bandung Fifteenth Battalion camp, two of the three from the Chinese school, who were berthed near him onboard.

19 Oct. '42 We lie at anchor just outside Singapore. It is very warm in the overcrowded holds: a small old transport ship with 2200 prisoners. Tomorrow morning we have to pack and disembark.

<u>Thurs. 22 Oct</u>. Dear Nel and youngsters, That 19 October, we remained lying in the suffocatingly hot and dirty holds. The next morning: disembarkation and loading onto trucks in groups of 50. One could see clearly how Singapore had suffered from the bombardment!

We are now sitting in the former British barracks on the Strait of Johor (to the north of Singapore Island) [actually, the northeast end]. Concrete buildings. Beautiful view. Sleeping on concrete. Plenty of muscle aches, little sleep. I don't think we'll be here long. Bye for now! Kisses from father and husband! Your loving <u>Wim</u>.

Taken over by the Japanese, the immense former British Army post stretching roughly eight kilometers north to south, and three east to west, had become a staging area for the distribution of thousands of prisoners of war to work projects throughout the Pacific. The red armbands they had received in Batavia apparently identified them as technically skilled and bound for the Japanese mainland,[4] likely by an old troop ship like the derelict that brought them from Java—unmarked by Red Cross insignia, and thus subject to Allied attack.[5]

Despite its hardships, the Changi camp seemed preferable to a long voyage on a crowded and filth-laden vessel. Suffering from dysentery, Lindeijer had begun requesting a move to the camp hospital, hoping to make inquiries about joining the staff there, along with Gribnau and Stenfert.

[Roberts Hospital, Changi] <u>Sat. 24 Oct</u>. '42 This morning, I transferred to the British Hospital. There are 3,000 sick in a camp of 4,000. I have dysentery. The care is very good, I believe. I already feel myself improving.

[*Tofuku Maru*, Singapore] Thurs. 29 Oct. The hospital was disappointing. Luckily, I still have some [medicinal] powders, myself. We (Gribnau, Stenfert, and I, a good group) have now been back on that ship (about 5,000 tons) for two days already, together with 1200 hundred English, Americans, Australians, and Dutch [prisoners], and 1,000 Japanese. Fearfully hot. Waiting for convoy.

3. Transport Overseas, 1942

Map of Southeast Asia. De Jong, Louis. *The Collapse of a Colonial Society: The Dutch in Indonesia during the Second World War* (Leiden: KITLV Press, 2002. Xi).

> I keep thinking of how it will be when I come back to you. Bye! Kisses from father and husband! Wim.

Fear of another transport had given way to fear that his friends might be moved without him. Pressing for early release, he managed to return to the barracks to join them—and not any too soon. By noon on the twenty-seventh of October they were once again loaded on trucks and headed back to the Singapore docks to re-embark.[6]

An elaborate delousing procedure temporarily raised hopes of sailing under improved conditions this time, on a reasonable vessel. However, within hours, they learned otherwise. Their transport was to be on the same ship that brought them to Singapore,[7] despite its not having been cleaned properly after their first voyage.

Scuttlebutt was that a British major's protest over its "absolutely filthy" condition had gone entirely unheard.[8] And when, during the two-hour embarkation process, some among their number resisted the order to descend into the already crowded holds, they had been driven in by brute force, at the point of the commander of the guards' sword.[9]

<u>Monday, 2 Nov.</u> We left Singapore on 30 October. We may be going to Saigon. It's getting better now that the heat is over. Bye, kisses from Wim!

The space he shared with three others, this time in the back of the ship, was insufficient to lie down at full length, and barely allowed sitting up. His predominantly Indonesian Dutch group of five hundred (apparently, the majority of those who boarded the train at Cimahi),[10] with a handful of European Dutch officers and medics like himself, was packed into what he could only surmise to be a lower deck of the first after hold. The British, because of their numbers, were likely to be in the same hold, though not so far down. Their total of more than six hundred would have meant overflow into the second, smaller after hold. Most likely, in this same smaller hold, at a level similar to his own, the combined group of eighty or so Americans and Australians slept as the Dutch did—on top of the bauxite cargo.[11]

Formerly allies in war, they surely needed to be allies now. The ladder up the hatch of the hold Lindeijer was in allowed only single file access to reach an insufficient number of latrines hanging over the starboard side of the main deck. Access from the other after hold was no doubt the same. The hatch was also the opening through which their food was lowered in buckets three times a day. They could ascend to the main deck only by permission, which at times was denied.[12] And in any case, despite the ladder's being mounted on a bulkhead, for anyone weakened or ill, the distance from the lower hold to the main deck amounted to a precarious climb.

Dear Nel, boys and Joke, Wednesday, 4 Nov. '42

We lie idle on the Saigon [Mekong] river, close to the city. At least something to see. Yesterday, we lay near a beautiful little French island [Cape St. Jacques] with engine trouble, owing to which we lost our convoy. We are doing relatively well, but the food is bad, and bathing nearly impossible. Today I just managed to grab a small bowl of water: my first "bath" in a week.

In small numbers at a time, they had been allowed freer access to a cramped area of the main deck aft the bridge, between the latrines on one side of the hatches and the so-called "kitchen" on the other.[13] Yesterday's abrupt departure of their convoy of three to four other POW ships and an old oil tanker had been disturbing,[14] as had the slow progress of their disabled vessel making its way upriver this morning. Within proximity of the city, however, the distraction of new surroundings outweighed their concerns over the condition of the ship's boiler. The Americans from Texas, in particular, had been cheered by the sight of a familiar red and white Texaco sign at a bulk oil plant near the spot where they anchored.[15]

A number of these Americans from the USS Houston, along with Australians from the HMAS Perth, had performed brilliantly in the Battle of the Java Sea, only to have their ships torpedoed while attempting to escape through Sunda Strait. Those who survived the ships' explosions had been captured after swimming to Java, or while still floating about at sea. The soldiers from Texas, he'd learned, were part of an army unit that had been on the ground in Java. There were also British and Australian army troops on board—the Australians from "Blackforce," the formation under Brigadier Arthur Blackburn, with which the Texans had been allied. And British and Australian air force personnel: RAF members who fled south just before the fall of Singapore, and Australians from an RAAF squadron who had been captured in Java by the first days of March.[16]

In this present instance, the Americans' cheer was largely bravado, however. Virtually none among the prisoners failed to recognize the crisis they faced. Their food, never adequate, had initially included at least a few vegetables with a small ball of rice; now the rice was accompanied by watery soup with little dried fish. Water was rationed to a half canteen cup a day, with none for bathing. He had "grabbed" his small bowl by collecting steam from taps on the winches, in secret.[17] Most alarming, in the holds, men lay in spaces some forty-five to fifty centimeters wide, with virtually no room to turn over at night.[18] Conditions had worsened drastically. The first cases of acute diarrhea had broken out yesterday.[19] To change focus, he turned back to addressing the family.

> I'm more generous with paper again, aren't I? That's because I received a blank exercise book from a good neighbor. We're helping here as much as we can with a makeshift clinic. How is Wim doing in second grade? I have every confidence that you will get through this, Nel. That is a great comfort for me.

Yet, thoughts of the family in context of an episode earlier in the day called for a pause and discussion with Gribnau and Stenfert. One of the two Indonesian Dutch doctors, Lieutenant Lutter, had requested that an RAF corporal by the name of Allan be removed to a hospital in the city; otherwise, the man would surely die. The request was denied: "I am sorry, but let him die."[20] Appalled, and struck with the increasing precariousness of the situation, the three medics decided on an exchange of addresses that might later allow them to contact one another's families. He had asked them to inscribe their information at the point of his unfinished entry.[21]

H.V.A. [Compagnie]
W.G. Gribnau
Ond. Tindjowan, Sei. Bedjankar S.O.K.

J.H. Stenfert
Ond. Dol. Sinsembah Perlanaän, S.O.K.

Both had fears for a wife left at home, and a child, or children, who might forget them—Gribnau, a small son and daughter, and Stenfert, a one-year-old son.[22] *Finding words for their common ordeal helped restore equanimity. Before putting the notebook away, he completed the day's entry.*

Herman is surely still going to pre-school. I'm wondering if he'll find a good little friend. How I would dearly love to play with the children again! Freddy would join in nicely, I think. No doubt Joke is walking like anything now and giving you a few headaches, Nel! I do so hope that you can stay in our house. Bye for now!

Kisses from father and <u>Wim</u>.

Dear Nel and youngsters,   Sunday, 8 November '42

We left Saigon the day before yesterday, and yesterday passed that "little island" once more. We're in convoy again, now with 11 ships and 1 destroyer. We had rough weather again last night, about as bad as we had that time on the Indian Ocean. I feel healthy, despite the poor quality food.

We have now been put on regular duty for the care of about 20 sick. Horrendous, for those fellows: little if any medicine, bad bedding, food, and the like.

The rough weather reminded him of his experience en route to Java with Nel—but then the sole menace had been the ocean itself. Now, submarines plied the waters from Indochina all the way up the China coast, and dysentery or something very much like it spread in their hold. The cases so far were British, with a few Dutch. Since the fifth of November, he, Gribnau, Stenfert, and a young British medical orderly named Jimmy Garbutt[23] *had been assisting the Dutch medical officers, Lieutenants Lutter and Van Slooten, during round-the-clock watches.*[24] *But the medicines the two brought on board with them would soon run out, and requests for more had met with refusals.*[25] *The single Japanese doctor confined his efforts to a detachment of returning Japanese troops and the merchant crew, in the areas off-limits to the prisoners, the bridge and forward of the bridge.*[26]

The situation made the summons he'd received the previous evening all the more strange. One of two medics on duty, he found himself taken with little warning to an upper deck of the prohibited world. He nonetheless thought to bring aspirin and bandaging cloth with him as he made his way with the guard up multiple ladders. Reaching the merchant captain's cabin, and recognizing the occupant's need to be examined, he felt a degree of relief. The man suffered from a sexually transmitted disease and was clearly ashamed.

Sensing the awkwardness of the situation, he had done his best with the remedies at his disposal to relieve pain and wrap the afflicted member. When finished, he had been surprised to comprehend, with his limited Japanese, that he could ask a favor. But what favor, without the appearance of collusion? His inspiration had been to ask for a bath—aware of the irony that he would be unable to share this bit of luck with his friends.[27]

Afterward, he was left with a conundrum. The master of this inhuman ship, whose decks and holds aft the bridge were perpetually soiled with slime and human feces,[28] and whose washing facilities were accessible to the Japanese, but denied the prisoners, had allowed him a freshwater bath. This captain, whom his own superior officer, Dutch Captain P.C.F. Meys, had tried to contact without success to lodge complaints,[29] had acknowledged weakness and even shown gratitude. The incident required description in the most guarded terms in his diary.

> Yesterday I had the watch. I hit the jackpot in the evening when I was allowed to take a warm bath with the Japanese as a reward for the medical help we gave them. The ship's crew is a lot more approachable than the soldiers!
>
> My English raincoat, which I received in Bandung, is just the thing for me here. My pajamas, on the other hand, are now threadbare. My thoughts are often with you all. Bye now. Have courage and trust. We are in God's hands. Kisses from husband and father! Your Wim.

> Dear Nel and youngsters,   Saturday, 14 Nov. '42
>
> We are in the vicinity of Formosa [Taiwan], but it seems that we'll be sailing on to Japan. We hope so intensely that the sick can go ashore here, because their situation is horrible. Helping is almost impossible because of the lack of water, medicine, and such. I have night shift soon. Thank God, I am still healthy. Bye for now. My best wishes for all of you! Kisses from father and Wim. Bye!

The RAF corporal, Allan, had died on the ninth of November.[30] Thereafter, one bad piece of news followed another: reports of American submarines nearby, and boiler trouble again, with Japanese in the engine room injured. Toiling along at four knots on the remaining boiler, they lost much of their convoy, including the destroyer.[31] Then, in what seemed an ominous pattern, a Dutch prisoner who died on the thirteenth was sewed into two gunny sacks as Allan had been, with bauxite added for weight. Following a brief prayer by a compatriot, his body slid from a board into the sea. Meanwhile the ship continued at "full" speed.[32]

50 Part I: The Trauma of War

When Allan died, there had been forty-one cases of dysentery.[33] Now it was difficult to keep track. Rough storms kept them awake at night and resulted in seasickness for those not already stricken. All were weak, their food so inedible that for days they had eaten only dry rice. Another of the British died in the early hours of the sixteenth.

On one side of a sheet torn from his notebook and stuffed folded into a

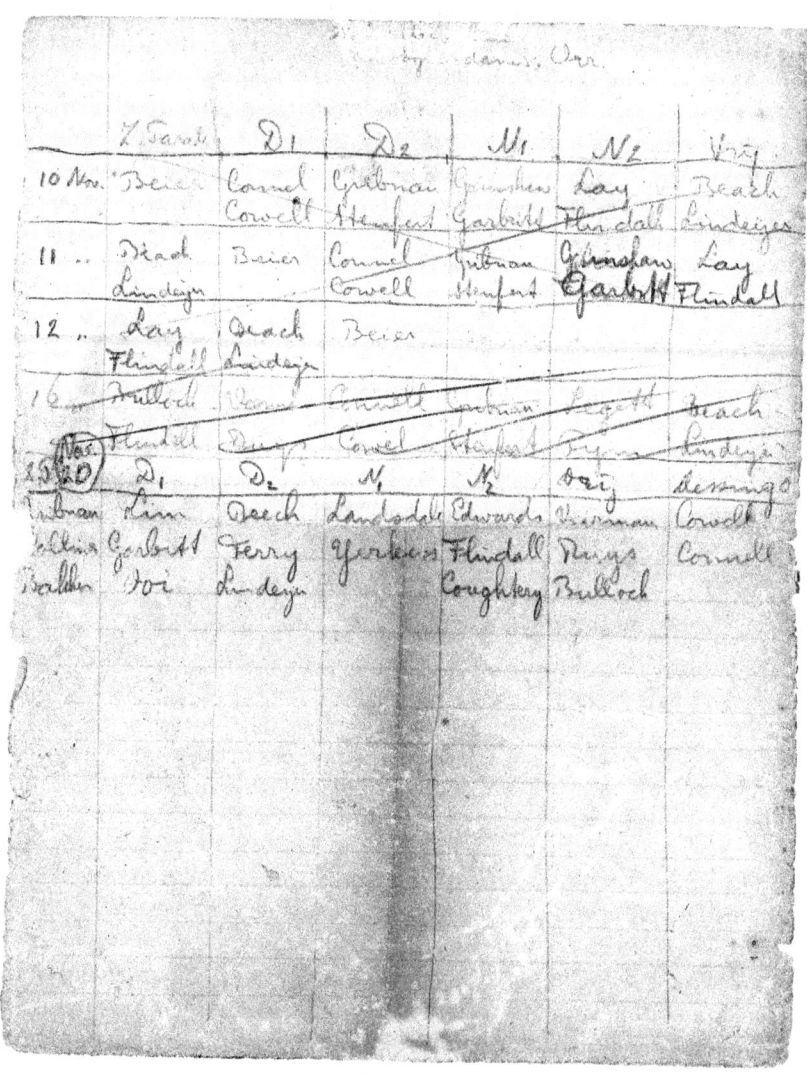

Lindeijer's schedule for the care of the sick on board the *Tofuku Maru* (Lindeijer Family Archive).

3. Transport Overseas, 1942

pocket, Lindeijer kept a schedule for the care of the sick; on the reverse, their itinerary, and the deaths by date.[34]

Monday, 16 Nov. Today, we're sailing into the port of Takao [Kaohsiung] on Formosa. A very beautiful natural harbor and a real sally port for Japan. We're glad to be lying idle after the stormy days at sea. Out of the 1200 prisoners, we have about 160 sick. Perhaps the serious cases will be taken to a hospital

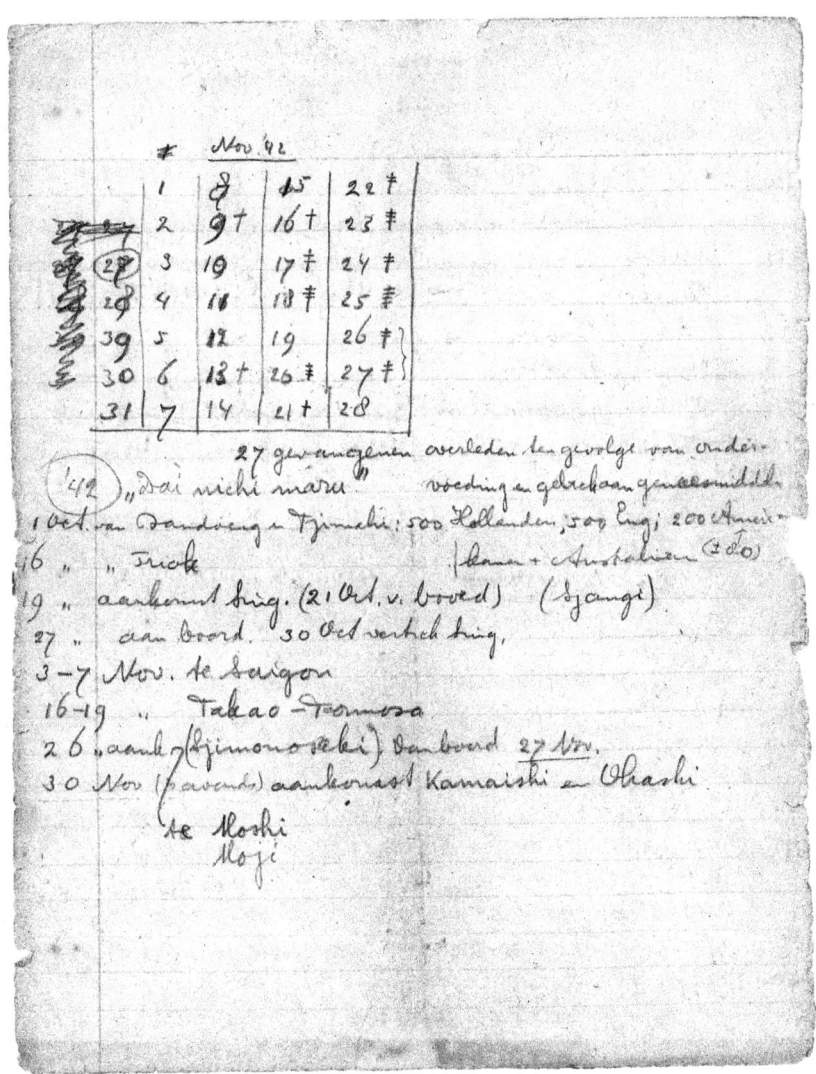

Lindeijer's itinerary of the overseas transport, with deaths by calendar date (Lindeijer Family Archive).

in Takao, and we may get medicines. There have already been three deaths between Singapore and here. Fortunately, the three of us [the Dutch medics] are still in good health and spirits.

While taking care of the sick, I work with an Englishman who is also a lecturer. Once we've arrived in Japan, I hope to work further on my English with his help. Onboard this ship, packed to suffocation, this is hardly possible!

Thurs. 19 Nov. We left Takao this morning and are now anchored at the northern tip (?) of Formosa. Possibly we await convoy. The utter violation of hygiene on board defies all description. No bathing or washing. In Takao we received no medicine! There are now 7 dead [eight, by this date on his calendar]. So-called "medical care" is incredibly difficult and deficient. Luckily, we were able to buy a bunch of bananas (40 cents) for the three of us, and we feel healthy, although really weakened.

Keep your courage up, won't you! How I would love to drop in on you all if only once. It's perhaps better not to think about it too much, as it makes one feel miserable! Now people, in spirit, a kiss for all of you from husband and father! Your Wim.

P.S. Not one of the sick was allowed ashore!

Requests by their officers and the Dutch doctors to have the sickest among them removed to a hospital had met with the same response as before: "I am sorry, but let them die." That was indeed happening, and with overwhelming frequency. The third prisoner death, on the sixteenth, had been followed by two the next day, and three the day after—by which time nearly everyone had dysentery. An American attempt to offer money to have medicines brought on board was refused by the commandant of the Japanese guards.[35] The prisoners could purchase a small quantity of fruit and the equivalent of a spoonful of sugar from the stores of fresh supplies taken in, nothing more.[36]

The collusion rumored to have taken place during the night of the 17th, between a handful of prisoners and a number of the returning Japanese troops, was odd then, if true. The latter, who were distinct from the guards, must have been desperate for vegetables too. How it had come about was unclear: the prisoners had apparently formed a line to steal daikon radishes from the piles of produce loaded onto the docks. A Japanese soldier stood lookout and motioned when the coast was clear. Then the roles had reversed, with the soldiers performing the theft, and a prisoner giving the "all clear." The group from the Houston, where the story originated, swore there was "cooperation there between the two."[37]

Apparently, there were more gray areas than one might have expected in the world forward of the bridge. There was little opportunity to examine the matter, however. By the time they pulled away from Takao, with their repairs complete, already five more of the British and Dutch had died. With the two doctors, Lindeijer's group of medics worked desperately to isolate the worst cases at the back of the British level of their hold, installing wooden casks as latrines for those too severely affected to make the climb topside. Even so, the seriously ill left trails of feces behind.[38] Attempting to help them where they lay, close together and nearly unreachable in their sleeping places, was further agonizing. On the twentieth of November, when their ship left the Formosan coast in a convoy of six transports and a destroyer, he had eleven deaths recorded.

For the remainder of the voyage disease was everywhere, and they as medics were at its epicenter. A day out from Formosa, cold winds and rough seas scattered their convoy,[39] leaving only two other transports visible. Soon after, cases of pneumonia appeared. Adequate isolation became impossible. As more men became ill, they had to lie on the oil cloth covering the hatches, and on the main deck itself.[40] Ultimately, highly infectious patients remained among healthier men in the holds. Not even the relatively less crowded American and Australian quarters were unscathed, on the twenty-second, experiencing the first diphtheria case.[41] The days that followed—continued cold, but with lovely sunshine[42]—had an eerie, spectral quality.

> Wednesday, 25 Nov. Tonight we entered the Bay of Nagasaki. We long to disembark. We are all weak and nearly everyone suffers from diarrhea; I, too, but not seriously. The others are doing most of the work for me. So very kind! The food is dreadful. One time, a Chinese stole fried fish for us. How we regaled in it! The condition of the sick is horrendous. So far 23 have died.
>
> It's becoming pretty cold. Almost no one has adequate clothing, especially the people from Java. The English have much better shoes and more substantial outer clothing. Fortunately, I have riding breeches and a double-thick, woolen Leiden blanket. I sleep with Stenfert under that blanket.
>
> Especially when using the dirt casks, the sick suffer considerably from cold, rain, and the roll of the ship. We as care givers can be of little help in this overcrowded mess, nearly without water or any other means to work with. The filthiness is beyond description! Many lie like pigs in their own excrement. On top of that, only a handful of people are willing to help. Often the "volunteers" don't show up, and we have the greatest difficulty, for instance, in getting food distributed to some 100 non-ambulatory patients out of a total of about 200. Medicine was exhausted long ago, naturally!
>
> At times we manage not to think continually of this misery. Gribnau and Stenfert are a couple of nice, sturdy fellows, both managers of palm oil factories in North Sumatra. Along with a few other chemists, we've agreed to form a professional circle as soon as we arrive at a camp. I succeeded in taking only one book out of Glodok Prison, namely, Crystal Chemistry. I still read from that often.
>
> And thus we wait with calm trust for what the future may bring. In the meantime, we hope intensely for a bath and a good meal. Well, my darlings, I kiss you all heartily, with my very best wishes! Your ever loving husband and father, Wim.
>
> Thur. 26 Nov. We steamed along a beautiful stretch of the Japanese coast.

Many rocky islands. We now lie at anchor at Shimonoseki [more accurately, Moji, across a narrow strait from Shimonoseki], an exceptionally beautiful natural harbor. The Japanese will soon be examining the stool of all prisoners, the same as in Singapore. A truly hypocritical farce. It's possible that we'll be sent to a quarantine station first. Both we and the ship are filthy; lots of cockroaches, rats, etc. Our berth [that of the Dutch medics] happens to be favorably situated against that vermin.

They were suffering from cold and malnourishment, but even more, from the loss of their friends. The British and Dutch had experienced the greatest number of deaths, from dysentery and pneumonia. But the other nationalities mourned also: the Australians, over the loss of two of their officers to diphtheria, and the potential loss of a youth who was unable to swallow; the Americans, over the passing of "Chief Alderman." Harmon Price Alderman, the radioman from the Houston, *was dead from dysentery and exposure, at virtually the moment of disembarkation.*

The news that to date seven Japanese had also died was further sobering—making profoundly bizarre the tale that on the night of the twenty-fourth, prisoners breaking into the ship's storage room found cases of Irish stew.[43] *What sort of authority, they asked themselves, with so many ill and dying would allow stores of food to remain unused?*

Someone, or some agency, had ordered technically skilled POWs brought from Java without reasonable planning, even for wartime. This was hardly the merchant captain or the sergeant major who commanded the guards. Rumor had it that a figure who remained nameless and unseen, a ship's commandant, was the official in charge—while an Army shipping command somewhere, in Hiroshima or Singapore, pulled the strings.[44]

Friday, 27 Nov. About 45 of our sick will be taken to a hospital. Rumor has it that we'll disembark this afternoon or tomorrow. We're longing for better food and water to wash ourselves and our clothes! The number of dead has now risen to thirty [twenty-seven, by the count on his calendar, taken earlier].[45] My diarrhea is a little less serious.

[Ohashi, Japan] Wednesday, 2 Dec. My darling Nel and children, So much has happened during the last few days! There was no time, or rather opportunity, to write in peace. We did indeed disembark that Friday afternoon and stood for an hour in the cold with our baggage on the wharf. The sick stayed on board for the time being. A little later, we walked to a large theater hall, where we received relatively good, although ice-cold food, for the first time (rice and vegetables with some fish in wooden boxes). We feasted!

Then each of us received a pair of discarded army trousers and coat, as if it was already 5 December [the Dutch Sinterklaas festival]! I didn't do too badly, but of course, the clothes are all too small! Then [after walking through a long tunnel or traveling by ferry to the opposite bay, of Shimonoseki],[46] we were guided to the railway station in pitch darkness. Again suffering from the cold.

3. Transport Overseas, 1942

Finally, on the train, we struck it lucky: a third class carriage with springs in the seats, and backrests. We left at midnight. We didn't sleep much, since we were sitting virtually on top of one other. In the morning, we looked, keenly interested, at the mountainous landscape, with rice paddies and bamboo, yet so strongly European, especially because of the pine trees and poor soil. We then heard that we would be sitting on this train for two days and three nights! You can imagine how miserable that made us, notwithstanding the small packets of cold rice and vegetables. Occasionally, we received warm "tea."

We passed through Kobe and Osaka, among other places, and the next night also Tokyo. Enormous cities, with only limited blackout. Factories everywhere. Also, a lot of new building.

We still didn't know what the Japanese wanted with us. We were split into three groups. We [Gribnau, Stenfert, and Lindeijer] ended up in the smallest, consisting of about 100 Dutchmen (nearly all Indo-European) and about 100 English, Americans, and Australians. This group would get off [the train] first. The others [including Captain Meys][47] would go on to camps in the more northern islands. A pity, these split-ups! Fortunately, Gribnau, Stenfert, and I stayed together. The other chemists disappeared.

Monday morning we finally stepped off [at Morioka]. Alas, only to board another train, from which we emerged only late that evening.[48] Yelled at by a mass of people (we continually attracted attention), we walked with our baggage, at the end of our resources, to the barracks where I now sit and write.

Fortunately, the bedding is all right here: mats on which there is a very thin straw mattress, then three ordinary blankets and one quilted. So that's plenty. It's also desperately needed, because there is virtually no heating. Today: 10° C [50° F] inside and 5° C [41° F] outside.

The sick, who have cropped up again in the interim (among others, Stenfert now suffers from a severe attack of dysentery) are somewhat better cared for. Today a Japanese doctor came and also had medicines delivered. We are again helping as best we can. The sick are getting porridge, and our food is also relatively good. Today, we even had Japanese noodles.

This land is a curious mixture of Eastern and western landscapes. During that last train trip, we went along a rugged mountain landscape with magnificent snow-covered peaks. Also saw Mount Fujiyama. With my Japanese, I could at times be of good service.

I almost lost this letter yesterday, during a rigorous inspection. I do so hope to be able to one day put it in your hands, Nel.

Thanks to the better food, the rest, and sleep, we slowly feel our strength recovering. We are all badly emaciated. How I would dearly love to have a pair of woolen socks, gloves, underwear, and watertight shoes.

Anyway, we can now wash our clothes in ice-cold water and sometimes warm ourselves at a tiny little stove. Last night, I even had a warm communal bath. Delightful! The first since the one near Saigon. Now I'm going to slip under my fine woolen blanket and remain there for a little while, thinking of you all. In spirit, a kiss for all! All the best wishes, you hear! Your husband and father, Wim.

Thousands of miles from Java, in a camp in a remote mountain village on northeast Honshu, he remained determinedly positive, at the same time keeping alive the memory of lost colleagues. Nearly fourteen months later, when directed by the camp authorities to report on his experiences in the war, he made use of the opportunity to shed light on the horrendous transport. In a voice that was civil yet uncompromising, he spoke for those whose lives he had tried to save, who could no longer speak for themselves.[49]

Name E.W. Lindeijer No. 121
Rank PRIVATE
Unit DUTCH ARMY JAVA (XVth Bat., BANDOENG)[50]

When the Japanese landed on Java, I was at that moment attached to the XVth Battalion of the Dutch East Indies Army, stationed at Buitenzorg [Bogor]. Two days afterward, we tried to retake the aerodrome of Kalijati. We were repelled [at Kalijati] and retreated to Cimahi. From there we were brought to new positions near Lembang, where we lay until our army capitulated. In both actions we were bombed continuously throughout the daytime and I never saw one Allied plane in the air. This fact [the bombing] was a significant drawback. It slowed every movement of our battalion and cut off our food supply.

From the 8th of March '42 to the 1st of October '42, I was a prisoner of war in Bandung. The first three months of the treatment was bad: we were crowded together in dirty barracks and the food was very poor, notwithstanding the abundance of food in that part of Java. There was also a lack of medicine.

My most terrible experience, however, came when we were transported to Japan. We started that [journey] on the 1st of October '42, and after several days of delays in Batavia [Jakarta] and Singapore, arrived the 30th of November '42 in Ohashi. Especially during the voyage from Singapore to Japan, the treatment was very bad. We were really starving, because the food was nearly inedible: a poor kind of rice with nothing else worth mentioning. Many men got sick, but we had virtually no medicine.

The two Dutch doctors could do nothing. They asked to bring the sick men ashore when we arrived at Formosa [Taiwan], but the Japanese commander refused. Also, medicines were refused. Even disinfectants were only given in very small amounts, although a dangerous and infectious type of diarrhea—perhaps dissentery [*sic*]—spread over the ship.

The men grew weaker and weaker. Several hundreds were attacked by different diseases. Nevertheless, we were compelled to work in the machine room in groups at nighttime, carrying coal, etc. Many times men were cruelly beaten.

Another trouble was the shortage of clothes and blankets. We left Java in tropical tunic, unaware of what the future should bring. Most of us had only one or two blankets. Between Formosa and Japan it grew quickly colder and the men were freezing. It was probably pneumonia that caused the death of several men. A diagnosis, however, was difficult to perform without the help of instruments, even a thermometer. Neither the Japanese doctor nor anybody else of the Japanese on board cared for the sick prisoners.

3. Transport Overseas, 1942

Drinking water or water for washing the patients or their utensils was very hard to get, and if possible, always very little. Only seldom was it possible to wash a patient. Since most suffered from diarrhea, it is readily understood that during the last week of the voyage, the patients as well as their sleeping places, clothes, and blankets, were dirty beyond any description.

In a stinking hold, about a hundred of the most severe patients were packed together, frequently shitting in each other's blankets. A dozen small casks were used as WCs [water closets, or toilets]. These, however, were very unsteady, and, during the stormy last two weeks, it sometimes occurred that both cask and patient tumbled over the floor. The slimy, bloody shit [then] covered a great part of the floor, dripping through the cracks between the boards into the area below, upon the heads and blankets of the sleeping men there. Impossible to clean anything. The orderly could only bring the staggering, dirty patient back to his sleeping place. Once, a patient occupying a cask dropped with cask and all into the area below and broke his neck. Only in the last two days the Japanese fixed [stabilized] the casks with rods.

No pen can describe the agony suffered in that hold. To perform a night watch among those moaning, vomiting, shitting, stinking, dying men is the most horrible thing I ever did in my life. I knew several of those patients to be honorable, brave men who did only their duty. However, after [they were] taken prisoners of war, the Japanese treated them worse than scoundrels and murderers. Thirty of them died on board that ship, but many more died after we went ashore, as a result of the bad treatment.[51]

4

Ohashi, Japan, 1942—Between High Mountains, Snow

The prisoners had arrived in Ohashi, a small hamlet approximately fifteen kilometers inland from Japan's northeastern coastal city of Kamaishi, on 30 November 1942. Their last ride, on a narrow-gauge train through snow-covered mountains, had brought them to a camp that was no more than "a new but shabby two-story barn-like building."[1] Its walls—thin boards with a lining of dried mud—had pencil-sized cracks that allowed them to see outside. And notwithstanding freezing temperatures, the few stoves that appeared belatedly the day after they arrived were limited to use at night. In the words of one of their officers, both "the space and the heating left much to be desired according to western understandings."[2] In the days since, the snow had fallen so thickly that from their barracks, backed up against the mountain on the village's north side, they could see only a few meters in front of them.[3] Bereft of their moorings, they were adrift—sealed off by a sea of whiteness in a far corner of the world. Lindeijer's positive tone in his letter written on 6 December was no doubt motivated in part by a desire for optimism in addressing his family even in a letter that he assumed would probably never be sent.

[Ohashi, Iwate Prefecture] <u>6 Dec. '42</u> The last few days I've remained in bed, warm between the woolly blankets, partly because of a cough and pain in my throat, partly because of the cold. Yesterday, my thoughts were often with you. I do hope that you and the children enjoyed a nice Sinterklaas [December 5, St. Nicholas Eve] celebration last night, Nel! Perhaps Wim and Herman made something themselves? (What a wonderful event we had last year, remember?) Or did the [Sinterklaas] costume remain in the cupboard this year? No, let's not be sorry that we purchased it.

I do have regrets, though, about not having been more generous with myself while in the POW camp in Bandung, because I have no use for my fl23.50 [Dutch East Indies guilders] here. Japanese East Indies money can be changed, but alas, I don't have that, and neither do Gribnau and Stenfert.

Apart from this we're doing fine here in the snow, between high mountains.

4. Ohashi, Japan, 1942

We sit here in Kamaishi [sic], 200 of us, surrounded by high-tension wire: 109 English, Americans, and Australians, and 91 Dutch (of which 87 are Indonesian Dutch).[4] Furthermore, an absurd number of soldiers are stationed inside and outside the barracks—a kind of territorial guard, with rifles and fixed bayonets.

In fact, they were located at the Ohashi inland mining component of an iron and steel complex whose coastal hub was in Kamaishi. They were likely replacements for the drafted Japanese, as well as the Korean mine employees, who had inhabited their barracks previously,[5] and as such destined for a role in supplying ore for the blast furnaces of Kamaishi.[6] The article of the Geneva Convention prohibiting their use in war-related or dangerous activity might have little meaning; the articles requiring provision of adequate food, clothing, and medical facilities had been violated repeatedly.

For now, they were glad simply to have a respite, however. Aside from the frigid conditions, sleeping arrangements in the shabby two-story building were compact but adequate. Their remaining officers—the American army Captain Zeigler,[7] now the camp's senior Allied officer, along with four additional Americans, two Australians, and three Dutch—were upstairs with the majority of the English speakers. He and his fellow Dutch medics were below on a cold concrete floor with the Indonesian Dutch enlisted men. Otherwise, the fourteen rooms on each level, with seven on either side of a central hallway, were nearly identical. They were learning to sleep on raised wooden platforms, eight men to a small room (four or five in a few).[8] The thin mattresses and odd little rice-husk pillows provided a degree of comfort; though, in one sailor's dark humor, "when you moved," the latter would predictably go "'Crunch! Crunch! Crunch!'" and "wake up your neighbors."[9]

The distribution of numbers to sew on their uniforms on the morning of 2 December proved prelude to a strict discipline, however. That afternoon, all of them, sick or well, had to gather their few possessions and march with them for roughly a kilometer up to a school ground. Once there, they had to lay everything out—including items as innocuous as his small eating pan—for inspection and what seemed senseless, even malicious, confiscation.[10] The diary and photographs escaped detection hidden under his shirt out of concern his field bag might be taken.

Meanwhile, disease stalked their hallways. They felt the loss of their medical officers, lieutenants Lutter and Van Slooten, who must have remained with the sick in Moji.[11] The rooms allocated as sick bays for throat afflictions and contagious and non-contagious stomach ailments were crowded with patients. Undiagnosed but confined to their bunks, he and Stenfert clung to the belief that they struggled with colds rather than something more serious. Gribnau carried on without them in assisting the visiting Japanese doctor, returning at intervals with news of life-threatening dysentery and everyone's "coughing and sniveling."[12] *The installation of a stove in each sick bay and another to supplement the existing two per corridor gave cause for celebration. Never mind that, as another wag put it, they "got more heat from the two hundred men in the barracks than [...] from all the stoves put together"!*[13]

The food is fairly good, but usually not enough. Never any meat, fat, or fruit; just little fish. The rice is mixed with barley. Although we still walk around with hungry stomachs, we are nonetheless improving. More's the pity that a Hollander (Wetters) has died here.[14] He was buried properly yesterday. Nice wreath. A few Japanese came to pray over the body.

We have good, regular medical care now. So, not much to complain about here. I would dearly love to have some more books, though. I am busy learning Japanese again.

August Valeriaan Hubert Wetters, age forty-one, died on 4 December 1942, of acute colitis according to the Japanese doctor.[15] *They thought dysentery more likely. That reservation aside, the care to date seemed reasonably satisfactory.*

Snow fell again that night, followed by a light rain for the next day's cremation and burial. The news of villagers paying their respects provided some uplift, which then dissipated following theorizing they may have acted out of superstition. The prisoners hardly knew enough of this alien land to give credence to one impression over the other. They knew only that the mountains were once again covered in snow, and their hoped-for recovery would be lengthy. They had diarrhea, bad colds, pneumonia, and dysentery.[16]

<u>Friday, 11 Dec. '42</u> The days pass slowly; always cold feet. If only I had my woolen socks and gloves. Another four men have died. Poor fellows. I've been to the funeral. My throat is a little better, a light tonsilitis. I'm taking powders for it. Besides that, things are going well: we have absolutely no news here.

Oh, but I did forget to say that I cut a length-wise strip from my Leiden woolen blanket. Enough for two scarves: one for myself, and one for Gribnau, which I gave him as a Sinterklaas present, complete with poem.

In the wake of more deaths, their pleasure over his poem caricaturing Gribnau[17] *was short-lived. He resumed helping in the sick room on their floor, pleased at signs the Japanese medical sergeant appreciated their efforts. Stenfert joined them for a day but proved too weak to continue and had to retreat to his quarters. Hardly robust themselves, they nonetheless portioned out meals, washed up, took temperatures, and coordinated with Jimmy Garbutt, the RAF medic upstairs. More nearly recovered, Gribnau served as interpreter for the German-speaking Japanese doctor whenever the latter was there.*[18]

They began to think the doctor concerned less with accurate diagnosis and treatment than with the appearance of competence in his reports. A

4. Ohashi, Japan, 1942

civilian employee of the mining company, he reflected its tight-fisted policy with medical supplies and tests.[19] *Further, they questioned his credibility in establishing cause of death. When the Dutch privates Ogilvie and Pfaff, and the RAF private Reeves (or Rees) died on the seventh of December, he cited "acute colitis" rather than dysentery, just as he had earlier in the case of Private Wetters. And despite concerns about lingering diphtheria, he termed the death of RAF Private Austin Black Noble, also on the seventh, the result of "acute bronchial pneumonia."*[20] *Whether intentionally or not, they feared he treated merely the complications of far more insidious diseases.*

A sense of vulnerability permeated the camp the morning after the deaths. The Houston *crewman Reynolds, assigned to cremation duty, predicted "more to come." The following day Lindeijer walked the two kilometers to the cemetery along with Reynolds and thirteen other prisoners. They stood in silence as Captain Edward Campbell, of the Australian Expeditionary Forces, read the funeral and burial services and a heavy snow fell and adhered to the frozen ground. "This is not our climate, treatment, food, or anything," Reynolds had said earlier, and no one present would have disagreed.*[21]

They were stunned, nonetheless, when a dangerous throat ailment struck the Americans Glenn Seidel and Gene Fanghor little more than a week later.[22] *The story making the rounds was that Fanghor's clothes had become badly soiled during the transport. Weak, but desperate to clean himself, the poor wretch had made a fatal error: almost immediately upon arrival, going down to the Dutch floor's bath house extension and washing in the ice-cold water.*[23]

Yet Stenfert's throat problems had also worsened dramatically, and another Dutch patient, twenty-two-year-old Hijmans, had difficulty breathing. Alarmed, on the afternoon of the nineteenth, Captain Zeigler sent word to the off-site commandant, Lieutenant Naganuma, of the urgent need for medical attention. However, this brought only a visit and no medicine. By evening roll call, the Americans and Hijmans had died.[24] *Stenfert's struggle continued.*

Distraught, the two medics had reason to believe—as Gribnau exclaimed—that they were "in a hot-bed of diphtheria without the Japanese doctor doing anything [about] it or being capable of doing anything or knowing how to do anything"![25]

Dearest wife and children,   22 December '42

We've been through terrible days. Last night [more likely, 20 December] Stenfert died from a throat infection. A heavy blow, especially for Gribnau, who was his closest friend. During the three weeks that we've been here, nine people have died already—and this despite our having left the sick and half-sick behind in Shimonoseki [Moji].

A frantic Gribnau had done all he could when Stenfert struggled for breath, prevailing on the doctor to order injections. The good medical sergeant, Neko, had come immediately when called during the last violent choking attack. But the order for medicine had come too late. Jürrien Hendrik Stenfert, born in the Dutch province of Gelderland, was dead at age forty-three, in Ohashi, Japan. The official cause of death was bronchial pneumonia. Rather, his friends thought, congestive heart failure brought on by toxins from the diphtheria bacterium.[26]

Gribnau and the senior Dutch Lieutenant Groeneveld spoke at the funeral, Groeneveld recounting the deceased's "work on behalf of others" while "already sick himself."[27] *The surviving medics carried on afterward in a daze. The number of patients had scarcely declined.*

Men not yet recovered had to work outside, cutting wood and clearing away boulders without sufficiently warm clothing or waterproof footwear.[28] *Lindeijer characterized the difficulties they faced:*

> It's easy to catch a cold here in these wooden barracks; plus the food is too little and nutritionally unbalanced. We've received bread only once—with nothing else—and so little that we suffered absolute hunger that afternoon.
>
> Yet, Gribnau and I can't complain since, as Red Cross soldiers, we're exempt from all other services and duties. Instead, we take care of the sick—which is no easy task either! However, we can stay inside for the most part, while the others have to work outside, carrying stone, etc., often in bitter-cold weather. Everyone is badly emaciated.
>
> We're close to an iron mine. Much of the work there is done by women, just as it was in the fields we saw from the train, for that matter.
>
> Gribnau and I sit for a glorious moment by the stove in one of the sick rooms, where it's relatively quiet. He wants to begin learning Japanese, too. I'm more than happy that we can do it together. I've started with the characters for writing. He's a fine, strong fellow. A great support for me!
>
> Oh, sometimes I long so terribly for home, Nel—for the quiet, loving atmosphere of our close family! How happy I would be with a little loving care from you! May God grant me the chance to show you that same happiness once more! The children will be so estranged from me. Wim and Herman—do they at times still talk about me? Oh, I cling to the belief that you are not doing too badly. One can live very cheaply in Java if necessary.
>
> Your last brave and cheerful letters (of 14 and 21 April) are a source of hope and comfort to me. On top of this, I saw you even later, so wonderfully healthy, especially on the third of August, in Riouw Street and at the BMC. Are Wim and Herman doing their best in school and do they like it? Freddy and Joke are surely becoming a handful, aren't they? Just watch that Freddy doesn't get under Joke's thumb! Well, it's time to distribute the porridge, which has just arrived, to the sick once again. Bye now! Many kisses from father and husband, Your <u>Wim</u>.

But within hours, his own crisis had come. What had seemed no more than a severe cold suddenly manifested itself as the same acute swelling of the throat and coating of the airways that had already suffocated two on board ship, and Stenfert and four others at the camp. As Lindeijer's temperature climbed to an alarming 38.9°C [102.02°F], a thoroughly terrified Gribnau gave him his last two dagenan tablets; then fearing demise himself, sat down to write a letter of farewell.[29]

Dearest Nel, Wim, Herman, Freddy, and Joke,   23 December '42

Last night it became evident to me that the same throat infection which killed Stenfert and others had infected me as well. It was devastating to think that I would never be able to see my beloved wife and children again. However, it appeared that God had so willed things, and I accepted it as established fact from his hand. Nonetheless, as Gribnau still had some medicines left, I began to take them. A miracle seemed to occur: my throat is less painful and breathing eases again. Oh, Nel, God in his great mercy may be giving me yet another chance. How deeply I now feel my shortcomings in light of the blessings we enjoyed in the past! How often we failed to bend the knee, whether out of false modesty or spiritual laziness.

I am, I believe, not completely out of danger, but I have great confidence that I may recover. The raging fever has gone.

I've promised to lead a service on the evening of Christmas Day. You know how difficult I find such things. It's not certain, either, whether the Jap. will give permission.

The work of our men has moved to the mine these days: for the time being, in two shifts, once every other day. Most don't consider it too taxing. Many even do it with a certain pleasure. The food remains too meager, however.

How will you celebrate Christmas now? You'll certainly do your best to turn it into a joyful day of celebration for our darlings, won't you, Nel! Will you be taking a bough from the pine tree in the garden? Decorating in itself is a pleasure, isn't it? And it may not cost you anything. Bye now! Wishing you happy days. Kisses from father and husband! Your <u>Wim</u>.

Dear wife and children,   <u>Christmas Day '42</u>

From my heart I wish you a blessed and happy Christmas. (Continued in the evening.) I know, Nel, that perhaps with tears in your eyes, you've tried to turn this into a happy day for our darlings: with decorating, singing and games, and, who knows, with some nice little snacks!

But, oh what joy you would have experienced, if only you knew that on this very day it became all but certain that I'm out of danger from that nasty throat infection. I've been without fever for 24 hours, the worst pain in the throat has subsided (I gargle vigorously!), and the Jap. who examined me for the first time today, found nothing wrong and prescribed no medicine. Our medicines (Dagenan and Streptosyl) might not have helped Stenfert, because he had weakened badly, and had been under that doctor's care for a long time already. Unfortunately, we have little medicine left. We've also finished a small bottle of cod-liver oil from Bandung.

The Japanese commandant declared today a day off (in response to request) and granted permission for a Roman Catholic night service and Protestant morning and evening services. The morning service was led by a seminarian from Salatiga [in Central Java]. Looking back, I'm glad that I didn't back down from my promise for that evening service. Really, Nel, I can say that a profound joy lay over this Christmas day for me. I hope that we may commemorate this later in thankfulness (God willing, next Christmas). Now, I must stop and get between the blankets. Bye, darlings! I wish you all a good night's rest. Kisses from father and spouse, your <u>Wim</u>.

Snow had fallen throughout the day. The toilet and washroom were iced over,[30] and they continued to have very sick patients. Other than the permitted services, the only organized "festivity" had consisted of an opportunity to purchase toothpaste and toothbrushes, and for the smokers, cigarettes.[31] In spite of all this, his renewed sense of gratitude persisted.

Dear Nel and children,   29 Dec. '42

I'm keeping watch over a seriously ill patient now, so I can write to you all in quiet, or rather, to you Nel. Yet I myself am not quite at ease because of something I heard from a soldier. Unfortunately, there always has to be an element of doubt as to the accuracy of such news. Yet, there is sufficient logic inherent in it, that in these final days of 1942, I can, as it were, sustain thoughts about it.

The "news" of a potential exchange of Allied prisoners for Dutch women and children interned in Java and Sumatra might amount to mere rumor.[32] Yet one could hope. With Gribnau and one other he was dividing the night watch over the twenty-two-year-old Dutch private Martherus. The youth was critically ill with supposed pneumonia and peritonitis. (In the words of the mining company doctor, there was "not a single case of diphtheria here, and never has been one either"!)[33]

Suddenly, all possessions which the Japanese here had taken from us were returned today. Furthermore, we were promised more food as of the 1st of January. We anxiously await confirmation, of course!! But in the meantime, I have my small eating pan and tennis shoes back.

A bit of bad luck is that Gribnau and I were passed over in the distribution of new shoes, because, as the Japanese officer said, Red Cross people don't have to walk outside. We don't get paid either, because only outside work is paid: 10 ct. per day. To make matters worse, our "friends" ["friends in arms"] stole the only 5 yen Gribnau still possessed. Since my Dutch East Indies guilders aren't exchangeable, Gribnau and I are completely out of money. Fortunately, two officers (Leent[34] and Groeneveld) are willing to lend to us. As officers, they receive more than 37 yen, net, per month. So being an officer is a great advantage. On top of this, they're allowed to shop by themselves in local stores.

The theft had been all the more disturbing because of its timing, the morning before Stenfert's death. The five yen note, which Stenfert and

4. Ohashi, Japan, 1942

Gribnau had purchased jointly during the transport, had been taken from the wallet in the dying Stenfert's pocket.[35]

The "friends in arms," a subset of the Indonesian Dutch group, had created havoc since the first of October, when the train en route from Bandung to Batavia had stopped in Cimahi to pick them up. Earlier word had been that Captain Meys had reports from a Dutch officer at the Cimahi camp that its "worst elements" had been selected for transport. A certain major had received an order from the camp authorities to designate roughly seven hundred technically skilled POWs for the first contingent of workers to go to the Japanese mainland. Unsure of what might become of them, he selected the most "difficult" of those who nonetheless could be said to have "some technical knowledge," individuals "from the city and from the lower echelons of Indonesian society."[36] *The revelation accounted in part for the contrast between the unruly group and the Indonesian Dutch with whom Lindeijer had taught in Bandung, yet failed to explain fully their resentment of Dutch Europeans.*

Today for the first time, some merchandise came in from which we could make some tea (very bad tea!). However, no one can buy bread, sugar or many other articles, most likely because these are being distributed among the local population.

I've mastered Japanese script—specifically, the katakana—now. I can also communicate a little with the soldiers but must still learn a lot more words.

Despite the relatively heavy night- and day work, I feel healthy again, and do it all with pleasure. I've also begun to long for my books again, which is a good sign. Bye for now, darlings. I do hope, for your sake, that the news is correct, and that you are all doing well. Bye now! Many kisses from husband and father! Your Wim.

The angular, syllable-based writing system was curious. The strokes were always to be made from left to right and top to bottom. Those that comprised each syllable had to be made in a certain order. In writing the character for the number ten, which resembled a "plus" sign [or more accurately, a cross +], you had to make the horizontal stroke first, then the vertical one. And for the beginning of the word for "earth," which was similar, the horizontal stroke came first, followed by the vertical stroke, which then received a slightly slanted longer stroke across the bottom.[37] *Seen against the white page, the black syllables slowly became intelligible, stimulating a question whether a similar intelligibility might emerge out of their surrounding snowy, white world.*

Dear Nel and children,   New Year's Eve '42 Kamaishi [sic]

Gribnau and I are sitting near the stove in the sick room again, while the others "rest" [in English] standing around the stoves in the corridor and singing something or other. Of course, our thoughts are mainly "at home." How lovely to believe that you may celebrate these days in freedom. And however sad the fact of our transport to Japan may have been, I'm nonetheless thankful that there is now, to some extent, a real end to our imprisonment in sight. I trust that '43 will see us reunited again, and that at our New Year's Eve celebration, we'll bend our knees together, to thank God for that glorious deliverance.

The possible "end in sight" arose from a rumor of the war's turning in the Allies' favor—one persuasive enough to cause speculation over the existence of an external source.[38]

Oh Nel, how I long for all of this, and also for the children and my daily work. Yet this time is so good for profound reflection on my (our) real task. What has to take first place in our work, the raising of the children, and our personal life, is our relation to God. Readiness to follow his will and to suffer and work for his Kingdom is what we have to prayerfully look for within ourselves, again and again. Only this can and will give our lives—however short—rich content, even in the presence of grief. I'm thinking here of the words: "Seek first the Kingdom of God and his righteousness, and all other things will be given to you."

That seriously ill patient I mentioned the other day died last night. Another of our patients, Lieutenant van Leent, is a pharmacist from Yogya [Yogyakarta].[39] A nice fellow. He's badly weakened and emaciated but is improving slowly. He's proposed inviting us—you and me, Nel—to "celebrate" over an exceedingly fine dinner at the Preanger Hotel,[40] as soon as we can move about freely in Java again. Van Leent is single, a gourmet who can describe all kinds of delicacies! We raise our spirits this way.

Oh, how gloriously we can talk here, on our empty stomachs, about delicious food and drink. I'm slowly beginning to realize that during the entire rest of my life I'll appreciate and enjoy virtually all foods. This evening, we received "a little extra" from the Japanese Army: a tiny fish and a small spoonful of caviar. However, the promised big improvement still has to materialize, tomorrow!

It's now about 9 in the evening and I'm not going to stay up: night rest is important here. All of you, an extra little kiss, and for Nel a firm embrace! Next year, better!! Your loving husband and father, Wim.

The faces in the photographs continued to inspire his most ardent thoughts. Yet coming to terms with his mortality and powerlessness in the hands of his captors made clearer than ever the extent to which reunion with them lay beyond his control: he could lose them as easily as his eating pan or the value of his Dutch East Indies money. Yet, that being said, his coping skills had increased. His experience during the transport had taught him the value of patient calm; his survival of the throat ailment, gratitude. And now, the blessing conferred by the memory of Sinterklaas celebrations past allowed him the hope of Sinterklaas celebrations yet to come.

5

Ohashi, Japan, 1943—
"We Rise in the Wind's Eye"

The prisoners who were well enough now worked outside in freezing temperatures at what appeared to be meaningless tasks such as moving boulders. Those in the sickrooms were hardly more fortunate, suffering from diarrhea or dysentery and lower rations. In either case, they felt the effects of the wind. It blew out windowpanes and howled through the walls of their small, crack-filled building.[1] "As cold as a polar bear's nose in a blizzard," someone had said. Notwithstanding the snow, the strong gusts continually whipped up dust to the extent that everyone developed chest coughs. "Another year here and all of us will have TB," Reynolds predicted. Even more disturbing, the effects of prolonged hunger and sickness eroded what sense of community they had. Two hundred distinct personalities, of more than a dozen ethnicities,[2] and they were barely able to survive each meal's food distribution. A recent fight between two prisoners had been over a spoonful of radish greens.[3] Others besides Lindeijer had to wonder how they would survive for the entire war. He needed an effort to address his family with good wishes for the New Year.

Dear wife and children, New-Year's day '43 Kamaishi [sic, Ohashi]

From the bottom of my heart, I wish each of you a truly happy New Year. And that I may also be a witness to your happiness! Perhaps even contribute a little something to that. How I would love to hear the slightest bit of news of you! I continue to hope that you still live at 121 Dago Road. Coincidentally, my prisoner number here happens to be 121 [on a strip pinned to the back of his cap], too.

This morning there was indeed more rice than usual, but this afternoon only a little piece of bread. Accompanied, however, by a smear of jam. So even here, '43 begins with good promises. Outside it's real winter weather: snow and frost. Luckily, the cold doesn't bother us as much anymore, thanks to the stove in the sick ward, where Gribnau and I are sitting now. Gribnau has made an undershirt from a blanket, and I hope to make a pair of long johns.

Wim and Herman will soon be going to school again, won't they? Freddy doesn't join the big boys yet? How I would dearly love to see Joke just once in her Sunday dress! Can you walk about freely again with the children, Nel? I really hope so! Oh, yes, and how does your denture suit you by now? Completely used to it, are you?

Gribnau has promised to cut my hair. That is badly needed, as it has not been done since mid–September!

The positive tone he adopted was hardly widespread. Increased inspections, now nightly, created new stress, and only the presence of the guards prevented spontaneous fights.[4] *An added daytime inspection by Colonel Hakatayama, the Hakodate area division commander, raised tensions on the fifth of January.*[5] *In the wake of his visit, the Americans Sparks and Goodson engaged in an extended battle—a draw in Reynolds's estimation—"over cigarette butts." Days later, Lieutenant Groeneveld smoothed over a precipitous incident: the dousing of two of the Indonesian Dutch when Kalinowski, of the* Houston, *stepped into a water bucket.*[6]

Lindeijer's colleagues were cold and unhappy and had little time for themselves. Those deemed even marginally well were sent out in miserable weather for the most menial of jobs—leveling ground, digging holes, or moving logs.[7] *Small wonder that they wore on one another's nerves. Lieutenant Naganuma's January 7 prediction of future work assignments suited to their technical abilities might help to some degree. The Americans' election, on the same day, of the* Houston *crewman Jack Feliz (who would later become their acerbic wit) as their "Master-at-Arms" of the barracks seemed a similarly positive thing.*[8] *A towering Californian, Feliz had apparently resented overweening authority even in his own country's navy: when a navy chief engineer had given him a shove, Feliz shoved back. After a summary court-martial, he was released for time served while awaiting trial and sent to the Asiatic fleet, claiming "they let me out of the brig to fight."*[9]

Dear Nel and children,   Sat. 9 Jan. '43

Gribnau has made good work of his task: I can leave my head of hair alone again for a few months. I also shave a little more often now, that's to say, once a week. So, I continue to look like a "gentleman." I'm finishing the large tube of toothpaste which I received from you while still in the Gas School, because we've been able to buy tooth powder here. Our luxury has increased nicely, hasn't it?

We're also getting more rice than before the first of January, although not enough for me because of this continuous craving I have for food, possibly a result of the cold. On Tuesdays and Fridays we get one little bread bun for a whole meal. That means hunger! Oh Nel, for the first meal at home again (!!), I'd go wild to have brown beans with fried bacon. The very thought nearly becomes an obsession in this fat-poor land. Foolish, isn't it? But everything here is so tasteless. To make things worse, our salt is almost finished.

5. Ohashi, Japan, 1943

Their food, prepared in a kitchen in the village, was primarily rice mixed with a gritty grain—someone's idea of added nutrition.[10] *The extra amount was hardly noteworthy; portions remained small, about six bites—if, as one of their number put it, "[they] didn't take too big a bite."*[11] *For breakfast and supper, they received a bowl of watery soup in addition, and for lunch a bit of fish.*[12] *Their respective weights, already dangerously low when they arrived, had scarcely increased.*

Fortunately, through Van Leent, we can buy curry powder and tomato sauce now and then. And following every meal in the ward, we reheat some of our rice with water so that we still have a warm little "dessert" afterward.

For Gribnau and himself, Van Leent's generosity was critical. Even those paid for work outside looked for ways to supplement their minuscule wage—some going so far as to scavenge cigarette butts from snowbanks and puddles. Once dried, pulled apart, and extended with old tea leaves, the used tobacco could apparently be recycled and sold. Not a smoker himself, Lindeijer could only applaud such resourcefulness. All of them were desperate for the wherewithal to buy tooth powder and soap.[13] *Out of necessity, they were learning new skills, sewing "patches on patches," in lieu of new clothes.*[14]

Oh yes, Nel, I've been busily sewing up a pair of long johns from a blanket! Don't laugh, because the thing is nearly finished. Tonight I hope to give it a trial run, although it still needs to be reinforced in the crotch. Nice and warm, though! The Japanese pants are completely threadbare, and too small.

These days, the seriously ill patients (four at the moment) get an egg now and then. Gribnau and I even received one once, but we of course passed it on to Van Leent, whose strength is severely weakened! My own feet are abnormally thick, perhaps from a nutritional deficiency; however, I do feel healthy. The pain in my mouth has also healed. I believe we've reached a period of recovery again! Oh Nel, I do so hope that we return to Java <u>this</u> year! Goodbye—a kiss for all of you from father and husband. Your <u>Wim</u>.

At present, they faced cruel weather and an appalling work schedule, however. On 10 January, Lieutenant Naganuma threatened no meal that evening or the following morning because too few men had gone to work outside. On the eleventh, most worked the entire day in freezing rain, despite the threat's failure to materialize. Those too unwell to go out found themselves forced to go out anyway, taken to the school ground for grueling exercise. By nightfall, the wind roared through their building "like a fire siren,"[15] *an omen of the next day's scenario. Starting at -10° Centigrade on the morning of the twelfth, they carried rocks balanced on poles slung over their shoulders, coolie style.*[16]

Dear Nel and children, Ohashi [Added in ink][17]   Wednesday 13 Jan. '43

We're sitting by the stove in the ward while a snowstorm rattles the windows. A comfortable feeling, that radiating warmth, especially when you see how the clouds of powdery snow swirl along the mountainsides. At the same time, you know yourself left to the arbitrariness of the Japanese Army.

"Jagen," his verb for "swirl," likewise denoted "hunt" or "shoot." The storm literally attacked the mountainsides, darting in unpredictable patterns, as if to disorient a quarry. On their upper floor, it had shattered the glass in a hall door, before blowing the door from its frame.[18] The capriciousness of its blasts heightened awareness of their own vulnerability.

Today we received only half our portion of rice because some of the men who work outside couldn't keep pace in the ice-cold wind!

Lieutenant Naganuma increasingly ceded control to his heavy-handed NCOs, further encouraging brutish behavior by the guards.[19] The working parties particularly suffered. Current scuttlebutt had Jack Feliz "beaten to the ground" for helping a local woman who attempted to bring the ditch-digging detail hot tea. When a dog knocked the teapot and cups out of her hands, Feliz incurred wrath for trying to pick them up.[20] A shipmate, Stewart, received even less warranted treatment. Badly burned during the Houston's explosion, and hampered by an arm that still "didn't work right," he had been set upon for lack of efficiency for the second or third time.[21] All this, in weather so cold that those who had been outside said they really hadn't even been able to think straight.[22]

Oh Nel, the worst [thing] is the awful longing for home, for the warmth of our close family. You know how fond I am of our youngsters—and here life speeds by without my seeing them or being able to take part in their upbringing. God grant that we may return to a free Java this summer! My wishes are really very monotonous, aren't they? But in such a tiresome existence as this, everything seems to focus, almost automatically, on a few deep-felt desires.

Otherwise, we feel healthy, though with occasional diarrhea due to the strange food. The doctor has diagnosed me with beriberi, so I take vitamin powders now.

Beriberi. The very word, Sinhalese for "I cannot, I cannot," was almost a taunt to his own repetition.[23] The lethargy and fatigue of this illness caused by the deficiencies in their diet might be handled gradually, as result of the powders received from the new doctor. Its psychological effects—malaise and irritability—were another matter.

Our aluminum eating utensils were confiscated, perhaps for the manufacture of airplanes. There are rumors of a Russian-Japanese war in Manshukwo [Manchukuo].[24] Gribnau and I were allowed to keep ours, because we need them to prepare food for the sick. Lucky, hey! Bye now, dear people, In spirit, kisses from father and husband. Your W<u>im</u>.

The days marched on, as monotonous as his wishes. The men continued their two-and-a-half-kilometer morning and afternoon trek to and from their job site, laboring for purposes that remained cryptic. Those marginally well in the barracks rotated turns emptying the "honey buckets" located under the benjos, or toilets. The cut in their coal supply on the sixteenth left everyone's skin cracked and broken, fostering ugliness, with the grapevine's report of "a Java nigger" stealing one of the Americans' mittens.[25]

Still, one couldn't help noticing small positive events that occasionally came into focus: the random guard who offered a small package of fish, or another with a cigarette to be passed around. Examined closely, the attitude of their captors was far from monolithic. In one case, a guard entered a room in the barracks and taught its inhabitants to write from one to one hundred in Japanese. From mere exposure, the prisoners were beginning to speak what they called "broken Nippon lingo"; most often "to understand enough of it to keep bumps off" their heads, in the words of Stewart. And Feliz wanted to be "into that damned language to where if I [got] in trouble, I would be able to talk myself out of it."[26] Even such limited understanding could have benefits.

Dear Nel and youngsters   Sunday, 17 Jan. '43

It was a busy Sunday! Everything had to be cleaned thoroughly this morning, because of an inspection by a high-ranking Japanese doctor this afternoon. We dare not say a word while that goes on.

The inspecting medical officer's remarks, in fluent English, had already become grist for the camp's bitter humorists. Feliz, one of the more prominent, caricatured the officer's pointing at each of the sick, with "You will live, go back to work with a natural recovery", or "You will die, but go back to work until then!" By the end of the day, a simplified version making the rounds seemed destined to be a classic: "You will live; go back to work! You will die; go back to work anyway!"[27] The Californian's provocatively defiant comedic sense, no doubt the result of his cattle ranch Spanish and Scotch Irish upbringing, was somehow curiously uplifting.[28]

It appears that we will be paid after all. Rather good, even though it won't be much. Diarrhea bothered me a lot this week. I didn't eat anything Friday morning; then in the afternoon, exchanged a packet of cigarettes for an extra roll, so that I could eat a good amount of toasted bread. The problem is nearly gone now, and I'm taking vitamin powders for the beriberi.

We continue to get relatively good portions of rice, but the taste is so monotonous without meat or fat. It appears that there isn't much one can get in Japan. The Americans are convinced that Japan will sue for peace this summer. My dearest wish! Meanwhile, we'll go and sweep the chimney again in the morning. Bye for now! A heartfelt kiss for everyone from father and your <u>Wim</u>.

The thiamine in the extra roll was one small step in the battle against beriberi. On the nineteenth and twenty-second of January, he was well *enough to think of others and visited Reynolds in the sick room upstairs, tempting the man's appetite from what remained of his supply of pepper.*

Despite bed sores, and leg cramps from beriberi, Reynolds was no less perceptive than angry: In the context of shortages, the rations of prisoners—even the needs of local civilians—received little or no priority. "Everything worth a damn" was given to the Japanese Army.[29]

The USS Houston *crewman might not have known something that Lindeijer was hardly authorized to tell him. A very few of their number, perhaps ten to fifteen—officers, petty officers, and a handful of others—now knew that an Allied counter-offensive in the southern Pacific had seriously weakened their captors' position. Japan's defeat in New Guinea and the Solomon Islands was all but certain. Lindeijer had learned only recently that the American officers had possessed knowledge of the war's status—including the Japanese defeat at Midway Island—as early as the previous June, while still in Java, at a camp in Batavia.*[30] *He and Gribnau were now privy to the intelligence by virtue of their association with Lieutenant Groeneveld. It came from an unknown source whose identity was fiercely protected. Someone, presumably an American, took an incalculable risk—listening at night via shortwave to Radio San Francisco.*[31]

> Dear Nel and youngsters   Sunday, 24 Jan '42 [sic]
>
> Gribnau was a bit sick today and remained in bed, so I did all of the most essential work. Except for my beriberi, I've recovered fully.
>
> Also, today an American patient (from Texas) offered to teach me English. Though his pronunciation is somewhat different ("slang"), you can no doubt understand that I accepted the offer with pleasure. Thus, in good spirits, I've begun to study again.
>
> We've made plans for lectures and courses, and for the latter, have 104 prospective participants already. I hope to give a course on electrochemistry.
>
> The problem, however, is that in this barracks there are only small bedrooms [available for classrooms]. On one of them, the hypocrites hung the sign "recreation room." We have no blackboard or chalk, either. In short, we rise in the wind's eye: we flourish under oppression.
>
> It is freezing, about -10° C again. A lot of snow. The work that our men are forced to do consists of a jumble of ridiculous tasks. It appears they're merely "kept busy." No one has received pay yet, except for the officers. The pair of long johns I made meets my requirements quite nicely: snug and warm.

In the Texan Hovis,[32] *he was finding an unlikely new friend with whom he could share bits of his past. The pair of long johns was a further plus. In contrast with the comfort they provided, that received from the radio had its sobering aspects, however. The first Allied ground victories of the Pacific War were taking place only now, after a six months' struggle on Guadalcanal, and two months' heavy fighting in Buna, New Guinea: Allied progress*

5. Ohashi, Japan, 1943

northward was likely to be hard-fought and lengthy. For the present, however, the prospects of improving his English and renewing his teaching identity were encouraging.

Dear Nel and youngsters 6 Feb. '43

Time passes quietly here, and ever more quickly. We're getting used to this mode of life, despite the severe pangs of homesickness that can suddenly burn in you. The owner of the English textbook on Physics, which I used for my English lessons, sold it to an American captain—so that the lessons no longer go as smoothly, alas.

For next week, we—that is to say, the Education and Research Committee—have put together a program for three presentations and two course hours, although we still lack blackboard and chalk, and have received no official permission. Yet we've been pressing for this for over a month!

We received a package of good quality tea for the sick room from that American captain. Nice, but of course we never have milk or sugar. Nor salt! Come to think of it, nothing special has reached us for more than two weeks now. The food remains fairly reasonable, but not enough.

Despite his attempts at equanimity, the forces that buffeted him and the others could seem unremitting. On recent days, they'd experienced an "ungodly wind" and a snowfall of over fourteen inches. A prisoner sick with beriberi who refused to go outside had his leg rapped twice with a broom handle; another with a bad foot who refused to go out had to take off his shoe and receive a "mashing."[33] By the night of the twenty-first, the tremors from an earthquake that rattled their windows could easily have been interpreted as an unfriendly universe's mocking them. The next evening, in the words of the Americans, it was snowing "like all get out." The men's gloves were so worn as to be useless, their hands cracked and bleeding.[34] And spring, at this high elevation, would hardly arrive early.

Yet from another angle, things could look somewhat different. Earlier, visiting Reynolds with a small cup of coffee, he had learned that the outside work, though brutal, at least had a rational purpose. The "jumble of ridiculous tasks" was actually site work for a new camp. Anxious to leave the sick room before he went "stir crazy," Reynolds had been out that day, "leveling off ground for a new barracks."[35]

New quarters or not, the winds of this war would continue to roil them. All he could do was to carry out small acts of civility to help limit its effects. In their own way, certain others among the prisoners would be doing the same; standing straight, even pushing back. Feliz came to mind, and almost as suddenly the name given him by the others in jest—"Big Wind."

6

1 March 1943—A Single Day's "Enormous Range of Thoughts"

The first of March 1943 was a poignant date for Lindeijer, marking as it did the one-year anniversary of the week-long defense of Java that had ended with his separation from his family. Yet his fellow prisoners in some respects were even less fortunate than he, as Lindeijer may well have realized. Men from the Houston *and* Perth *would have recalled the nightmare of abandoning ship after midnight on 28 February in Sunda Strait. News of their ships' sinking likely led to their families giving them up for dead.[1] Similarly, the Texans from the field artillery unit, abandoned in Java by the U.S Air Force's Ninth Bomber Group, would have been considered missing in action.[2] In contrast, his chance encounter with his former student on the railway platform prior to leaving Java provided him with an assurance that none of the other prisoners had. The young woman had promised to inform Nel of his imminent transport to Japan. Unlike any number of other wives left behind, Nel had good reason to believe she knew where he was: on the Japanese mainland, and alive.*

Comparing his situation with that of the camp's Indonesian Dutch would have easily shed light on an additional benefit that he had. Separated as he was from home and family, but less practiced in English, they suffered a degree of isolation that he did not. His new group of American and British patients had seen fit to rename him. Overnight, and almost without realizing it, he had become "Lindy."[3]

Whether as a result of such musing or for some other reason, he had determined to do something different for the day's entry.

My dear people!   1 March '43 Kamaishi [sic]

A long time of work and worry lies between this letter and the previous one. On the twenty-first of February I commemorated Ber's [his youngest sister's] birthday, and yesterday father's. But even more than to Holland my thoughts went out to my beloved children and their caring mother in Bandung. Thank God that I can't imagine anything other than your continuing to live in "our house," and doing well—so vividly has the memory of your cheerful faces on 3 August and other days stayed with me.

Their photographs lay before him, as usual. His diary had served as an escape hatch of sorts, from a squalid present to the safe haven of pages where, as though at home with them on the Dago Road, he discussed bits and pieces of his experience. For this anniversary entry he was resolved to make the door on the hatch swing the other way. Rather than retreating to the past, he would bring the family into his daily life, creating a composite day and casting in relief moments whose significance might otherwise be missed. Particularly some associated with a fascinating new acquaintance—one Hiroe Iwashita.[4] He resumed writing.

At some future time, you may have difficulty imagining our life here; and because of the sheer number of impressions, my memory may later be insufficient to provide a reliable picture. Even here, life is full of the enormous range of thoughts and deeds which we, as God's creatures, display. I will therefore try to describe an entire day: a day like so many over the past months, yet, regardless of its apparent uniformity, holding its own distinct experiences and possibilities:

I'm sleeping on a mat, hidden deep beneath some five blankets. Gribnau lies next to me, totally invisible, like the other six fellows in our room. Now and then one climbs out of his "submarine," slips quickly into his old Japanese soldier's coat, and runs as fast as he can to the water closet. For a moment he has to cross some "open air," where an icy snowstorm blows through his underwear. After completing his mission, the shivering victim of watery soup and porridge returns, and crawls under the warm blankets again.

Normally, I awake early and lie here a little longer enjoying "my very own" Leiden wool blanket. At 5 ½ hours [5:30 a.m.], an Englishman gives my legs a push—and with a "Thank you," I quickly start dressing: an old pair of Japanese trousers over my homemade long underwear, woolen stockings, two or three pairs of socks, Jan's [the Dutch army's][5] green shirt with the Red Cross arm band, an American pullover, and around my neck—last but not least—the wool muffler which I cut from the Leiden blanket. I wake Gribnau, and quickly fold my blankets together. Then I slip my feet, layered thick with socks, into the slippers I made once upon a time in Singapore from a tropical hardwood.

My first move, of course, is to the WC [toilet], because I still suffer from diarrhea almost constantly, even though my stomach is becoming used to the strange Japanese food. A frightened rat runs along the corridor and into one of the bedrooms. We were already well-acquainted with these creatures on board the ship!

After visiting the "benjo" [night stool], I enter the territory that occupies us daily: the ward. Our admirable American, Hovis, has already placed our dinner from the previous evening on the stove and finished sweeping the floor. Indeed, we sometimes receive a lot of pleasure and help from our recovering patients! Van Leent, Coughtry, and Zerbis are awakening. Rijnders, with his curly little red beard, comes in and asks timidly for a light: he pushes a tiny bundle of firewood into the stove, and once that burns, goes to light the stove in the corridor with it.[6]

The engine of the food catering van interrupts my English conversation with Hovis. Upstairs they're shouting "chow down," and downstairs, "eten halen" [Dutch for "pick up and eat"]. The English food distributors are already running down the stairs when the Hollanders [Indonesian Dutch] wander out of their bedrooms with sleepy heads, or hang about the stoves. I happen to be a food distributor today, too, and help to bring the food upstairs. I quickly divide the porridge between "upstairs" and "downstairs," [then] put some lobak [vegetable/turnip mix] in a small dish and take it to the ward. Gribnau will distribute it further among the patients. Meanwhile, he goes outside to get the "soup," while I take charge of the side dishes and parcel them out for our two rooms. This is a thankless task: many hungry, hypercritical eyes follow your every move. Selfishness and greed, cheating and theft are rampant here. Fortunately the spirit among the English and Americans is much better.

I put the portion for Gribnau and myself in a small aluminum pan (from Jan) and escape back to the ward again. The whole company (five sick) is already eating, thanks to Gribnau's good care. We now tackle ours too, which I again portion out. Oh, I do hope to have as good an appetite back in Java as I always have here! The portions of rice are pitifully small again because our 15 "mine workers" receive extra large portions. It's lucky for us that there are sometimes leftovers from the patients. The Japanese guards are shouting in the corridor: mineworkers' roll call!

As soon as we've finished the food (rice with some brown soja lobak soup),[7] I go to empty the two "benjos" (night stools): a dirty orderly's job, like cleaning the bedpan, of which Coughtry makes frequent use! Fortunately, I got used to that in Bandung.

Gribnau is washing the small Japanese bowls and plates. Hovis is helping him with it. So far, I've managed to leave my chopsticks in my field bag. I proudly use my beautiful "Sola-Massief" [a brand of Dutch silver] spoon which I hope to bring home again!

Now and then a Japanese sentry with rifle and fixed bayonet comes and peaks around the corner. This contingent of guards has only been here a few days and is still curious and suspicious.[8]

"Lindy, give me the pan, please [in English]," Coughtry asks suddenly. I quickly fold back his blankets, lift his painfully swollen hips as well as I can, and slip the bedpan in place. A dirty little square tin is placed on top of the pan as a urinal.

While Coughtry thus "occupies his throne," as Gribnau calls it, and various sounds are produced, a small Japanese man enters, dressed in black, with a little white kerchief tucked into his belt in back.[9] He's apparently an official of the mining company who likes nothing better than to write novels. Perhaps he wants to collect material for a new story! He knows some English and French and is very impressed by our linguistic ability. German doesn't interest him at all. At times, Gribnau or I must correct his written English, as well as orders, etc., that the Japanese commander will read to us [prisoners]. This puts us in

6. 1 March 1943

a rather special position, which can occasionally come in handy. The aforementioned mine supervisor may at times bring pepper, salt, and cigarettes along; one time, even about five potatoes, on which we feasted as if they were a delicacy.

For Lindeijer and Gribnau, the man described was Iwashita, or even "Iwashita-San," whose intellectual curiosity outweighed any official role the mining company might have assigned to him. A civilian employee of the company's labor branch, and apparently serving as its liaison between the prisoners and the camp administration, he had begun stopping in regularly to see them. For the outside workers, with whom their new acquaintance had limited contact, he was "Smitty the Spy."[10] As sickroom medics who saw him more often, they considered him a revelation; the earnestness with which he practiced his French and English with them, completely genuine.

Nearly thirty-three years of age, he had completed three years of preparatory study at Hosei University in Tokyo before (surprisingly to them) embarking on the study of English literature. No more than a year later, domestic responsibilities forced him to take the clerical job with the mining company from which he had been transferred to his current assignment.[11] His continuing interest in the novel—in their minds, a western genre until relatively recently, and one focused on the experience of the individual—fascinated them.[12] Added to this something else resonated: his life, like theirs, had been turned on end.

Most humanizing of all from their point of view: though he spent most of his time at the camp, their liaison had a wife and two children, and a domicile in Tokyo.[13]

On rare occasions he asks Gribnau or me to go walking with him. That's not to be sneezed at, because then we can buy something. The other day, I bought from <u>his</u> [black market] shop[14]: a packet of tea, a tin of coffee, a small bottle of Vitaray (vitamin) tablets, shaving blades, and two small packets of curry powder. Of course not all for myself! I'd received five yen from Van Leent, which were very nearly spent in full. Otherwise, we can't buy anything. Sometimes a sentry can be tempted to "sell" a pack of cigarettes at a good profit. All food and tobacco are under controlled distribution, and therefore, typically beyond our reach.

Admittedly, there was an element of self-interest on either side of the growing acquaintance (or was it friendship?). Yet beyond the "tit for tat," possibly some sort of middle ground was reached ... The ironic humor of the bedpan scenario broke off his train of thought:

Meanwhile, Coughtry has finished: "Take me off, Lindy."[15] I again lift the heavy body with much difficulty, while he cleans himself. I straighten and smooth his clothes as best I can, while he lies down exhausted. He is a good fellow, but we fear for his life. When I pull him up into the improvised pillow and straighten the blankets, he says "Tuck me in, Lindy," and is thankful for a good tucking in around his neck and back. Meanwhile, our Japanese visitor has fled the stench, after a chat with Van Leent in French and with Gribnau in English. I go to clean the "pan and can."

We put on water for tea, and take turns chopping wood. In fact, the stove has to be fueled with wood for the most part because of late we've only been receiving one box of coal every two days. The English and Americans bring wood with them from their outside shifts, something the selfish Dutch never do![16] In our attempts to eke out sufficient rice, soup, and fish for the sick, these hyenas cause us endless difficulties. Unfortunately, our Lieutenant Groeneveld is no match for them.

For this morning we have as our special duty the cleaning of Van Leent's berth. He can sit up for a sufficient length of time now, in a chair by the stove. In the meantime, we're taking the bedding outside, shaking it out, and once the area has been swept thoroughly, putting it all down in order again.

It's nearly 11 a.m., and I start cooking. We always save our food for the next mealtime so that we can heat it up before the stove is needed for the patients. We boil our rice with water, as well as the soup or the fish. Today we can mix in some salt and finely crushed black pepper corns! We put a bucket of ice water on the stove for cleaning the dishes later.

The engine of the van and the "chow down" call me outside again. I carry the vegetables (slices of lobak) and porridge (white rice) upstairs and divide the latter. [The Indonesian Dutch] Bertsch intends to portion out the lobak, but gets into a quarrel over it with an American: later, they fight it out![17] Later still, we hear that the fight was reported in the Chihaya[18] [newspaper] in Kamaishi.

In the afternoons, we have no soup, only rice with some fish, sometimes of good quality but usually bad, hard little things. We "fry" the latter by letting them burn a bit on the stove. (We never see oil, fat, or meat here!) That way they acquire a bit of taste.

At 1 p.m., the workers, who'd returned at around half past eleven, depart again. Gribnau and I used to pick up coal at 2 p.m. in "the good old days," but unfortunately, since the rationing, this is no longer necessary.

After lunch, Gribnau is called downstairs to fold powders [medicines] into packets, with the Japanese orderly [medical sergeant]. When he returns he tells me that the doctor will come this afternoon. Quite an occurrence, because lately he only comes once every 2 or 3 weeks. Consequently, we continually have half- and seriously sick people who are forced to go and work outside. Naturally, only this Japanese doctor (a poor excuse of a fellow) can give permission to stay indoors.

I go downstairs to update the temperature and pulse charts. One of the bedrooms is half empty and doubles as a "consultation room," where Gribnau translates the patients' complaints into English, which the Japanese doctor understands a little. The doctor is always accompanied by two female nurses in wide black trousers and a type of apron, who give an injection here and there.

I straighten up the ward a bit before the doctor comes for his cursory visit. This evening we may have little bottles and packets of medicine to distribute

6. 1 March 1943

again. The English have been alerted and come down the stairs in droves to join the "sick parade."

After the doctor and his party have left, the bucket of water we put on the stove after lunch is just warm enough. Thus, I can nicely finish washing the clothes we put in soapsuds yesterday, partly ours, and partly those of the patients. Immediately, a new bucket of water has to be put on for washing dishes. We let the laundry dry in the ward; there is no other way.

It's already time to go for food and cook again. The soup in the evening is usually a little more plentiful and tastier than in the morning. It tastes extra good after a busy afternoon. There isn't much to do most afternoons [however]: we read a little. I try to learn some Japanese or English. The last few days I've been reading to Coughtry, who has very poor eyesight, from "Peter Simple" by Captain Marryat.

After dinner we're busy: taking temperatures and pulses, doing the dishes, and sometimes (2× per week) I give my course in electrochemistry, which generates a lot of interest.

The books I've mentioned are from the YMCA, which managed to send some English novels here via the Swedish Consulate. Never would I have thought, as a student, that I would be a prisoner of war and the subject of the "relief work" that I heard about at the time. As it happens, our own NCRV [Dutch Christian Student Association] was a member of the YMCA and performed the same work in association with the YMCA during the world war [World War I].

"Tenko" (roll-call) is at 8:30 p.m. I just go to our room. (One of us is allowed to stay with the patients.) Fortunately, the "visitors" disappear, and after "tenko" we have our quietest hour: Van Leent gets his little bowl of soup and we also eat something. Afterward we stay for a sociable chat and think of home; make plans for the time when we'll be back in Java. Van Leent wants to give Gribnau and me each a lasting memento of this time. I suggested a camera, for us, but he was afraid that in Java, after the war, there wouldn't be any of good quality for sale.

Tonight it's Gribnau's turn to watch half the night. Hovis will do the other half. Sometimes Riedé and Mulder, both former patients, help out with these watches, which are necessary for Coughtry and Van der Veen; otherwise, it would be too taxing for us in the long term.[19]

So I go to bed and fall asleep, after a fervent prayer for your well-being. One of the few things that the Japanese Army has given us is a good set of blankets. Despite the cold of -10° C [14° Fahrenheit], it is warm under the "wool," and we sleep delightfully.

I haven't been able to tell you much, but with the above it will surely be possible to recall a lot later. In the meantime, it has become 16 March, and tonight the thaw has finally begun. People are saying that we'll be moving to a larger camp near here on 1 April. Understand that we are expecting a lot from that camp, as well as from the summer.

His account had not left much out. Inadvertently, he'd missed mentioning Iwashita's role in bringing books from the YMCA in Tokyo.[20] And strategically, he couldn't have mentioned the risk taken by the Japanese medical sergeant and his wife in purchasing medicines for the prisoners on the black market.[21] How to reconcile such kindness with the havoc wreaked by certain of their own "comrades in arms" among the Indonesian Dutch? The fight written up in the Chihaya, between Bertsch and the American guardsman Rich, was but an example.[22] Admittedly, the group selected for the transport was less highly educated than his mixed-race colleagues at the Lyceum. And His valued Thurner, Rijnders, Riedé, Nieraeth, and Mulder were exceptions that clearly stood out.[23] Forming a conclusion on the matter was hardly straightforward—as so often the case in this disruptive, confusing war.

But on the whole his entry accomplished what he intended. Addressing the family was a rhetorical technique, but one that would involve them in his camp life at some future date. Just as critically, it was a way of signaling, perhaps to himself, that without diminishing in any way his identity as "Wim," he could also be "Lindy." From the start, the implied familiarity of the name, and the English speakers' tendency to associate him with aspects of their own experience—"Lucky Lindy," and the popular "Lindy Hop"—was completely disarming. In accepting the name, he was effectively coming to terms with himself and his camp situation. The realization itself was liberating.

The context of his photograph of Nel and the children had perhaps also changed as a result of sharing it with so many. Had he shared it with Iwashita? There was no way to be certain, but if so, this would have been a different moment from the one in which he shared it with Gribnau and Stenfert, or even the American Hovis. The man had a family, with its own story; something to ponder.

For now, it might be enough to have enlarged his personal narrative in a manner that made room for hope, and even a bit of humor. His mood would lighten further upon hearing Reynolds's comment on their rainy weather: "booger wooger."[24]

> The Americans are very optimistic: definitely, home for Christmas! There are rumors about an attack on Italy from Turkey. In a two-month-old Japanese newspaper we read about the American landing in Morocco. The Germans are being pushed back from Stalingrad, Charkov [Kharkov], and Rostof [Rostov].[25] Good news; we keep good courage. If only my darlings in Bandung are doing well too!
>
> Bye now. All of you heartily kissed by husband and father. Your <u>Wim</u>.
> PS The day before yesterday I wrote a short letter home. The first!![26]

7

Spring and Summer, 1943— "It Lasts So Terribly Long"

Spring found the Ohashi prisoners mired in place psychologically as much as by the season's mud. Men between the ages of twenty and fifty-eight grew old in attitude as well as body, with "nothing to talk about that we haven't already told [to the extent that] every man in the building knows the others' life history."[1] They were cold, perpetually wet and miserable, and lacking sufficient footwear. The old saw of "patches on patches" had returned, as they tacked tops onto shoes, and mended what remained of their socks. "Really," to paraphrase Reynolds, after so many patches, "there were no socks left." Weakened and despondent from the work outside, the normally stoic crewman had become "so mad" from "talking to the Nips [sic] about the shoes," that he "had tears in [his] eyes."[2]

Ever so imperceptibly, the weather did ease, however. Busy in the makeshift clinic, Lindeijer focused on improvement in his patients.

Dear Nel and youngsters! Kamaishi [sic]   21 March '43, Sunday

Spring today! Although there is still snow here and there, the daily frost is apparently over. Our sick are improving so rapidly that, as of a few nights ago, we no longer have to keep watch. It is a miracle the way Coughtry has slimmed down: his thick, doughy, swollen body has changed into a lean one within 2 weeks. The improvement began suddenly, and no one knows why. He is so fortunate! Even his eyes seem to be getting better. I showed him the photo of our family, and he responded with a promise to send each child silk pajamas!

For everyone who saw the photograph, it had somehow struck a chord. His separation from the young wife and children pictured no doubt played a part. Conversing over it aroused empathy that could lead to relationship even with near strangers.

We now fuel the stove with wood because we no longer receive any coal at all! Fortunately, we only need it in the daytime. A few days ago, for the first time, the Japanese gave us an opportunity to buy certain things. I bought a pair of socks, a packet of curry, and some cayenne flakes. People are saying that we may move to the new camp on 28 March. We'll believe that when it happens! I've been darning my stockings with a vengeance, and still hope to reinforce the soles with some strong material.

My dear people,   Monday, 29 March '43

Just a few words to you all before tenko [roll call], and then under the blankets again, because it's still very cold. We receive just enough firewood to fuel the stove at mealtimes. Thus, we chop wood three times a day; sometimes substantial logs, with a crooked pickax! Heavy work! Our rice rations are again as small as they were before the first of January. We only hope that things will improve when we are in the new camp. At least we no longer have to keep watch overnight; the patients in our ward are all improving. Coughtry's recovery is amazing! The other day we were able to "do some shopping" again. We each bought a can of pineapple for 50 cents apiece, the swindlers! We're suffering an attack of lice just now.

*Nearly as bad as the cold, the small rations, and infestations were the anger and resentment these generated. A corrupt administration forced them to purchase out of their minuscule wage items already intended for distribution.³ The prospect of the new camp helped somewhat, as did their own dark humorists, who scarcely missed a beat. Ohashi had "ten months of winter, and the other two [were] extremely cold," according to one's sardonic banter; and "it wasn't any crime to get [the lice]," but it surely was "to keep them," in the catchphrase of another.*⁴

Dear Nel, Wim, Herman, Freddy, and Joke!   Sunday 4 April '43

We're sitting here in the new camp: with more space, our own kitchen (the food, however, is still nothing in particular), bath facilities (not finished), and hospital. The hospital has 12 patients, including myself. I'm experiencing a severe attack of diarrhea and need to stay in bed for a few days. Our hope for more time off proved unfounded; we are busier than ever. All healthy men have to work outside from 7 a.m. until 5 p.m., some 20 of them in the iron mine. They have an arduous task! We'll still have many patients, I think.

The clothing supplied by the Japanese Army is very bad. Up to now we have received one pair of socks and have been able to buy one pair ourselves. I began to sew a pair of slippers in bed this afternoon, because wearing shoes is not permitted inside. You understand how I long for my beautiful leather slippers. Right now, I have an enormous craving for a mug of warm chocolate milk. The food, rice, always with the same "aquarium soup," as Van Leent calls it, is tasteless, and all we have besides this is water to drink.

We moved on 1 April. Fortunately, Gribnau and I could go with the patients on the truck. Yesterday, we each received 3 yen 10 cents; so 10 cents per day over March, for the first time with no reductions [for sickness or infractions of the rules]. However, for the time being, we cannot buy <u>anything</u>.

As their liaison, Iwashita had managed the move, in sunny weather.⁵ The new camp was lower down in the valley, three or four kilometers east

7. Spring and Summer, 1943

of Ohashi,⁶ and the men had to make multiple trips on foot—first bringing their belongings, and then their bedding, before returning an additional time to clean up the old barracks for the Korean workers who would inhabit it next.⁷

Gribnau and I had a stroke of luck with regard to a sleeping space: a separate little room in the hospital. Despite the bare boards and lack of table or chair, a rare privilege of privacy. More's the pity that nothing will come of giving or taking lessons in this camp. Everyone has to work too hard, except the officers. You know how I regret that! Well, dear people, Wim's birthday is in sight. I will think about that, perhaps too much!

The "hospital"—an infirmary for ten to fifteen sick—was constructed of wood like the rest of the camp buildings, with a tin roof. Aligned with the camp office and a guard house, it stood on one side of a small parade ground. He and Gribnau were fortunate in living here, along with their RAF counterpart, Jimmy Garbutt.⁸ Opposite them across the parade ground, a forty-five by eight meter barracks housed everyone else—"pushed up together like sardines" in a single long space, without privacy partitions even for the officers. The men termed their new building "the hut."⁹

Two rows of "double-bunks"—really two-tiered platforms—ran the length of the barracks, with a four-meter walkway between. Sleeping places on the two-meter-wide platforms were perpendicular to the wall, restricted to less than a meter per prisoner. A narrow overhead shelf held belongings. Reaching a place on the upper level necessitated climbing one of six ladders arranged at intervals along each row of bunks, then making one's way, bent over (with headroom at little more than a meter on either level), across the space of others. Likewise, it was a long climb back down again and out one of the doors at either end, to get to the "benjo," or toilet, a twelve-man latrine located behind the barracks, in alignment with the camp kitchen. Behind it stood the bath house, unfinished.¹⁰

Lindeijer hardly needed to record any detail of the new 70 × 110-meter compound; already it was etched on the prisoners' consciousness.¹¹

Days passed. The discontent over quarters gave way to assessment of their new work assignments' relative risks: the workshops of the mine (electrical, mechanical, carpentry, and others) depended on the temperament of one's (usually civilian) Japanese supervisor. Labor in the limestone quarry was preferable to work in the mine itself. The latter, in multiple shifts, was to be avoided—by demonstrating technical skill put to better use elsewhere, or (a desperate last resort) pleading sickness.¹²

Sadly, sickness more frequently produced rage than an exemption.¹³ Thus, groups of ailing prisoners trekked five kilometers to a location farther west and higher up than Ohashi, where four levels of horizontal shafts

The Ohashi Camp, likely summer 1943. Photo by Hiroe Iwashita, signed on the back with his name and Tokyo home address (Lindeijer Family Archive).

opened into the mountainside.[14] *Assigned to one of the levels, they raked and gathered by hand the ore blasted loose by Japanese workers—each attempting to load the equivalent of fourteen ore cars a day into a hopper. Any who collapsed in the process had to be carried back down the mountain by others. Men despondent over their chances of survival began filling the hospital.*[15]

Lindeijer was grateful to be of help, by the eighth of April no longer a patient himself. Once more in the room he shared with Gribnau, he focused more easily on another matter that troubled him. In his absence, the six-year-old in the photograph was turning seven. Lindeijer's letters to the family had become his dialogue with himself over how best to deal with his past life with them, and with his present. Distilling his perspective into terms a seven-year-old could understand might be the most valuable gift he could give to his son. Taking notebook in hand, he composed a letter that integrated his identity as Wim, with all that he had become as "Lindy."

Dear Wim, on your birthday, Kamaishi [sic]   8 April '43

It's for the first time, Wim, that I write to you! But it's something very special to become seven years old, isn't it? I congratulate you, you hear, and hope that it will be a nice day for you and the others. You are old enough now to understand how very glad I would be to be back with you, especially on your birthday. I often think how happy I will be when I rush into the room again

7. Spring and Summer, 1943

"English, Dutch, and American POWs at work in the iron mine, Ohashi, Japan" (Lindeijer's notation on the back of the photo), likely in spring or summer 1943. Hiroe Iwashita photo (Lindeijer Family Archive).

and we—the six of us—dance round and round [a family birthday tradition in which the celebrant stood in the circle of family members].

Until that time, I hope you will grow up into a <u>good</u>, <u>strong</u> boy. I still remember well, how my mother (your grandmother) wished me the same thing, so fervently. Whenever you are sad or disappointed, you should think back to this heartfelt wish from your father.

To be good does not mean to be a little "softy" who allows himself to be pushed about, but to be ready to help others when they really need it, regardless of who it is or how much trouble it costs you.

To be <u>strong</u> means, first of all, to have courage; not to boast and show off, smoke a lot, or curse and swear! No, it means to have the courage to act in such a way that you know is good and reasonable. For that you think of the example of someone you look up to and deeply admire.

I certainly hope that you will find real friends; boys who themselves try to walk the right road and have faith in their lives. But the best support in overcoming the difficulties you encounter in search of that road is your silent prayer to God. Before him, we can never lead a double life, for he knows us better than we know ourselves. If we pray in absolute sincerity to God, we learn to see our pettiness and faults in the proper light. But God's Holy Spirit also thus shows us the way we have to go. The understanding of that gives us the courage and strength to walk this road according to his will. Don't think little of this, because I am convinced that it is God's will that we all develop fully according to our abilities in every direction of our lives.

So don't fear to take up something new or out of the ordinary when you know that it's right and believe that you should do it. First consider it well, of course, but then grab hold of it and persevere. Begin to do this in small things, so that you will be successful in important matters later. This is what I mean by being strong. Do all this with a praying heart and you will be a worker for God's Kingdom. This is the highest achievement that anyone can have in life.

Well, dear Wim, I trust that you will one day read this letter, and also that God will allow me to return, and play and work again in our happy family. A kiss from your <u>Father</u>.

PS. My friend Gribnau (another orderly) opened his small tin of corned beef in honor of your birthday. He'd saved it for 14 long months. We feasted on it. Nice of him, wasn't it? I think that mother will have prepared something nice and tasty for you too. Bye now; see you later. A kiss from your <u>Father</u>.

He had written his first direct expression of the credo he himself had adopted, and apparently felt strongly that whenever the letter did reach his son, the words about helping "regardless of who it is or how much trouble it costs you" would stand.

Dear Nel,   9 April '43

It may have been a sad day for both of us, yesterday. Wim begins to develop spiritually now, and you know how I would have loved to join you in that experience. Last year he stood alongside the road to show me his colored pencils. Did you give him something from me again? Yesterday, it was a dark rainy day here; today it's radiant weather. May that be a symbol of our present and our future! Once we work together again for the happiness of our children, it will be with more joy and understanding than before the war, don't you believe so, too? We know better than ever how we need each other, and how best to express our love to the other. May God give us that chance again! A kiss from your <u>Wim</u>.

He chose not to mention that they now failed to salute and bow at their peril. Their new camp was more rigidly military in character. At last, on the eleventh of April, however, a hot bath! And on the sixteenth, shoes for the outside workers; poorly made, of canvas, but shoes, no less![16]

Dear Nel and youngsters,   Easter '43 (25 April)

Especially today, I must think of you. Will it be a festive day for you? I certainly hope so! I am of course hugely curious about everything that concerns your daily life. Joke is almost 2 years old. She can walk about quite nicely, can't she? And then those boys! I so dearly hope that you still live at 121 Dago Road. We heard rumors about American bombardments of Java. Perhaps our bomb shelter will still be useful!

7. Spring and Summer, 1943

I suspect that things are not going very well for our enemies, especially in China. Our poor boys [Dutch] and also the Americans now have to work in the mine day and night, in three shifts. I am afraid that we will have casualties.

The food situation did not improve! Luckily, the cold is practically over. It's sometimes nice outside in the sun. Someone brought cherry blossoms for the patients. And yet the trees on the mountainsides are still bare, and we still have to fuel the stove. Sawing and cutting wood with a small impractical little hand saw and a caricature of an axe is not easy! Well, there is no shame in calloused hands, if only we stay healthy. The officers have to gather wood from the neighboring mountain slopes. They also have to prepare a garden.

Reports from the mine had grown worse. The men moved "stones" weighing as much as 70 kilograms [roughly 150 pounds], often working for whole shifts in areas where they couldn't stand at full height. Reynolds told of an older Indonesian Dutch prisoner who couldn't keep up; the man had been sick with diarrhea for two months. Guards drove him "extra hard," and at times pushed him down. A prisoner on the same shift "ruptured himself," while another was "spitting up blood." The remaining men were "wishing for a medium sized rock to break an arm or a leg [...]," in hopes of getting a respite. Word circulated that the Australian Captain Campbell was preparing a protest that all their officers would sign. While deriding the possibility of its having an effect, they clung to the hope that it might.[17]

Meanwhile, in the conversation of visitors to the hospital, he found hope of a different sort: In the case of the abused Indonesian Dutch worker, Reynolds had been motivated to help, lifting the larger chunks of ore, and leaving the smaller ones for the other.

Dear people,   1 May '43

This time I'm in bed writing and thinking about you. Yesterday was our Princess Juliana's birthday, and our best wishes went out to her and her family.

The day before yesterday was the Japanese emperor's birthday, and thus we had a "yasumi" [free time] day. Gribnau and I were looking forward to it, but by the time we finished our regular morning chores, we were ordered to go to Ohashi, about 3 km. from here, to bring back a scale [for weighing people]. Four days' diarrhea and no appetite had made me very weak, but as I expected, the Japanese soldier in charge was not impressed. Moreover, that cast iron scale was so enormously heavy that the assignment turned out to be much worse than anticipated. It was a terrible exertion, especially for me, even though Gribnau carried the heaviest end. We were both completely exhausted when we finally reached the camp and fell onto our beds.

An hour later I felt feverish and it developed that I had a temperature of 38.8° C [101.84°F]. Gribnau alerted the Japanese orderly, who gave me a shot and some aspirin. In the evening, my temperature rose to 39.3 [103.28°F]; the diarrhea became more violent, and I had pains in the back, stomach, and head. I felt terribly sick and didn't sleep much that night. Yesterday morning the fever had dropped to 37.8. I stayed in bed, of course. Last night, again 38.8, and this morning 37.6° C.

So, I am improving, but still very weak. That, I think, is not so much the result of the fever, but the miserable food.[18] In the previous camp we received a mixture of barley (large grain) and rice with—now and then—a good sajoer [a vegetable mix] with a reasonable portion of fish. At this camp, with the exception of the Japanese soldiers, whose food is cooked separately in our kitchen, everyone gets only barley and a weak sajoer (with seaweed or sometimes pieces of potato). Never any fruit! In the afternoons, sajoer is replaced by *not more* than a small teaspoonful of fish! There is nothing extra for the patients, who actually receive less of everything. The message is clear: being sick does not pay. Unfortunately, healthy orderlies are simply counted as sick, since they belong to "the hospital."

Since my stomach and intestines have been out of order again for the last four days or so, I couldn't eat more than just a bit of sajoer and my portion of fish. Well, we keep courage. Sometimes, I long for a glass of milk or an egg, not to mention a slice of bread and butter!! It's a good sign that I am hungry, but at the moment my body does not agree with the food. Yes, I know that I am complaining too much this time, but I *must* write down these pent-up feelings of indignation over the outrageous treatment by the Japanese Army.

> *His stomach, like everyone else's, could only tolerate so much barley. A last line of defense, their humorists struck back admirably: Feliz, with a characterization of the barracks at night (one row of bunks sending forth "a loud roll of a drum sound" followed by a responding "loud blast on a bugle—toot-toot" from the other)[19]; Reynolds, with a pithiness that was equally off-color. (There was "no nourishment" [in the barley] that he could see "because it all goes to farts.")[20]*

Recently, two of our elderly people were beaten in the face for over 15 minutes because they couldn't go outside and work. All officers filed a written protest against the dangerous work in the mines, which is in fact work for the war industry. The scallywags answered that they had no business with the Geneva Convention, and that the Japanese POWs in America had to live in pig pens.[21] (Their previous stories reported leaking tents, but they had conveniently forgotten that.) All of the officers ought to stand before a Japanese court-martial for their "disobedience."

> *The protest had been filed on the twenty-second of April, with a request that it be forwarded to the area camp commander in Hakodate. In the interim, Lieutenant Naganuma issued a refusal to stop the mine work without orders—along with scathing remarks and a threat of courts-martial for the officers. By the morning of the twenty-eighth, word had returned from Hakodate: Japan recognized neither the Geneva Convention nor The Hague Treaty. Called before the camp office, the officers were threatened again with courts-martial.[22]*

7. Spring and Summer, 1943

The rest of the camp felt threatened with them. Even prior to the protest, "sick call" had been worse than a farce: after the morning departure of the working groups, two of Lieutenant Naganuma's sergeants would comb through the barracks for those who remained in their bunks. Typically, the sick had to drag themselves out to the parade ground where, in Feliz's inimitable terms, "if you were bleeding or had a big swollen problem, then all you [might get] was a whack alongside the head with their fist. But if you had something internal [...] like dysentery, or any other kind of a damned internal problem [...], you never got a chance to express yourself." In short, you were first beaten, and then sent to work. Lieutenant Naganuma stood on the edge of the parade ground and watched.[23] After the failed protest, such treatment seemed destined to intensify.

Meanwhile, the Americans are convinced that Japan will be blockaded by submarines this summer, and moreover thoroughly bombarded ... with us at home again for Christmas. In which case, it won't be any better for us in the near future; but many of us wouldn't be able to survive a second winter here, either!

The trees begin to bud and the famous cherry-blossom is to be seen again.

Again, the Japanese authorities didn't keep their word: we were denied permission to write home. Well, if only the first epistle arrives! Have you ever heard anything from Wim Swaan? He belonged to the infamous [Dutch] demolition unit![24]

For the first time I started to read English detective novels. It's a pity that I don't have "Think fast Mr. Moto," which I received from you some time ago.[25] But don't let me get started on self-pity again; there is always a glimmer of joy to be found. We'll remember Joke's birthday well on the sixth of May, won't we!!

On the second of May, the barracks reported a peculiar absence of bashings.[26] The number of those who stayed in was checked; but no one was forced out to the parade ground, where what Feliz termed the usual "racking and stacking"[27] took place.

3 May This morning, the second official postcard written to you; hurrah! Unlike some 25 other cards, I didn't get the latest one back. It may have gone through. Fortunately, I recovered just enough to write to you that I am healthy!!

My dear folks   6 May '43

These days, Nel, I am planning a course on Differential and Integral Calculus, and although there are no books, I succeed much better than I dared to hope. Funny, isn't it. We enjoy more leisure now, which I will spend as usefully as possible! Bye now, I wish you all the best, <u>Wim</u>.

Work on the calculus course kept his spirits up, and might help in finding a postwar teaching position, possibly in an English-speaking country. Envisioning his two American students as future contacts, he asked them, *along with his Indonesian Dutch student, to record their addresses in his diary:*

George Zerbis	Howard C. Hovis	H.F. Meijer
c/o 1978 Canalport Ave.	Wichita Music Co.	S. f. Poerwaasrie[28] Kertosono
Chicago, Illinois USA	Wichita Falls, Texas	

Dear Nel, boys and Joke,   12 May '43 [Kamaishi, sic]

The last few days have been quite "shocking." Twenty-nine of our people left for Hakodate and 39 British POWs from there arrived here.[29] Almost all of them have skin diseases. Some are literally covered with ulcerating wounds. Terribly dirty.[30] It took us a long time to pull the wounds open with pincers and clean them. There are hardly any wound dressings. This morning we repeated the treatment outside in the sun. That will do them a lot of good, I think. From one of those who left, I bought for one yen a nice book to read, with the name and address of the Barends in it!

They would scarcely have believed the conditions of another camp to be worse than their own. The May 10 arrival of the thirty-nine RAF personnel—labeled "the Hakodate boys"[31]—proved them wrong: loading and unloading ships in freezing weather at the northern industrial city's docks had been "hell on earth." Deaths had been commonplace—"five on the worst day"—along with "dysentery, bad food and working conditions, [and] septicemia." Space was made at the end of the barracks to accommodate them, as far from the others as possible. "I can well understand," one of them said, "at seeing our condition [...]."[32]

In such circumstances, the Barends' name and address in the book he had just purchased took on more than usual significance. It had been Daan Barends, his teaching colleague at the Lyceum, who smuggled the photographs in to his camp in Bandung. What would Barends make of their trajectory thus far?

His attention was diverted just then by news brought by visitors to the hospital.

Red Cross packages from America arrived here this afternoon with $KMnO_4$ [potassium permanganate, a disinfectant] and bottles of cod-liver oil. There should also be small packets of sweets for us. We keep our fingers crossed! In addition to that we received extra fish this evening and we could buy cigarettes. Word has it that we are going to have some bacon tomorrow. We are both excited and flabbergasted! Besides that it's very quiet for Gribnau and me. Lots of leisure time, which I use for reading and math. In the meantime, my thoughts are with my beloved five! Bye. All of you a kiss from <u>Father</u> and <u>Wim</u>.

Dear Nel, Wim, Herman, Freddy,   Monday, 17 May '43
and Joke, Ohashi

The camp is jubilant today! The long-awaited Red Cross packages are suddenly being distributed. I've just opened mine. A real Sinterklaas-treat. I've already munched one sugar cube and one biscuit. Seventeen items, including a chocolate bar, tea, soap, cans of milk, sugar, pasta, pudding, tomatoes, jam, bacon, and meat were packed in a strong cardboard box of 30 × 20 × 10 centimeters. In the meantime, I've just polished off another biscuit... Oh, I am definitely planning to take it easy with this ... [suspension points in original]. In the Hakodate camp, almost all prisoners became sick the day after they received the packages. It is indeed a giant temptation after yearning for such a long time for something sweet and something spicy.

The package was sent from London on 21 April '42 and contains things of the best quality. I consider it an expression of thanks for the Spitfires we sent to England, previously.[33] How nice it would be if we could <u>all</u> feast together!

There are rumors about American action in the Aleutians, and it's certain that they are doing excellent work in China.[34] Will this year bring us deliverance? That is the question that keeps us preoccupied. Well, dear Nel and children, from this cold room, wholehearted wishes for your well-being. God keep us for each other! Many kisses from husband and father. Your <u>Wim</u>

Dear Nel, Wim, Herman, Freddy, and Joke,   1 June '43 Tuesday

Not much has happened since I wrote previously. From time to time, Gribnau and I open a little tin and feast exquisitely. We are not yet halfway through the package.

The Japanese guards have been terrible for a while: lashing out at the slightest opportunity. After a complaint from our officers they suddenly became more reasonable. The day before yesterday, yasumi day,[35] some sport was even allowed. In the morning we went to the graves of those who died here. It was Memorial Day for the Americans, and Gribnau and I laid flowers on Stenfert's grave.

> The "lashing out" had actually been a long period of beatings. One of the "Hakodate boys," Stranks by name, had loaded the Ohashi camp's packages for shipment prior to being transferred. Aware that the number of packages received was many times fewer than those shipped, he alerted Captain Zeigler. The captain, in turn, refused to sign for an incomplete shipment. Lieutenant Naganuma then handed over more, but not all of the stolen packages. The men had bottled up anger over the loss of quantities of the long-anticipated supplement to their diet. The perpetrators were furious at their exposure. Stranks was taken to the camp office and beaten unconscious, in some reports. Then rage unleashed on the rest of the Hakodate group spilled over onto the entire camp. There wasn't a man, the consensus went, "that hasn't been bashed at least two or three times."[36]
>
> One could find "good guards," of course: one who helped several men get little pies baked with beans for fifty cents, and another who gave out the equivalent of two packages of cigarettes.[37] Such small gestures helped.

My course on Differential and Integral Calculus is now half completed, including the English translation. My students (now 3 of them) are studying arduously. Luckily, the cold seems to be over now. I don't have to tell you how much I think and worry about you. All sorts of plans whirl in confusion through my head. God grant that I can still do something for you. Bye, dear Nel and children! All the best to you. A kiss from <u>Wim</u>.

Roll call on the thirteenth stood out from the blur that was the rest of the month: at the direction of Lieutenant Naganuma, Iwashita had taken their photograph. Assembled in rows in front of the camp office, they were instructed by the lieutenant to "look happy." The men privately fumed. "Who in the hell could be happy under these damned conditions?"[38]

Their frustration was hardly with their liaison. Iwashita clearly thought for himself, and though he had to take direction from the camp office, managed somehow to remain a benign influence. His primarily logistic duties (accounting for their wages, arranging transport for supplies, and the like) allowed him to operate with a degree of independence. By now, even the working parties considered him innocent of reporting against them (though neither did they expect him, as a civilian, to attempt to intervene in cases of their mistreatment). In the summation of Feliz, who genuinely liked the man, Iwashita "generally knew what was going on, but it was only hearsay that he ever implicated anyone."

The fact remained that he had a wartime assignment in support of the perpetrating authorities. Further he was loyal to his country and its people, if not its army.[39] *For a number, Lindeijer, Feliz, and Stanbrough among them, Iwashita was hardly the "Other," though neither was he someone who saw the world through the same lens as a western Allied prisoner. He was an individual whose "otherness" they could acknowledge and respect, and from whose acquaintance they might learn something.*

The month drew to a close. News from the secret radio had the Allies advancing to New Georgia in the Solomons. Word circulated that Prime Minister Tojo had made a speech about the need to economize on food. A kindly supervisor in one of the workshops who protested shortly after that his workers received too little was threatened with a beating.[40]

Dear Nel and children, Ohashi   1 July '43

Today is our wedding day and we'll think of each other even more than ever. I just reread what I wrote to you on 1 July '42, Nel. The separation was already very difficult then. Now I would be grateful if I knew for certain that we would be together and home again in July next year. Yet, I quietly hope that it may be earlier. We haven't seen any newspapers for more than a month now ... [Slightly more than three lines of text has been erased here, either for personal reasons or safety.]

The food only consists of groats and watery "soup" or a small piece of dried fish. Gribnau and I opened our last can of bacon [in honor of the wedding

7. Spring and Summer, 1943

anniversary]. Do you take something special too? Oh, by times I worry so much about you. It lasts so terribly long. If only I could have some message![41] I hope that my postcards have reached you. We have not been allowed to write again since 3 May.

The entire Hakodate camp may be brought over here. For that, large barracks must be added. How busy it will be then! (500 men instead of 200!) Today, high-level inspection by a big gun! The officers seem to get separate barracks. Well, let's wait and see.

Reynolds had entered the hospital, badly swollen with beriberi and experiencing kidney trouble. He spoke with dread of the mine, and dreams in which he tried to "get away from the Nip [sic] guards."[42] Lindeijer likely worried over possible similar traumatic effects of the war on his young family.

Dear people   3 July '43

Today is our youngest son, Freddy's birthday! Already four years of age now! How happy he will be to celebrate that with his brothers and sister and, not to forget, his mother. In spirit, an extra birthday kiss to you from me. I am already brooding now about what I will bring home for all of you. Oh, it's trust in the future that keeps us going. I do hope, though, that we will be spared sudden calamities, and you, from a long time of poverty. Driving the Japanese Army out [of Java] could still mean a lot of danger to you!

Wim and Herman are now home on holiday, of course. I hope that the little school can continue to operate. That would be a help to you, Nel! Joke is over 2 and walking about, of course. Such a cute age. She will keep your hands tied with work. I have a quiet hope that you once in a while manage to write about your experiences with the children. We may be able to laugh about those later. Bye for now, I wish you all a truly nice and enjoyable day together!

He balanced worry over his family with concern for his patients in the camp hospital. Of the current fourteen, a majority had lost the will to eat. Circulating a cookbook with mouth-watering pictures, he worked at stimulating their appetites.[43] Such effort was only moderately successful, however. On the morning of the thirteenth, British Corporal Leslie Merralls, R.A.F., age thirty-three, was found dead. The causes given were colitis and perforation peritonitis.[44] Others swollen from legs to trunk, as Merralls had been, took notice. Price, from the Houston, *entered the hospital in his place.[45]*

Dear Nel and children,   15 July '43

It has been very warm for a few days (now 88° F [31° C]); so, warmer than in Bandung. Yet, the hospital is full and an Englishman even died here yesterday. There is still one serious patient left and two boys from Java have tuberculosis, according to the Japanese doctor. They have a separate room. Van Leent is still in the hospital too, but almost well again, apart from the pain in the joints. He provides us with money now and then, which we can hardly use, except for some smuggled-in "mochis" (some dough with beans) and cigarettes for Gribnau.

The Japanese soldier guards are now gone. We are still "guarded" by some old discharged servicemen. Unfortunately, it is quite impossible to escape here in this country.

Their strict military guards had gone off to war, replaced by scarred veterans—some missing an arm or a finger, or otherwise partially disabled. Officially, these were "the Honorable Men"; unofficially, in the barracks' terminology, "the pole vaulters," in recognition of the wooden sticks they carried.[46] *Lieutenant Naganuma and his NCOs remained in charge; even so, the barracks harbored hopes based on these older guards.*

We are fine except for my intestines which are often upset. The course on Differential and Integral Calculus is now finished, including the English translation. Four students work hard. Others gave up.

Oh, I sometimes long so bitterly for you. Still continuously without news; no newspapers either, since mid-May! Bye, kisses from <u>Father</u>!

"No newspapers" also served as code for the absence of recent news from the secret radio. In the relative seclusion of the hospital he had become privy to another secret that was open to guarded discussion, however. Reynolds also kept a diary. The crewman's purposes differed greatly from his own: tracking cases of mistreatment for use in possible war crimes trials.[47] *Lindeijer had hardly considered such an activity himself. Yet querying the man revealed him to be motivated more by a desire for justice than revenge. He was careful also to record every act of kindness reported.*

Reynolds had long called him "Lindy." Taking a risk, he asked the American popularly known as "Red" to sign his day's entry.

James E. Reynolds, c/o Miss Leona Cahill
1769 West 36th Place
Los Angeles, California, U.S.A.

By 16 July, Reynolds's approach might have seemed to have merit. An Australian named Drabble, who fell out of line while forced to march single file and sing Japanese songs, was beaten unconscious with a rake handle. Captain Zeigler had finally stopped the perpetrator—a civilian supervisor of the kitchen.[48] *While dreadful, such incidents clearly related to their perpetrators' concerns about the progress of the war. Reynolds, who was receiving regular visitors, reported that "a Nip [sic] told one of the men today that the English and Americans had pushed the [Italians] back ninety-five kilometers in Sicily."*[49]

Meanwhile, another of their outstanding personalities, Jack Feliz, had entered the hospital. The normally strapping, over six feet Californian was down to 63 kilograms [139 pounds] and had narrowly missed "getting patted in the face with a goddamned spade" on the parade ground. Sergeant Neko, now head of the hospital, intervened, telling the officer in charge, "Jack's not lazy. He's sick."[50]

7. Spring and Summer, 1943

Darling Nel and children,   3 August '43

Naturally, I can neither stop thinking about you, nor can I stop writing on this day. I think it is difficult, Nel, to tell the children that it is their father's birthday. Last year you managed to make such a great happy day for me. I remember that with pleasure now. How dearly I would love to know whether you can still display those same happy faces. If all is well, Wim and Herman must have moved on to the next grade, but I am so afraid that you cannot afford it anymore. Oh Nel, there are so many things I am worried about. Thank God, it looks as though the war won't last much longer: Italy capitulated.[51] Yes, I trust I'll be able to celebrate my 36th birthday at home, albeit that we'll still have to endure another dreadful winter here.

We're having a quiet time here, but it's said that an American doctor with two sergeant orderlies will be coming. That last could mean no improvement for us [it could impact his and Gribnau's hospital positions], but a "real" doctor is badly needed. We do get our regular 10 cents per day paid (minus "costs"). We would receive more if we could prove that we belong to the Red Cross. Unfortunately, my registration booklet does not show that![52]

I tried to keep my birthday secret, but Van Leent remembered it. Huininga [a Dutch officer, along with Van Leent and Groeneveldt] brought a mochi [dough with beans] and asparagus along as a special treat, and as soon as my stomach is back to normal, Van Leent will treat us with a tin of asparagus.

Yesterday we could buy small, tasteless cookies from a Japanese soldier. Oh yes, one nice thing to report: I'm busy writing a high school textbook on Chemistry, totally based on Modern Chemistry. Unfortunately, we have no literature, except English detective stories, but perhaps that is an advantage.

Oh Nel, in what condition will I find you? I am so anxious at times, that I will not see one of my loved ones again. It is so difficult to maintain confidence without any message. Bye now, From my heart I wish you God's blessing.

                                 Your husband and <u>Father</u>.

He continued to keep balance by helping those close at hand: on the fifth of August, giving half his noon ration of "rice mesi paste" to Reynolds; on the seventh, taking tea to the sick forced to sit in the hot sun; and on several more occasions managing to obtain extra food for the patients or giving away part of his own.[53] To some extent, he was following his own advice: helping those who really needed it.

On the eighth of August, blackouts and air-raid alarms began[54] as the hospital prepared for the new doctor. The arrival of the U.S. Navy medical officer, James Eppley, close to midnight on the ninth,[55] came too late for British LAC Harry Jackson, RAF, however. One of the "Hakodate boys" who had been beaten unmercifully despite being "a mass of sores," Jackson died at age twenty-seven of colitis and malnutrition, hours earlier.[56]

Life—and hope—had to go on. Lindeijer recorded the name and address of one of Reynolds's visitors over the last several days, Franklin Erving "Curly" Curtis, at General Delivery, Decatur, Texas.[57]

Dear Nel and youngsters   11 August '43

    Several days ago, some Americans received a kind of telegram-letter in answer to their letters of half March. Oh, how happy I would be with any news at all from you! Are you still living at Dago Road or did you have to move to some institute, packed together with other families? How is your health? What is the attitude of the "Inlanders" [indigenous Javanese]? Did you find good friends? Sometimes, the life here is oppressive; what wonderful possibilities there were in the freedom we enjoyed earlier, almost without noticing. But most of all, I miss the comfortable warmth of home and the play of the children. Whenever I think of them I see them in front of me as they were in the past. They will frighten me, I think! But we will also have changed a great deal, Nel! Who knows ... [suspension points in original] perhaps to our advantage.

Feliz was one of the recipients of the telegrams[58]; *thus, the* Houston *crewmen's families now recognized that they were alive. Lindeijer made an effort to focus on good in the present.*

    An American doctor arrived here yesterday. He was taken prisoner on Guam on 10 December '41. Also 2 sergeant orderlies, one from Kisha [sic, Kiska], in the Aleutians. We may get a busier life now, but that doctor is good fortune for the camp. Gribnau and I are lucky to stay in our separate little room in the hospital. We are freer here with more space than in the barracks, less chance of theft. I write now on the edge of my bed. We also eat there and sometimes play chess. There is no chair or table and we are not allowed to make those. We do enjoy our mosquito nets this summer. Lots of midges and flies. I received a striped blanket from Van Leent from which I hope to make a dayshirt for winter. In general, one expects that the war in Europe will end this year, and here in the spring of '44. The end comes in sight. Hope is life! All of you, a kiss from <u>Wim</u>.

    For practical purposes, the month continued much as it had begun. A Swedish Red Cross visitor arrived, but was primarily kept drinking tea in the camp office.[59] *On the twenty-sixth, as punishment for some minor infraction, Lindeijer was forced to stand at attention for the entire afternoon, and by five o'clock had collapsed.*[60] *Recovering, he learned that Reynolds and Feliz, both still in the hospital, had argued and nearly come to blows, then negotiated an interim truce: "under the circumstances," they had "dropped [the matter] with the agreement to finish it when [they were] in better shape."*

    Prolonged privation had worn the best of them down. Yet had Lindeijer reread the letter to his son from the beginning of April, he could hardly have considered the entire spring and summer a loss. Its advice had much in common with the positive and modulated approach that he and others had developed with Iwashita. The admonition to be a friend and help implied empathy, yet was clearly distinct from overdone sympathy or loss of one's

7. Spring and Summer, 1943

own point of view. It was rather a delicately balanced "middle voice" that allowed for considering other perspectives and possibly expanding one's own.

In the ward, Reynolds still studiously avoided Feliz while making wooden checkers in his hospital bed.[61] Strong differences could arise even between friends. The two men should have been playing chess.

8

Kamaishi, Fall–Winter 1943–44— A Space Where There Was None

At the end of August, cooler nights and the beginning of blanket weather aroused the prisoners' apprehension over their ability to survive a second Ohashi winter. Some speculated on the possible lack of a need to do so, based on news from the secret radio: Allied air power, both in Europe and the Pacific, was now superior, and together with a submarine blockade, the effect on Japan's shipping and troop movements would be devastating. Yet such intelligence could hardly dispel their anxiety. An Allied advance northward would mean hope, but simultaneously pose the danger of being caught in the approaching war. Aggravated by their most recent plagues—biting flies by day, and mosquitoes and fleas at night— they waited. Everyone felt the strain; most of all, the British prisoner Stanley Elvy, RAF, who on the morning of August 30 attempted an escape. The poor fellow was brought back to camp by evening, caught as a result of becoming sick to his stomach: traces of his illness had left a trail for his pursuers.[1]

As if to compensate, on the 31st, all the Dutch in camp, the Indonesian Dutch included, wore their green uniforms in honor of Queen Wilhelmina's birthday.[2] *Lindeijer also honored his wife, who he hoped celebrated her own birthday and continuation of life.*

Darling Nel and children　　　　　　　　31 August '43

More than ever my thoughts are with you. Are the boys and Joke happy for their mother's birthday? And yourself, are you too in good spirits, Nel? I can't put away that oppressive feeling that you cannot and will not continue to be well. Except for some Americans, we have received no message from home yet. We were told [by the Red Cross visitor] that there are a half a million letters waiting in Tokyo. Perhaps mere conjecture.

It seems that the Americans are gaining ground, but it goes terribly slow. The last newspaper, of 13 July, reports about the landing on Sicily and fighting in New Georgia. The Japanese have built ever more houses here in the valley. Some are already occupied by women and children: people evacuated from

8. Kamaishi, Fall–Winter 1943–44

Hakodate. There is also a second railroad under construction from the mine to Kamaishi and the nearby blast furnaces on the coast.

The relocations from the strategic port city of Hakodate further sensitized the prisoners to their own vulnerability. Hokkaido, the island to their north, on which Hakodate was located, not only supplied food to the main Japanese island of Honshu, but coal and limited oil for fueling its war industries.³ The evacuation of civilians, together with recent air patrols, indicated high-level nervousness over the area's security. Not so far away, in Ohashi, the prisoners hoped that the mountains that had long isolated them might yet be their sanctuary.

A few days ago that civilian Japanese [whom I've mentioned] showed me the laboratory of the mine and the working of the iron ore. He saw me developing the chemistry course and asked me whether I would like to work in the laboratory. You understand that it suits me to do chemical work, but I have not decided yet. I would have to forego [sic] many advantages; I would have to move to the barracks. The lab is also small and poorly equipped.

Iwashita had been stunned at the relative sophistication of the technical content that Lindeijer, a lowly army private, was creating for his chemistry course. Apparently, in Japanese military culture, a graduate level education was inconceivable for anyone beneath the rank of officer.⁴ Lindeijer's explanation that the haste of the draft in Java had ruled out officer's training did little to lessen the other's incredulity. Nonetheless, both the exchange and the offer to transfer to the laboratory had been interesting …

An Englishman walked away yesterday morning but had already been taken prisoner again in Kamaishi in the evening. We don't know what is going to happen to the poor man.⁵

The food is very insipid and meager again. Yet I feel relatively well. Sometimes, we can buy a small, hard cake, or we get one from the Jap. orderly. The American doctor does good work here. He has already saved one life with an appendicitis operation. There is no Jap. surgeon!

I made a shirt with long sleeves from the blanket I received from Van Leent, so that I am fine now on underwear. I also made new wooden slippers and washed the blankets, etc.; all that for the winter and a possible move.

Now, people, I so dearly hope that this day will pass enjoyably. Perhaps good friends will come to visit. I am also interested in how the Lindeijers [in Holland] are doing. Bye for now. Kisses for all from your <u>Wim</u>.

During the first days of September, the new doctor's ability to effect improvements helped to lift spirits. The man "knew how to exert influence on the Japanese camp staff," as Lieutenant Groeneveld observed: their diet seemed better, a bread oven was under construction, and a revised policy allowed them the freedom of the camp between supper and roll call. A demonstration of surgical skill in which he removed the American George

Stoddard's appendix in thirty minutes apparently worked wonders to convince the authorities of his usefulness.[6]

By the third of September, attention in the hospital turned to something additional, however. More intelligence had emerged about the war's going well in the Allies' favor. Lindeijer was unable to detect a source. By all appearances, Reynolds was now well-connected; Feliz, perhaps better.[7] In any case, he was grateful to be informed, despite the double edge to one late-arriving report: in Europe, the German bombing of London was being reciprocated by the Allies. In attacks on the city of Hamburg in late July, as many as forty thousand had died; the implications, momentous for populations on either side.

At midnight on the fourth, with Gribnau and the two American orderlies, he assisted Dr. Eppley in taking one of the Indonesian Dutch, twenty-one-year-old Klaas Feenstra, to the hospital in Ohashi. The doctor attempted to remove a tumor from the youth's kidney but failed after nearly three hours. The tumor was entangled, and too large. Unaware of the outcome, Feenstra would have a limited time to live.[8]

> Monday, 6 Sept. Today, we scrubbed [hospital] rooms and corridors: we simply threw buckets of water onto the planks, and dirt and water flowed away between the chinks! ...

[Original double-sided pages numbered 59–62, accounting for autumn through at least late November, are missing.]

Lindeijer was to say little after the war about the interval represented by the pages missing from his diary, except to trusted intimates; to them he related details of an unexpected night visit that he received from a Japanese officer, which led to his lengthy absence from the Ohashi camp. The visit, likely on 12 September, may have resulted from well-intentioned reporting by Iwashita to his superiors: a prisoner writing a high-level chemistry text might be put to better use in the laboratory, and the prisoner himself, perhaps pleased. Lindeijer recorded the surprise visit at the time, but apparently later decided that its entry and at least one that followed would be better destroyed.[9]

In the days leading up to the visit, nothing suggested that anything other than the proposed transfer to the laboratory might lie in store. The time passed unremarkably, with the exception, on the ninth, of what Reynolds termed "the best of rumors," which proved to be the news of Italy's surrender, announced over the radio on the eighth, after taking place on the third; not in August as he had thought earlier.[10]

Lindeijer was unsettled, therefore, by what took place on the night of the twelfth. As he sat in the ward writing and keeping watch, a high-ranking Japanese Army officer—a colonel, if he remembered correctly—opened the

8. Kamaishi, Fall–Winter 1943–44

door and entered the room behind him.[11] Turning, he identified his visitor, sprang to his feet to perform the requisite bow, and stood at attention. The officer approached with some accompanying troops, curiously absent the usual fanfare. Lindeijer was thankful that he worked on the modern chemistry course that evening, less dangerous by far than the diary.

It had been strange how the officer scrutinized him, picked up his work and examined it, and began asking questions in German. What was his background, at what university had he studied, and what aspect of modern chemistry was his specialty? Lindeijer's response that his undergraduate and PhD work had been at the University of Leiden prompted a nod of recognition. Like many of Japan's high and mid-level officers, the man was likely educated in Germany, and thus aware of Leiden's reputation: impressive in chemistry, and perhaps third in the world, after Göttingen and Copenhagen, in theoretical physics. Lindeijer's dissertation, on the explosivity of gas mixtures, overlapped chemistry and physics, and provoked interest,[12] perhaps too much.

The officer's use of German was telling. Gribnau, the ward's other German speaker, had already retired for the evening. The interview was clearly designed to prevent its ultimate topic—the time needed for the United States to make an atomic bomb—from being understood by the room at large. Fearing coercion to work on a weapons program, Lindeijer began with a high estimate of three generations, or seventy-five years, based on time needed to enrich the uranium.[13] The officer pressed, negotiating further to a minimum of twenty-five; then confiscating a sample of Lindeijer's papers, quietly departed with his troops.

Had it then been two weeks or three before he received the order to pack his things and be ready to leave? The move, when it came, had been in darkness, to a house in an unknown location which he guessed to be on the outskirts of Kamaishi. It was to be a long time before he would write again to his family.[14]

[Unknown date; late Nov. or early Dec. 1943]

... writing, just like I did when I began these letters on 15 May last year. I suspect that you are sleeping soundly right now. In spirit, I send a kiss and wishes for God's blessings, from your father and Wim.

For a period of weeks in October he had been interviewed, first by army officers and then two scientists, about the same question raised during the night visit. There had been no possibility of documenting the experience as it occurred. He managed this only in late November or early December, sometime after being dropped off at a newly established camp near the blast furnaces on Japan's northeast coast, in Kamaishi.[15] And only much later still, he had second thoughts about having done so. The entire sequence, reaching back to 12 September, might too easily be misconstrued. Removing the entries, he would have noticed that the last lines of the sequence flowed to another page. Happily, the fragment announcing his ability to write to the family again could remain.

What little he did say about the interval after the war was always curiously lacking in detail,[16] though in human terms wholly clear:

Inside the house in Kamaishi, he had been greeted by several mid-level army officers in German and English, who queried him as the colonel had, but in the context of shared meals and a warm fire. The hospitality unnerved him, but even more so the frankness with which they acknowledged that Japan was losing the war. Concerned that he was being manipulated, he wondered whether to trust their apparent openness as real.

Yet keeping his composure, he evaluated what they had to say in light of information he had from the secret radio.[17] Most likely, the loss of New Georgia Island, effectively isolating their base in Rabaul, would have figured in their conversation: the route was now open for an Allied advance toward their homeland. Likewise, in Europe, the surrender of Italy, and particularly the devastation of Hamburg—a major port, with radar and anti-aircraft defenses—would have disturbed them. No city in their own country would have seemed untouchable.

More than by the corroboration of their facts, he was convinced by the distress in their voices, however, and in the end could only judge them sincere.[18] Apparently assigned to fill time with him prior to the arrival of the two scientists (his "real" interviewers), while waiting they pursued an agenda of their own, expressing their concerns about the war. They also had family ties, and in this non-military setting, spoke primarily for themselves. Whether he showed them the photo of Nel and the children was immaterial. It was perhaps a sense of kinship in this regard, and importantly, his experience with Iwashita that prompted him to feel empathy for these officers, despite the differences he had with them. In the space of time before the scientists arrived, he found himself in real dialogue with them.

What he was clear about regarding the episode in the postwar was the value he placed on the human communication it represented. One can only conjecture whether he gained insight into his own assumptions in addition to those of the officers. Since the Japanese invasion of the Dutch East Indies, he had viewed the citizens of his own society as victims. The officers likely saw them collectively as Western (and white) colonial overseers. One needed only to think of the status of the multiracial Indonesian Dutch—Dutch citizens under the law, but less equal in financial terms or the eyes of society—to recognize the truth in this.[19] The indigenous peoples were another matter altogether, receiving even less equable treatment.

8. Kamaishi, Fall–Winter 1943–44

Whatever the details, the sense he would convey later was that in the end nothing, and yet everything, had changed. The officers had remained captors, and he their prisoner. Yet empathy and mutual concerns allowed them to suspend judgment and listen for a while.

Finally, the two scientists arrived. He was surprised by their youth and even more by the ease (or was it relief?) with which they accepted his estimate of twenty-five years for atomic bomb making. Their own senior scientists had already refuted the idea that any country could produce such a weapon during the current conflict. Despite this, the two found themselves assigned to an Army project in Tokyo intended nominally at least for this purpose.[20] Without going so far as to antagonize their escorting officer, they projected a realistic pessimism. They had virtually none of the equipment or resources needed; most critically, enriched uranium. Clearly reluctant to embrace their military's objectives, they departed, his interview abruptly concluded.

Afterward, adjusting to the new camp, Lindeijer might well have asked himself: to what extent did Iwashita's independence of mind reflect other Japanese? And how, after his exchange with the officers, was he to regard his family's suffering, and his own colonial Dutch identity?

Dear people, Kamaishi   19 December '43

I'm still detached [in the military sense, of being sent away from one's unit] to this Dutch camp.[21] It's a difficult time. There are now seven people dead, six of them of pneumonia. Right now we have 25 sick, 17 of whom have pneumonia. The last group has to be helped with everything and is very restless: winding their bedclothes into a ball all the time and wanting to get up, while complete rest is prescribed. Although their number is still growing, there are fortunately some showing signs of recovery.

Ironically, since his announcement of his ability to write again, he had been too busy to make another entry until now. The dust-ridden environment of this camp for Nippon Steel[22] produced high numbers of patients. The return he had requested to Ohashi was unlikely to take place soon.

23 Dec. '43 Yesterday, some frightfully high-ranking officers, Big Shots (perhaps they're called something else in Japanese!), were here, with a lot of brass on their chests. However, their "inspection" turned into quite a drama for them. We had everything neatly cleaned, but by the time the "gentlemen" appeared, a little storm broke loose, covering everything with a thick layer of dust. Finally, a strong gust of wind unhinged windows and doors and blew half the roof over the fence.

After the initial shock, we extinguished the stoves, carried the patients, beds and all, to the barracks, and as well as possible, picked the glass splinters out of the blankets. Fortunately, no one was injured. So long as it did not harm the patients, this could not have happened at a better moment. The Big Shots could only inspect the rubble. Dozens of Japanese [regulars] helped and worked hard, so the patients can probably be returned by this afternoon.

Alas, it looks as though I will have to be here for Christmas. It's very busy with two- or four-hour shifts per night, but the work here is more satisfactory than in Ohashi.

<u>28 Dec.</u> Kamaishi. Christmas has passed already. Naturally, full of sad thoughts. How are you doing? This war seems endless. There are rumors flying about over the capitulation of Germany. Oh, how I long to see you again! I imagine that you celebrated a happy Christmas in the camp. Perhaps with a Christmas tree and some presents.

He had learned definitively from his interviewers at the house: the Dutch women and children in Java were in camps. He wanted desperately to believe the assurances of one officer in particular, that as such they were "under protection" and safe.[23]

Even here, some people made a little Christmas tree with handmade candles and bells. The "tree" was also brought to the hospital, where we sang carols. With gratitude I recall my recovery from that terrible throat disease a year ago now.

The work here is frantic and sad. There are twelve dead now and 24 sick. Fortunately, 6 have recovered from pneumonia. There is progress! From my heart, God bless you all!

31 Dec. '43 New Year's Eve. My fervent wish, written down a year ago, that we would be together again by now is unfulfilled. We still moil and toil from one month to another, languishing for family happiness. It is difficult not to complain. And yet, what a privilege to be healthy. If only I could say the same of you; now I can only pray for it! In my thoughts you are all heartily kissed. Your loving husband and father, Wim.

1 Jan. '44 Dear Nel, Wim, Herman, Freddy and Joke, Kamaishi

Wholeheartedly, I wish my beloved five a very happy New Year! Of course, above all with the wish that we may see each other again this year. But also that our boys and daughter may grow up prosperously. Your task, Nel, will be demanding again this year, but I do hope that you'll remain spared great sorrow. Who knows whether we can still bring some joy into the lives of others. God will then bring joy into our hearts as well.

For the time being, it seems that I will continue to be put to work in Kamaishi. Although I miss my friends and spare time in Ohashi, the work suits me better here. I enjoy the confidence of Doctor Pijma[24] and carry out more responsible tasks. Among other things, I have learned to count white blood corpuscles. It seems that the most serious disease period has passed, which makes our work lighter, too. We work in three shifts of 3, so there is some time off. Unfortunately, the doctor is not very tactful and he quarreled with two orderlies, who had to be replaced. One of these is [Dutch seaman J. G.] Becker, a former student at the Lyceum [the high school in Bandung].

Can Wim and Herman go to school? I suspect that classes will have been

8. Kamaishi, Fall–Winter 1943–44

formed in the women's camp. Freddy is already 4 1/2 now, and Joke nearly 3. When and how will I see you all again? It's a pity that I can do no more than wish you much blessing and happiness. Kisses from husband and father Wim.

8 Jan. '44. A few days ago I heard about an exchange of Japanese prisoners for Dutch women and children from Java. The latter would be sent to South Africa. To be honest, I hope that you are already there, sound and well. You would be safe there from the days of war that Java may yet have to experience. You would be certain to have it best there. You once said that you would love to go there (though not in this way, of course!). It even entered my head that you could settle there and I could look for a job.

Someone here saw how the Japanese Army destroyed a great deal of glassware in the Chemistry classroom of the Lyceum and burned books there.

The 14th prisoner died here today. The doctor wanted to conduct an autopsy on the body. At his direction, another orderly and I opened the chest and abdomen. The doctor showed us the most important organs. Lugubrious, but interesting!

[Ohashi] 17 Jan. '44. I returned to Ohashi yesterday. Happy to see old acquaintances again, especially Gribnau. I didn't like abandoning the work in Kamaishi, but I had to make a decision. I did mainly microscopic work: urine analysis, counting of leucocytes, differential counts on colored blood slides, blood residue, etc. I'll try to persuade Gribnau to ask the "hancho" (the Japanese sergeant orderly, Neko) to allow us to work together in Kamaishi. It's colder here than in Kamaishi, but also less dusty. So there are advantages and disadvantages. Well, we'll see. At the moment the frost could be worse: -3° C [26.6° Fahrenheit] inside our small room this morning.

Last night I had to make the trip here on top of a small open utility vehicle. I nearly died of cold, especially because the departure, for which I waited for more than one and a half months, came suddenly: I had to pack in two minutes with no chance to put on extra warm clothes. Besides that, I was spoiled by the stoves in Kamaishi—three there, one here. Upon arrival, though, I was warmed with the news that I could write home again. Naturally, I did so again, but it's so sad to never receive an answer. Several postcards have arrived here from Java, which has boosted our hope, of course. Among others, de Vogel[25] received two. Bye darlings, kisses from <u>Wim</u> and <u>father</u>.

His desire to return to Ohashi had decreased somewhat as the work in Kamaishi became more gratifying. Still, when he was forced to decide quickly, something pulled in the direction of his former community—his friendship with Gribnau, but also with others, as he had mentioned. He remained conflicted; yet Ohashi was the setting where his identity as Lindy had developed. It might hold unfinished work of a different sort. In any case, determining whether he was to conduct microscopic investigations for Dr. Pijma again would now be a matter for the authorities.

Some aspects of the place to which he had returned were all too familiar: the howling wind, the news of Clarence Bolt's beating over stolen food (termed by Reynolds "the worst I have ever seen anyone receive and live"), and the cavalier shuffling of personnel. Thirty-eight prisoners had been transferred to Hakodate in mid-November.[26] Of the forty Dutch transferred in to replace them a month later, already one, Private Jacobus Hilling, age forty-eight, had died.[27] Another (number 549) had been identified by the barracks as a spy.[28]

Even so, the camp had been spared the numerous deaths of the previous winter. And the holidays brought a touching surprise from one of its "honorable men." On the twenty-fourth of December, the one-armed guard known as "Wingy" had asked about Christmas, and some in the barracks had explained. In response, according to the Texan Ben Kelley, this guard who had been disliked at first ("the one-armed bandit," who "would trade you out of your shirt"), went into Ohashi and returned with enough oranges to give one to each prisoner, "his gift for Christmas." Reynolds pronounced that Wingy had "changed all around." One orange was "not much but there's two hundred men here. A pretty nice thing for a common guard to do."[29]

Resuming his prior duties at the hospital, Lindeijer could only have been reminded of his gratitude for having survived the terrible throat disease of a year ago. As if an omen, during his absence, Feliz and Reynolds had made up. Encountering each other by the fire late in the night of January first, the two had shaken hands and apologized, agreeing "to start the New Year off right." Reynolds had said that he couldn't explain the feeling this had given him. But he would always remember it.[30]

9

Ohashi, 1944—"Quite Something Has Emerged"

Lindeijer had scarcely settled back into his routine at the Ohashi camp hospital when he received the directive that was to result in the two reports that he wrote for the camp administration, on the defense of Java and the overseas transport. Only he and Reynolds, who frequently visited his friend Grant in the hospital, had been singled out, so far as Lindeijer knew, to write in English about their experience during the war, including their most negative experience.[1] Unsure of the authorities' motives, he confided in his fellow medic, but found it reassuring to be reminded of Gribnau's having responded to a similar request without consequence just over a year prior, on 16 December 1942. Lindeijer and Stenfert had been ill at the time with what they had thought were colds. When Stenfert died, the two remaining medics had forgotten the matter—until two months later, when Iwashita surprised them by returning Gribnau's submission, along with the initiating directive.

In light of the present request, they examined the earlier one. Handwritten in German by someone comfortable with the German script, it bore the clear imprint of the Japanese Army.[2]

1. die Eindruck über diesem Krieg [Your Impression of this War][3]
2. die Folg in diesen Krieg [The Course of this War]
3. die Eindruck des Nippon Soldaten [Your Impression of the Japanese Soldiers]
4. die Eindruck im Nippon [Your Impression of Japan]

(Am merking: Schreiben sie inst Deutsch) [Remark: Write in German]

Newly arrived in Ohashi, Gribnau had responded in German as directed, but with caution.

1. My impression of this war is that we were overrun by Japan's military force so quickly that help from England and America—

without which we never would have risked war against Japan—could not be there in time ...

2. ... For the world war as a whole the fronts in Europe and North Africa are very important ...

3. Until the fifth of March 1942 I was still a civilian and was only then registered as a soldier, therefore I have not been on any front and have met no Japanese soldiers in combat. After four days I [became a prisoner] and saw the first Japanese soldiers in the camp in Bandung. As [one] militarily uninitiated, I can only say that Japanese soldiers are, in my evaluation, tough and well disciplined ...

4. During the journey I saw the many factories from the train window and towns which point to a rather technical lifestyle, so Nippon must have an extensive technology ...

With the reassurance Lindeijer had received, the present request far more than the previous one seemed an opportunity to give testimony about the wartime suffering he had witnessed. His mention of the matter to the family was low-key but conveyed a sense of possibility.

<u>7 Feb. '44.</u> Twice again, letters arrived from Java; unfortunately, nothing yet for Gribnau and myself. Several Americans received private [personally addressed] packages.

A few days ago, we received relatively good clothes (trousers + coat). Together with my homemade underwear, I won't be too cold. I must often repair that underwear, but the many added patches keep me nice and warm. I often repair [knee-length] stockings and socks also, because clothing is a real problem. Perhaps I can show you the results one day, Nel!

We did have -10° C [14° F] in our little room, but now it is around 0° C [32° F] again. The winter could be worse; except that we've been without water for about five days now (frozen pipes, etc.), and have to carry it from a nearby source. There have also been many cases of pneumonia here, and while I was in Kamaishi, one even resulted in a death. No serious cases anymore, fortunately.

What a treasure this wholly intact new notebook is! I rustled it up in Kamaishi.

Strangely enough, the Japanese asked us to write about our war experiences, including our most unpleasant experiences, during our time as prisoners of war. You understand that quite something has emerged—especially in regard to this last [the request to write about their worst experiences]! I've done my best to contribute something about the battle of Bandung and the overseas transport.[4]

In general, we have no complaints about the treatment and the food these days.

Indeed, quite something had emerged; alternatively, in Dutch, "a beautiful thing had shaken loose." Someone in a position of influence was interested the worst of their wartime experience. Responding on the twenty-sixth of January, Lindeijer made an effort to place the authority he addressed nearly "in the shoes," as it were, of those whose suffering he had witnessed.

Reynolds, in a report the same day, took a dramatically different but no less spirited tack. In his "opinion of the war and some of the battles [he] was in and what [he] saw," the feisty crewman made no bones about putting "the Nips [sic] on the losing side of everything." He might "get a kick back on it," he said. "The Nips are pretty riled up over something these days." On the twenty-seventh, directed to rewrite with supporting detail, he was undeterred: "Boy I really put the detail in this one."[5]

10 Feb. '44. Dear people, Today we are allowed to write [home] again. Since there is always a small chance that it will arrive, I do it, of course. But it's so discouraging when you never hear anything in return. Mail, letters and Christmas cards, has just been distributed; nearly all for Americans. The Christmas cards were sent in November '42 and arrived here too late for Christmas '43!

Within a short time, his attention had shifted to something seemingly positive, however. Reynolds had heard nothing further about his submission, but in Lindeijer's case, Iwashita returned both of his reports. Whether the annotations in Japanese that remain visible, even today, on every page of the report on the battle of Bandung—penciled in above the English— were the work of Iwashita himself or someone in the camp office, possibly with Iwashita's help, cannot be known.[6] (There were no annotations on the report about the conditions of the transport; sadly, the authorities' interest had apparently been a purely military one.) Nor can it be known whether Iwashita might actually have sat down with Lindeijer in the camp hospital to talk over the reports in person. The inquisitive liaison had addressed spirited questions to Gribnau in a written response to the latter's submission the year prior, however. At a minimum, Lindeijer's awareness of that interchange would have made it inconceivable for him to believe that Iwashita had not read the two reports that he, Lindeijer had currently submitted. And in reading them he would have encountered new perspectives on the war, perhaps causing him think twice about officially sanctioned views ...

In the earlier case, Iwashita had sent Gribnau a letter dated 22 February 1943, handwritten in (self-described) "inadequate English," expressing consternation over one of Gribnau's statements.[7] "It distresses me," Gribnau had said, "never to have been able to send a message to my wife and children in Deli (Sumatra), nor to have received any message from them, so that I do not know how they live." Astounded not so much by the sentiment itself as by what he perceived it left out, the Japanese civilian fired back: It was "an incomprehensible thing for us [Japanese]," he said, "that you did not [say] a *word about your fatherland in your note. You wrote only about your family and [earlier, about] your compatriots."* Quite naturally Gribnau was concerned about his wife and children; Iwashita himself had a family whom he valued, and for whom he worked every day, "hoping to make their life happy." Yet one's fatherland was "more precious than our private life." If his government were to draft him, he would "manfully respond to its demand."

Gribnau attempted an explanation via return note: *"You are right Sir, in saying that one's native country is more precious than one's private life. But what if one's private life cannot possibly be offered any more? When one is a prisoner of war one has to wait for peace, and one's mind turns to private things more than before. But that does not mean that I should have forgotten my fatherland. The reason for [our difference] in this respect is that you can speak as a free man, a member of a fighting people, for whom war is in full swing."*

His interest thoroughly piqued, by March 1943, Iwashita was stopping in regularly to see the Dutch medics—who likewise had more to learn about him. What were the implications of "more precious than our private life"? Did Iwashita really believe that the policies of the state, however unreasonable, merited the unconditional support of its citizens? Did he accept his government's propagandized view of its aggression, as necessary to free the Pacific of Western domination and promote "co-prosperity"? More likely, he was caught in a double bind. His government and military had started a war that might be impossible for them to win. Yet in the event of a threat to his homeland, he would have no choice other than to join in. "It is said," he had written, "that the Greater War of East Asia is the greatest war in the history of our country." "If we should be defeated by our enemies, we [Japanese] could never rise again."

Now, a year later, it was fair to wonder whether their liaison no longer accepted unquestioned an agenda-driven version of events. Double-bind or no, was he coming to grips with the war himself?[8]

8 March '44 A time lag of a month! This way it appears as if time goes faster. There is, however, not a day that I do not think of you. Can Herman still draw so nicely? He certainly did not inherit that art from me! Wim becomes 8 already and is in the midst of his mental growth. You know, Nel, how I miss the children! Oh, and it's always painful to think of home. Today, the capitulation [of the Dutch East Indies] is two years old.

He was hardly alone in marking the anniversary. *Men from the Houston and Perth recalled their furious engagements off Java's coast. By now, most of their group had the "dope" (code for intelligence from the radio) that their other survivors, last seen at Singapore, had been sent off to work on a railroad in Thailand or Burma "or somewhere." They believed that by now nearly all were dead from mistreatment. On 2 March, the American lieutenant from Texas, Maxwell Humble, led services in the bath house for the presumed lost.*[9]

Thoughts of the lieutenant prompted a new topic.

Except for two [Lieutenant Humble and the American Captain Zeigler], all officers left for Hakodate and from there, possibly for an officers' camp. A pity that Van Leent is gone. I hope to see him again in Bandung.[10]

The departed officers would be greatly missed. Still, the list of Ohashi camp grievances they took with them to present to the area commander might bring improvements.[11] *In the meantime, Captain Zeigler was proving dexterous without their support, the nighttime incident in which two of the Indonesian Dutch were caught urinating into the water barrel being case in point. Rather than turning them over to the Japanese for beating "within an inch of their lives," the captain put them in the hands of two of the Houston crew, Godfrey and Rich. Reynolds recounted the result: "They didn't put up much of a fight. Rich knocked his out with one punch and Godfrey knocked his down three times. Later, the captain, Rich, Godfrey and the victims all shook hands."*[12] *Lindeijer could only applaud.*

Yet more than this might be needed for relationships to move forward. The incident triggered memory of a challenge from Iwashita's letter to Gribnau: "It seems to me," *the liaison had written,* "that you despise Indo Europeans very much. There is an antagonism between pure Dutch and [the Indonesian Dutch]. From [what source] does this antagonism originate?"[13]

"I do not at all despise Indo Europeans," *Gribnau had shot back. It was not Indo Europeans in general, but some in the resident group that he did not like.* "...I do not know why just these men were gathered together in this camp. They have bad manners, make troubles enough among themselves and sometimes one fights another." *Even some members of the group might have wished for better company, themselves, he concluded.*[14]

Yet the question nagged, most recently, in regard to a book that Iwashita brought from Tokyo, which currently circulated in the hospital, The Conquered, *by Naomi Mitchison.*[15] *Reynolds had pronounced it* "good." *Its central character, a slave, had a master who was at the same time his rescuer and benefactor. Giving the loyalty he owed meant denial of his own identity. The situation was that of the victims of dominating societies in any age. Who was "the conquered" in the present narrative? Iwashita's question forced recognition of tacit complicity with a level of oppression in Lindeijer's Dutch Indies prewar society; oppression with a racial dimension that had ramifications in the larger war and in Ohashi. Unlike his valued, mixed-blood Dutch teaching colleagues in Java, the Indonesian Dutch in the camp had originated in the poorer areas of Java's cities.*[16] *Inequality and deprivation might have contributed to their resentment.*

A few weeks ago, I applied for a transfer to the Kamaishi camp. The work there gave me a lot of satisfaction: more responsibility, and so on, as I wrote you earlier. Hakatayama has refused, however. It doesn't bother me much, because here I have more spare time and the camp is nicer. Not so dusty, and consequently healthier.

There may have been another reason that had to go unexpressed. In beneficial ways, the prisoners' relationship with Iwashita had changed them both. It was likely important to see where it might lead, despite the challenges it could raise. Having grown used to thinking of Iwashita as the one who needed most to enlarge his perspective, they could be startled—as in the matter of the Indonesian Dutch—to discover areas in which they needed to grow themselves.

On 5 March, the American Red Cross surprised us with another package. It contains butter, cheese, sugar, coffee, chocolate, cigarettes, jam, corned beef, bacon, meat pie, dried prunes, salmon, soap, bouillon, powdered milk, and vitamin C; all of it exquisite stuff. I hope to enjoy it for at least one or two months. I have already bartered 6 of my 10 packages of cigarettes for salmon, butter, and bread. Approximately every three days, we get a bread meal and that is quite a treat, especially now with the [Red Cross] package. I just ate my best meal of the year: four slices of bread with butter and jam. I never knew how delicious that could be!

Astonishingly, this time each man received his full package, with no items missing. More astonishing, even their regular food was better than that of the Japanese.[17] *Cynics in the barracks attributed the change to Lieutenant Naganuma's sense of a shift in the winds of war.*

Since the worst of the cold is over, I can sit in our little room again, as I do now, at 4° C [39.2°]. Also the small textbook on Chemistry grows again. I'll try to spell it all out, although there is many a point that does not satisfy me. I may be able to use it later as basic material, perhaps. Once in a while there are letters coming in. Coffield [one of the American medics transferred in with Dr. Eppley] received 14 letters in one batch! Full of envy, Gribnau and I still await the first! Keep courage!

He spoke too soon about the weather. By 12 March, they had snow five feet deep with ten-foot drifts, and the electricity was off.[18] *The prisoners might have been downhearted, had the air not been alive with rumor. Everyone, including the Japanese camp personnel, seemed to grasp that the American counter-offensive was working. Lessons learned during the amphibious landings at Tarawa in the Gilbert chain had been put to good use in the Marshall Islands. The Marshalls, once the outer ring of Japan's island defenses, were now in the hands of the Allies. The Marianas, critical to the inner ring, would surely be next.*

The effect on the camp's Japanese workers was striking. Hunger and shortages were taking their toll, along with news of the defeats and heavy casualties (8500 in a single recent battle, according to a speech by Tojo, the Prime Minister). Individuals previously silent about the war muttered opinions out of earshot of their superiors. An employee in the mine's electrical workshop allowed to Captain Zeigler that the war would end soon; he didn't "know [what was] holding Nippon up right now."[19] A mine supervisor confessed to one of the RAF men, Frank Planton, that Japan had been "silly" to start the war.[20] Most arresting of all, a bus driver from Tokyo, in an appearance at the mine's 350-meter level repair shop, was scathing in his contempt for the situation. Entering the shop, and engaging Reynolds, whom he had never before met, the man reportedly "threw a broken pair of pliers down [...] and said disgustedly, 'Made in Japan.'" No doubt many more had opinions of the war they weren't free to express. The camp's personnel were proving to be more varied than the prisoners would have guessed. "These people are tired of this war too," Reynolds said. In another speech, Tojo had advised the population to prepare for a five-year war. "My God," the red-haired American exclaimed, "they aren't getting enough to eat now."[21]

13 March. Today two Hollanders were allowed to send a telegram. Gribnau and I were the lucky ones. It was about a year ago that we wrote for the first time, but it is quite possible that this telegram will arrive earlier.

The day before yesterday, I began doing microscopic analysis here. I am happy to do that.

16 March. This evening we were taken by surprise with a distribution of clothes by the American Red Cross. Gribnau and I each received a thick woolen pullover, a towel, and a pair of stockings. Others received underwear, a thick cap, gloves, or summer clothes. I later exchanged the towel for a warm American cap of very good quality. The distribution is quite arbitrary, but everyone has something of excellent quality, of course. It is forbidden to sell or barter outside the camp. Both the Japanese and the accomplice prisoner will be punished if a Japanese is caught with Red Cross clothes.

Such trading did take place, of course. Particularly their older guards, the "Honorable Men," were eager to obtain goods that they could sell at a profit on the black market. The prisoners benefited: to protect themselves from being reported, the Honorable Men found it prudent to protect the interests of the prisoners. Upon learning of a coming inspection, they might rush through the barracks shouting "Search! Search! Search!"[22] To some extent, a community of mutual interest was developing. Prisoners who had things to conceal during an inspection were known to give them to the Honorable Men to stuff under their shirts. Following the inspection, the Honorable Men would give them back.[23]

Quantity-wise, there is plenty of food these days. Flavor is added with the small tins from the packages. On night duty I enjoy eating toast with butter + jam or cheese and a cup of coffee!

No warning had been needed for the inspection on 25 March. The camp office announced that Colonel Hakatayama, the area commander in Hakodate, had been promoted to general, and was being replaced. Lieutenant Colonel Emoto, the new commander, would come to inspect. He was well educated and spoke English "as fast and plain as Walter Winchell," the men said afterward. But he was too stern, telling them they needed only the most basic food.[24]

28 March '44 The day before yesterday, a new doctor arrived here (American, from the Philippines) with four orderlies. Medically speaking, totally superfluous [because we already have enough staff], but we must wait and see what the Japanese have in mind. This doctor (Tucker) seems nicer to me than his predecessor (Eppley). Of late, I have enjoyed the work much more; I get more microscopic work to do now, thanks to what I learned in Kamaishi.

This morning, I scored a nice success: I found little eggs in a patient's feces, which Tucker thought to be tapeworm eggs. Now I'll try to find the worm segments.

The new personnel, men who had served on Corregidor and Cavite, brought fresh intelligence that quietly raised morale. Manila was a deserted city; the Japanese there anticipated attacks "any day." Further, the 17–18 February Allied attack on Truk Island had been a particular triumph, equivalent in magnitude to the Japanese attack on Pearl Harbor. Formerly the key airbase that supported Japan's outer defenses, it had effectively been neutralized without an invasion. Even prisoners who already knew of the attack were cheered at hearing the number of planes downed and ships sunk: "These guys say we pulled a Pearl Harbor on Truk."[25]

On the morning of 31 March, one segment of the barracks received a boost from another source. During a surprise inspection, they had next to nothing taken. "Wingy," the one-armed guard, who had distributed oranges at Christmas, had conducted the search.[26]

2 April '44. There were no segments of a tapeworm, but what I [had] found was a roundworm. In the body of that worm I found hundreds of the same eggs that I also found in the feces. So those were roundworm eggs. Besides that, I have now found two other types of eggs, but nothing yet about the corresponding worm types.

We have two patients in isolation, who need to be cared for night and day. Thanks to the four new orderlies (total of eight now) we each take only three hour shifts. I was very fortunate. My watch is in the morning from 6 to 9; thus, immediately after breakfast (we get up at 5 a.m.). After that, I go to work with the microscope; then, in the afternoon, read, write [the chemistry text], play chess, etc. A Japanese mine employee whom I helped once with his mathematics promised to do what he could to buy a textbook on Differential and Integral Calculus for me. I do have money because I sold my raincoat for 30 yen. Oh, how splendidly I could spend my time nicely on mathematics!

9. Ohashi, 1944

8 April '44. <u>Ohashi</u>. Dear Nel,

I find it difficult to write today: the birthday of our eldest son. I know how sad this day must be for you too, and yet the children expect a happy face. Yes, that is what they would want to see from me too—people always expect that from you—but for children, it's different; for them it is a deep-felt need. Joy in life is what they need for their spiritual growth. Everyday I worry about how our children are growing up. How I do wish you strength and wisdom in these sad times, Nel! I cannot write Wim as I did last year. I am too possessed by sorrow and hate.

The Japanese become disgustingly friendly. Even for a serious infringement they no longer utter a harsh word, where earlier they would have nearly killed you for it. They come with presents and have stopped stealing Red Cross things. Yes, they know now that they are losing the war, but it takes terribly long! I don't believe that we will return this year. Yet when we do, our lives will be much happier than they ever were before the war. We will be less afraid to face difficulties, and more grateful for our lives.

Meanwhile, I hope that you have received my first postcard. In spirit a kiss from <u>Wim</u>. Also for our loved ones, especially for our Wim on his birthday.

16 April '44

We are allowed to write [a postcard] home again. I'll start [today's letter-entry] with this [fuller version of the card]. It's so difficult to find suitable words that will pass the censorship. Luckily I can report that I'm doing well. The day after Wimmie's birthday, each of us received half a Red Cross package; a nice replenishment of the almost-empty box of 5 March. Sometime thereafter many, including Gribnau and I, received a pair of American army boots from the Red Cross. Magnificent shoes with leather soles covered in thick rubber, much stronger and less heavy than the English army boots.

This morning, we went to the graveyard and placed 12 new crosses on the graves of the deceased prisoners. The original crosses may have been used for firewood by the area people. There are still long rows of small wooden houses being built in this valley, probably for evacuees.

This evening we all receive an egg! Our first in Japan. I plan to devour mine tonight during my watch duty, with some bread I saved.

My little Chemistry textbook is ready; that is to say, the organic part. I will leave it at that, except that I'll finish the English translation. In order to use it for school, I'll certainly have to recast it, but this can serve as the basis.

With others, he monitored results of the change, on 21 April, in their camp's jurisdiction. They were no longer Hakodate Branch Camp Number Two, but Tokyo Branch Number Six. A new camp commandant, Sublieutenant Inaki Makoto, replaced Lieutenant Naganuma.[27] The thought of oversight from Tokyo was a worry. Yet by 30 April, their consensus was that Sublieutenant Inaki was "not a bad fellow." He had put up volleyball nets, played ball with the men, and refused to allow the guards to beat them. They could scarcely believe their good fortune.

Meanwhile, those in the hospital saw a positive trend of a different sort.

Reynolds was back as a patient, after an appendix operation with a spinal that "barely took." Sufficiently recovered to hold court, he was receiving visits from his "Dutch friend Dias"; Van Room, the "Balinese kid"; and Becker, "the Dutch office orderly."[28] *Just possibly, a new little society was forming. Iwashita, chatting with their perennial patient, Grant,*[29] *was no doubt pleased. Reynolds was emerging as a friend of the Indonesian Dutch.*

> <u>2 May</u> <u>'44</u> Dear Nel and youngsters, An unpleasant change took place yesterday. I am dismissed as an orderly and now must work with the others outside. Fortunately, not in the mine, but in the so-called "Denki," the electricity workshop [of the mines]. The work yesterday was not heavy, but it makes you terribly dirty. Fortunately, I still have an old Japanese suit which I can use. This sudden change is by order from Tokyo. All orderlies who cannot prove by their documents that they belong to the Red Cross must go and work outside. It's a pity that my field papers don't confirm that I am a Red Cross soldier. Well, we will see. We are happy with the approach of summer. Kisses from <u>Wim</u> and Father.

His training as a draftee for the medical corps of the KNIL had necessarily been sketchy. As a prisoner in Bandung, he attempted to compensate by taking classes for Dutch "Silver Cross" certification with Red Cross equivalency, but the October transport had cut this short, leaving him without

The "Denki." Hiroe Iwashita photo (Lindeijer Family Archive).

official papers from the Red Cross.[30] *He would need to move to the barracks and would now see much less of Gribnau. The latter's extensive translation work for the camp office had resulted in an exception that allowed him to continue in the hospital.*[31]

<u>6 May</u>. Dear people,

Today it is Joke's birthday, 3 years old already. How plucky she will have grown in the eyes of her mother. In my eyes, too, when I think of her, and that happens a lot these days. I am afraid she will be too much of a darling to her mother. You know, Nel, how readily I would have loved to celebrate this day with you and the children. Yet, I do hope that it will be a nice birthday for our little one, be it with or [more likely] without the tarts, I guess.

It's fine here. Usually the work is not hard and I received some sort of overalls to protect my clothes. I hate the dirty grease and tar, and whatever else it's called. Yesterday, something funny happened: I noticed that the Japanese cleaned their batteries and topped them up with what they thought to be sulphuric acid, but it was nitric acid! They and the Americans who worked with them were baffled that the batteries failed so quickly! More than 30 batteries had already been ruined.[32]

I suddenly acquired a good reputation with the Japanese. The [workshop] boss came to me later and asked whether I could cut a round of glass out of a glass sheet. However, there was nothing for cutting glass. So I said "ashita testo" ["tomorrow, a test"],[33] and went to Gribnau to get a "glass-knife," with which I'll start the job this morning.

Well, people, I must stop now. Kisses for all of you, especially for Joke on her birthday, from husband and father, <u>Wim</u>

The barracks' complete lack of privacy took some adjustment. He was crowded onto the top tier of the row of bunks nearest the parade ground, at the "American end," close to the front gates.[34] *The "American group" (which included the Australians, he soon learned) numbered the smallest, with roughly a dozen men on each of the two tiers on either side of the aisle; at this point in the life of the camp, forty-seven in all. The ninety-three Dutch occupied both sides of the middle section; the fifty-six British, both sides of the far end.*[35]

The divisions were more than spatial. Too often a tendency arose to regard another nationality—or even a subset of one's own nationality—as "other." In most cases, the differences could be smoothed over: as in the case of the American and Australian tendency to see the British as "stuffy"—something that no doubt dated from the latter's having administered the camp at Changi for the Japanese—or the American Navy men's occasional resentment of army Captain Zeigler's seniority.

Discrimination against the Indonesian Dutch was more serious, however. Here and there, a westerner still cast a slur: expressing dislike, for example, of bathing in the large bathhouse tub after "the Black Dutch" had used the water. Distrust was another problem ("*for a bowl of rice, they'd tell [the Japanese] everything they knew*"). Granted there was an informer in the group. Gribnau had been called to the office this spring to translate some fifth column material.[36] But tarring all ninety-three over the misconduct of one or a few was hardly humane or reasonable.

Facing the aisle, Lindeijer found himself at the intersection of two groups: Americans on his left and Dutch on his right. The Allied officers— Zeigler, Humble, Eppley, and Tucker—were some distance away, at bottom left on the other side.[37] From where he sat in this barracks of 196 men, the potential for incivility could be considerable. At the same time, after his experience in Kamaishi, this might be the next phase of his education; he might find friends here who would become allies in dialogue throughout the camp.

> 16 May '44. It was more than two years ago that I started these letters. On 15th May '42, you told me, Nel, that you had enough money to continue to live at that level for another two years. In the meantime, I hope that you have moved to an acceptable camp. No doubt life will be even cheaper there, and perhaps safer too. There may even be little difference between "freedom" here and at the Dago Road. In addition, it may be possible to improvise some schooling for the children in a camp.

The seers of his own camp predicted fifteen more months of imprisonment. His family's health and meager resources might have to stretch that long. Meanwhile, on 13 May, Colonel Emoto's tenure as area commander had ended, and a colonel from Tokyo whom the men proclaimed "no damn good" replaced him. The new colonel said they were getting "too much to eat." Their food, already decreased in quality, suddenly became poor. During a visit to the hospital, Iwashita reportedly told Larry Grant that "it wasn't fit for human consumption."[38] Apparently, there were limits on what their own commandant, Sublieutenant Inaki, could do.

> The last five days I remained inside, because I developed a few large pustules on chest and belly. They are almost gone now, but gave me some extra time, which I used mainly to translate the Chemistry course into English. Now still 70 pages to go, and [I have] to write a course on French. (Surprised?!) At the HBS [*hogereburgerschool*; middle school and high school equivalent] I hated French, but I am about the only person here who still knows something of its grammar, etc. Pupils enough! Beyond that, I read "Little Man, What Now?" ("Kleiner Mann, Was Nun?").[39] Perhaps tomorrow, back to the Denki!

Despite his move to the barracks, Lindeijer was determined not to give up his relationship with Iwashita. Given the liaison's interest in French as the language of the novel he wanted to write, with any luck the grammar Lindeijer was developing would prompt him to stop in at the Denki.

9. Ohashi, 1944

In addition to allowing for work on the grammar, Lindeijer's confinement to the barracks was profitable in another way. It allowed him close observation of the guards, who—he now knew—invariably entered the building through the door nearest the back end of the compound (the one used by the prisoners to visit the latrine or go to work), then walked straight through, and departed from the opposite ("front") door.[40] Aware of their irregular appearances, he worked quickly to establish a new hiding place for his diary. Recalling a conversation with Reynolds about the latter's own diary, he examined the loose ceiling boards overhead. Removing one, he tucked the diary between the ceiling and the roof, and then replaced the board. Reynolds had described keeping his manuscript "in a hole in the attic over [his] bunk," where he trusted that it would be "fairly safe," adding that if it were taken, "you can rest assured I won't be left to worry about it."[41]

At present, Reynolds remained in the hospital. He would return to the barracks soon, to a sleeping place no more than three or so spaces to the left of Lindeijer's own.[42] By now, a scan of the area and reasonable conjecture would have allowed Lindeijer to develop an intriguing hunch. Reynolds's possession of intelligence from the radio had always been noteworthy. If the radio truly was operated by an American, its location had to be on this tier, somewhere between Lindeijer's bunk and the barracks' front wall. The individual who took the great risk almost certainly occupied one of the ten to eleven spaces to his left,[43] Lindeijer by now could easily guess.

18 May '44 A big mining disaster happened today. Thank God, none of the prisoners have been seriously injured, but the number of dead among the Japanese and Koreans is estimated at fifty, and further, very many wounded. It seems a miracle, the way our people escaped. A whole shift of our men had been delayed and given extra rest, which saved them from being crushed.

Two of the five mines,[44] each above the other, excavated [horizontally] in[to] the mountain, collapsed. The air pressure was enormous, and the stones [that were] dragged along with it killed many people. Two of our boys could save themselves by pressing against the tunnel wall. At 1.5 meters away from them a Japanese was killed. Another was blown over and a Japanese fell on top of him. At the same moment a piece of ore fell on the Japanese and broke three of his ribs. The prisoner underneath (Kent)[45] came away unhurt. For the time being, the production of the mine will be decreased! It is crazy indeed, the way the Japanese take the ore out and hollow the mountain without any propping.

The number of Japanese deaths was sobering. Some Japanese at the Ohashi camp were cruel, but many were kind. A few were a wildly incalculable mix. Sasaki, the kitchen supervisor, widely known as the perpetrator of the Australian Ross Drabble's beating, was a prime example. This same Sasaki had announced only yesterday that he was conducting a recipe contest, of all things. Every prisoner was to turn in a recipe, and he would award a prize to the best three.[46] One hardly knew whether to cry or laugh.

Lindeijer was recognizing, however, that he was hardly unmixed himself. A recent insight, that too often in his marriage he had failed to respond to an undercurrent in Nel's voice, was causing him grief. His growing awareness of the role of listening in developing the empathy needed for understanding was one of the greatest lessons of his imprisonment. He could only hope that it was one that had not come too late.

Dear Nel, 25 May '44

I am tired from writing! One can never express well what is really going on inside. Nothing can replace the spoken word from mouth to mouth. What greater happiness than to speak and understand each other. I'm thinking of the happiness I envisioned for married life, before we were engaged. It is really true that we will begin a wholly new life after this war; whether we like it or not, it will be new.

Oh Nel, that gives me courage, that makes me happy. Forget about old mistakes and begin a new life! Earlier, my thoughts about marriage were vague and confused. Now, I think of you. When we are comfortable with each other and find each other's love, then we will be happy, whatever social position we are in. Then our children will have a truly good home; the best that we can give.

What he could not have known was the extent to which his unsent letter was to resonate poignantly with a letter similarly unsent that Nel addressed to him from a camp in Java:

If I reflect back on our years together, I feel that there has indeed been so very much for which we can be thankful! [Yet] also, I often think with remorse how little of our deepest feelings we have given each other! When I brood over all that and search for the cause, I can only find that it has to have been due to a certain shyness! Also, it's so difficult to express your deepest feelings in words! To be sure it has not been a failing in love for you! However, often I longed for more warm-heartedness. I even believe that you have never said that you still truly loved me a lot, in all those years of our marriage, Wim. And yet every woman has a need of that, where the daily drudgery and sitting stuck in unimportant small things takes so much out of you! "Let us, if we may start together again, above all try to support each other by being 'open' for one another."[47]

Far away in northeast Japan, Lindeijer could only draw a line across the bottom of his entry, indicative of his determination after the war to make a fresh start.

For the present, he might find allies in suspending judgment and listening at the Ohashi camp, Iwashita among them. The liaison's overnight accommodations seemed in some way symbolic. Rather than in the quarters above the guardhouse, where the administration slept with a degree of comfort,[48] he lived in relative isolation: according to Jack Feliz, in a small hut located midway between cemetery and camp.[49] There was more for Lindeijer to learn about this complex man, and in the process about himself.

10

Ohashi, June 1944–April 1945— *"Amicitia Vitam Ornat"*

Though still new to the barracks at the beginning of June, Lindeijer could hardly have been unaware of the location of the Americans' secret radio, if only by virtue of its proximity to his sleeping place, which itself was near the "American end" of the top tier of bunks on the side of the building nearest the parade ground. Hidden behind a loose ceiling board a short distance away on this same side, and above the bunk nearest the barracks' front gate,[1] the prohibited set was easily accessed by its operator, the bunk's occupant, a sailor from the Houston named Jerry Bunch.[2] Known for his lighthearted pranks and signature Dutch army hat, Bunch was perhaps deliberately the antithesis of the larger-than-life Feliz, his best friend. He managed to go largely unnoticed in the taller man's shadow.

Only a close observer from a nearby location such as Lindeijer's would have noticed Bunch take the set down during the raucous hour after supper and listen with the man next to him, Jess Stanbrough.[3] (Once when a guard entered, just to be certain, another prisoner had held up a blanket to obscure vision.)[4] Moments before lights-out, the two quickly disseminated the news: Bunch, to Feliz and the American lieutenant Maxwell Humble, and Stanbrough, to two others. Feliz passed it on to five from the Houston; Lieutenant Humble, to Captain Zeigler and four others. Stanbrough's two likewise each told five. Those "in the know" were primarily Americans and Aussies.[5]

The British—at the far end of the barracks and considered "dirty" by the other prisoners as result of skin disease acquired while working in the cold at the docks in Hakodate—were not included; likewise, the majority of the Indonesian Dutch. Lindeijer and Gribnau were exceptions, as Europeans. Were the whole camp to be more cheerful than it should be, the secret would be out. Bunch and his collaborators might be executed.

By mid-June the exciting intelligence of the week prior could be shared as common knowledge, however. Even the camp's Japanese were aware of the

10. Ohashi, June 1944–April 1945

Allies' June sixth crossing of the channel (code named "C.T.C" by Reynolds and friends, who had placed bets in advance on the date).[6]

15 June. Finally, news has reached us about the [D-day] landings in the North of France. Thank God. We can be optimistic again! Let's hope that this is the last storm over Europe. What will remain of Europe? And of our poor country? What's going to happen there now is quite terrible.

People here think that the war in Europe will be over before September, and that it will then last only a short time thereafter in Japan. The Japanese become increasingly more mild-tempered. We have also received better clothes, and even two cakes of soap, the first this year! Sometimes cigarettes (1 × per month), and tonight apples ($\pm$ 5 per man). Three serious patients have been transported to a hospital in Tokyo; among them, Feenstra…

Last night, an air-raid alarm! That is for the second time now.

At the sound of an approaching guard, he had crumpled his entry to fist-size.[7] *The increased Japanese "friendliness" was due, on the part of some, to fear of punishment for war crimes should theirs be the losing side. It wasn't safe to talk, let alone write, about the war.*[8]

As Allied raids moved closer, the prisoners monitored the effect on their captors. During the nights of the fifteenth and sixteenth, American B-29s based in China bombed northern Kyushu, near Moji, the location where the prisoners disembarked two and a half years before.[9] *The next day, one of the British threatened his Japanese boss that their roles would soon be reversed. Reynolds reported the commandant's giving him "six days in the brig. But he received not a single slap."*[10] *Those with diaries considered it better not to take such risks. Lindeijer was writing less about camp events, which were better stored in his head.*

1 July '44 Dear Nel, Today, we have been married for nine years, two of which have been in purifying separation. We may have to add another year to this. Such an awful separation must surely produce hearts of gold! Yet there is already good reason to be grateful. The 200 new prisoners from Singapore who were to come a few days ago have not arrived. One cannot bear the thought that their ships may have been torpedoed! Fortunately that's one danger I've escaped.

Oh, I long to see how you manage with our boys and Joke. I often lie awake nights for hours and think of you. I begin to remember the past ever more clearly. How we ate at the table, sang at the piano, put the children to bed, and walked and played in the Juliana Park. Actually, I cannot imagine how I will return to an altogether different world. Also between us, Nel; but I cannot describe that now!

The work in the "Denki" [electrical workshop] suits me. Yesterday I completed the English translation of my Chemistry textbook [there]. Great! Bye, dear Nel. A kiss from your loving <u>Wim</u>.

The Denki had become his sanctuary. He could find moments for his mathematical work provided that his productivity otherwise satisfied

Kato-San, the shop's reasonable boss.[11] *Equally important, he could visit with Iwashita, who stopped in and occasionally brought books for him, as well as for Bunch and Stanbrough, who were in the adjacent shop for broadcast band radios, and for Feliz, in the machine shop across the way.*[12]

With the exception of the searches ordered by Tokyo, their current commandant Inaki's reign was relatively benign. (Recently, he had ordered a guard who hit one of the Indonesian Dutch to apologize. Per Reynolds, "I guess we have a good commadant [sic] now."[13]*) Iwashita's activity in the prisoners' interest increased. Twice on yasumi [free] days, he'd brought—on his back—a Victrola in a three-foot long wooden cabinet, and two bags of his own classical records for their listening enjoyment.*[14] *More striking, in guarded circumstances, he was talking about the war; in late May, telling Grant, in the camp hospital, that 150 Allied aircraft had bombed Wake Island. Reynolds, Grant's visitor, reported Iwashita's laughing about "the [propaganda] pictures that were up in the mine yard."*[15]

> 3 July '44 Our Freddy is five years [old] now! An extra birthday kiss on this festive day, my dear boy! I can hardly imagine how big you are already. From my heart I hope that it will be a celebration for your mother, brothers, and Joke. That will mean that they love you very much, and that you are good to them too. How I would love to be there on your birthday and join in your play. Perhaps Mother has prepared a surprise for you! Are you going to school already? Bye for now! Best wishes from your father!

By the eighth of July, the camp's Japanese were understandably irritable. A signboard in front of the electrical shop read literally, in Japanese, that Saipan had "died." Stewart, who worked in the shop, stood in front of the sign long enough to interpret this much, but attracted the attention of an employee from the camp office. The next day, the text was gone.[16] *The circle around Japan was closing. Saipan would be an important base for Allied attacks on the Philippines and the Japanese homeland.*

Iwashita nonetheless kept his composure, on the twelfth, telling the still-hospitalized Grant that "Saipan was finished, and the Americans [were] going strong."[17] *The prisoners had known about Saipan. It was their liaison's straightforwardness that surprised them.*

> <u>31 July '44</u> At last, today (yasumi day) we are allowed to write again, and, practically without limit, quantity-wise. Only, the subject matter is very restricted. We received another cake of soap, too. The course on Trigonometry is ready. Only the English translation still to do.

Lindeijer could hardly have recorded the ruckus during their 2 August inspection. Douglas Fyvie, a Scot, had authorization to drive the camp's motorbike, accompanied by an official escort. With the inspection ongoing, Fyvie had set out on the bike for an errand with the Honorable Man they called "Bird Legs." A new group of soldier guards had stopped them, and reportedly "given them hell." To the prisoners' delight, "Bird Legs" retaliated, marshaling the Honorable Men versus the soldiers: "a little revolution in camp," as Reynolds described it.[18]

Had the authorities only known: rumor had it that during a previous inspection, Fyvie—alone among the British with knowledge of the radio—had driven a general around on the motorbike, with the radio under its seat.[19]

<u>3 August '44</u> Dear Nel and children,

In thoughts, I receive your good wishes [for his birthday]. I cannot really imagine what you have done with this day, Nel. I mean, what you would have told the children about it. Talk about that father who is sliding slowly away into the past must be really unpleasant for the children, and at worst, stir painful thoughts or strange impressions in the two youngest. How can you celebrate this day other than alone? This time, I haven't told anyone here. In any case, it's not the right time for it either.

Last night, it was announced that the Japanese Army would be confiscating all our possessions, including our Red Cross clothes. Early this morning, before work, everything had to be exhibited on one's "bunk." Everyone tried to hide what they could. I pushed books, my American pullover, gray-green clothes, and underwear under the floor of the barracks. Close to my sleeping place, there is a board that can be lifted at one end, thanks to the "solid" Japanese construction. These letters and my courses were there also. I wonder how many more times I will have to take such risks for them.

A warning from "Wingy"[20] *had enabled him to secure the letter-diary in a new place. (Unlike the concrete floor between their two rows of bunks, the floor under the lower bunks was dirt covered with boards, and never searched.)*[21] *In such context, the epithet "Wingy" was no longer derisive. As with "Bird Legs" or "Smitty the Spy," too many positive associations had accumulated. Stewart had told about the one-armed guard marching the men to work. When Wingy felt his rifle become too heavy, "he'd bring it over and say to one of them, 'Here, you carry it for a while.'"*[22]

I just reread my letter of 3 August '43. I expected to be home in '44, because of the fall of Italy. Now Germany is trembling, two months after the landings in the North of France, and the Russians are at Warsaw and East Pruisen [Prussia]. There has been an attempt to kill Hitler, and Tojo has stepped down [as Minister of War]. But Germany still stands! They say that after the fall of Germany, the fall of Japan is only a question of months. However, this country does not by a long way give the impression of being nearly defeated. Yes, everything is rationed, but there is no food emergency such as we experienced in Holland in '14–'18.

When I returned from the "Denki" at 4:30 p.m., I noticed that the scallywags had taken my woolen Leiden blanket, the American blanket, and my rucksack.

I only hope they return them before the winter. We recently got a new commander. A mean skulk, in my view. Now, dear people, I wish you all the best, with kisses from <u>Father</u>.

The new commandant, Sublieutenant Kawabe,²³ had taken charge on 28 July. The prisoners' consensus was unanimous: "No one likes his looks."²⁴ There were more searches, and Lieutenant Humble was "bashed."²⁵ Yet they had allies among the Honorable Men and their spirit was staying intact. Lindeijer was cheerful on his wife's birthday.

<u>31 August '44</u> Dear Nel and children,

This day, in spirit, I send you an extra kiss! You have not been spoiled with those of late, but I may get a chance to make up for that. Strength of body and soul, and above all, a healthy cheerfulness, are what I wish you wholeheartedly. You will certainly have found a few good friends who know how to keep your spirits up. Apart from all the worries, do you also find joy in our youngsters? You understand how I long for them. I so dearly hope that you will be saved from serious illnesses.

I myself am fine. My rucksack was returned, but my 2 good quality blankets may be gone forever, while the nights are already becoming fairly cold! Still a lot of fleas! We held a short remembrance service for the Queen this morning and sang the Wilhelmus. Thank God, there is good progress in Europe. I wonder how they are doing in Holland?

I've been able to borrow a book on calculus from a Chinese student from Formosa [Taiwan] for today (yasumi day). I'll try to borrow it every yasumi day. Nice to be able to study. The work in the Denki is not hard, but tough and relatively dirty. A couple of fellows study my Trigonometry course enthusiastically. Unfortunately, the days are becoming shorter again, which makes studying more difficult. Can the boys still go to school? I suspect that in the large camps a small school will be put together. Bye now. Keep courage! A kiss from <u>Wim</u>.

On 10 and 21 September there were searches for diaries.²⁶ Virtually no one was recording much, and Lindeijer himself was distracted. The Allies had been launching an ill-fated effort to seize bridges in the Netherlands as a way into Germany, and by the twenty-fifth had lost.²⁷ It was comforting, in such circumstances, to receive a letter from his homeland, even one over a year old.

26 Sept. '44. Today is a big day: a letter from Holland, from mother via the Red Cross, dated 1 July '43! She is "doing rather well [in English]," as are your parents in Oegstgeest [a Leiden suburb]. I am afraid that in general our elderly have a hard time these days, especially now that our country is the scene of battle. The mof²⁸ appears to be very tough again, and we must wait—endless waiting! And yet, we may be very grateful that we will win this war. Without this, I would certainly <u>never</u> return to Java again. Even now, I believe that we still have to make it through one more dangerous period.

10. Ohashi, June 1944–April 1945

Mother wrote that she celebrated her eightieth birthday in Amersfoort with 7 daughters and Frits. She lives with Ber [his sister] in The Hague, which I believe is very fortunate.

From here, I can tell you about a few good things, too. The beatings, which started with the new commander, are almost over now ... I work on [a borrowed textbook on Differential and Integral Calculus] with Horne, an Englishman whom I taught the fundamentals of the subject last year ... We haven't noticed much in the way of air raids. Bye now! ...

His technical work was viewed as harmless by the guards—or so esoteric that they considered him "baka" (crazy), and stayed away.²⁹ This allowed him flexibility to tutor others: in addition to Ken Horne, the Australian Keith Edmonds (in algebra), and a handful of young Japanese students (in math).³⁰ He was becoming known, once again, for help rendered. Typically, in the Denki, this could mean solving practical problems such as identifying hydrochloric acid or cutting glass, but it could also mean settling disputes. In one case, two sailors from the Houston *came to him with an argument over the value of "pi." Was it 3.1416 or 3.14159? He'd told them that the value 3.14159 was more nearly correct, but to be accurate required carrying it out fifteen places. Did they want him to name them? Unable to declare victory, one over the other, they said "No."³¹*

Through October and into November, he wrote furtive notes in his diary: about Herman's seventh birthday, his worries over heavy fighting in Holland, and the news of the "magnificent landing on 'P' [the Philippines]."

9 Nov. '44 Today 4 letters received: two short ones from mother and Frits and two long ones from Ber and Greet. Nice to read them. They sound like voices from a lost world. I also reread your letters which reached me in Bandung. Oh Nel, you were so full of good courage then. Much more than I, I believe. I long so much to be in your midst again. I would be grateful and ... *[The top of page 81 has been cut off; thus, the top of page 82, on its reverse, is also missing.]*³²

... I pray that things may go well with you and our children in body and soul. You are not one day out of my thoughts. What a lot of suffering there will also be in Holland!

The war grew ever more devastating. Germany was punishing lack of Dutch support with a blockade that prevented food from reaching the Netherlands' northwestern cities. In the Pacific the first B-29s based in the Marianas had begun bombing the Tokyo area. The noose was tightening on Japan and its prisoners.

It was perhaps time to reprise his entry of 1 March 1943, the "Single Day," and if only rhetorically bring the family into his time in the Denki, an important new phase of his imprisonment. His "Single Day" of 11 December

1944 would again be a composite of many, and again—but this time almost without conscious thought—place Iwashita at its center.

> 11 Dec. '44 Last evening the stoves in our barracks were lit for the first time [this season]. They are also allowed to burn in the morning when we wake up (0430) until we leave for work (0600). Although there is severe frost, it's now easier to withstand. There is no coal, except for some coal dust left from last year. This is mixed with sawdust and burned in a homemade stove of a special design. Beyond that, wood is used.
>
> With the Japanese commandant as our intermediary, we bought some forest nearby for 500 yen. Everybody paid 3 yen. That piece of forest is close to the camp on a steep mountain slope. Every free day, a "wood party"[in English] of approximately 15 men goes out to cut trees. On other days, and after our work, of course, we bring the wood inside the camp. This way we keep a good stock, which is distributed in daily portions over the stoves. (There are 5 stoves.) There is still some forest left, which we may cut the day after tomorrow (yasumi day).
>
> That work is not so bad, but what we hate is that we must also cut and carry the wood for the Japanese camp office and kitchen. The rascals have nothing to do and [could] easily form a regular full-time squad [to do it]. Now we have to drag wood, after a long day of heavy work … [The top of page 82 is missing.]
>
> … wait (one hour every two weeks) for it.
>
> Between half past 4 and 6 a.m., there is bed making, eating breakfast, tenko, etc. There is almost always half an hour for study. I've worked through 3/4 of "Advanced Calculus" [text title] now, but repetition is necessary. I like that study! I keep trying to buy books but have not yet succeeded.
>
> The workbell rings at 6 a.m., and after lengthy shouting of unintelligible orders, we (that is, our group of 23 men) walk off to the Denki. That ½-hour walk is our daily exercise; not bad, provided you are healthy and there is no driving snow!
>
> In the Denki, I have a privileged job: the wood lathe, of which I use a second version now (made entirely of steel), keeps me busy, or rather, I keep the Japanese busy with it. Besides handles for electric switches, soldering bolts, screw drivers, drills, etc., I'm making a chess game, which I hope to bring proudly home one day. These days, I've made three standing lamps, somewhat like the model of the lamp I received from you when I was still a student, I believe. The Japanese like them very much and act as if they have never seen such a nice thing before. I have already promised two of them a lamp, under the condition that they buy a book for me! You never know! Iwashita-San will try in Tokyo, where he is now.

*In addition to technical books, Lindeijer needed an English-to-French dictionary for use in producing the French grammar for Iwashita. The liaison would do his best to find one.[33] He was a reliable emissary, having already acquired through the black market a radio engineering handbook for Stanbrough, and an algebra text and English novel (*Anthony Adverse*) for Feliz.[34]*

10. Ohashi, June 1944–April 1945

The conversation resulting from such deliveries likely filled a need of Iwashita's as well as theirs. The Denki offered an out-of-the-way space for expressing his thoughts, which in some cases implied criticism of the government, considered treasonous by Japan's military police. "If they could read my thoughts," he had said, "I would be executed."[35] Thus, both they as prisoners and Iwashita, as a member of an oppressive society, engaged in humane conversation in the depths of a prison. They covered topics ranging from the best way to learn a foreign language to whether Russia might wage war on Japan—and if so, who would win.[36] Neither expected to know all that the other was thinking, or that the other would necessarily agree. They were, however, cultivating a humanized social environment. "Amicitia vitam ornat," Lindeijer might well have thought, before continuing to write. His Latin lesson prior to leaving Java was right. Friendship truly did adorn life: in this case, the life of their small community, despite a menacing authority outside.

> You must wonder how it can be that I have standing floor lamps to give away. Well, supervision is very poor here; partly, because of lack of organization, and partly due to the stupidity and laziness of the Japanese guards. I even managed to "pinch" an electric heater and keep it covered under my workbench. That way, I am not bothered by cold feet. It's quite lovely of course, that I can often work on "Calculus" when there is no Japanese guard nearby. The others make many pipes, tobacco boxes, and the like, which they barter in the barracks, and even with the Japanese.

Supervision was poor because their chief Japanese electrician had been drafted. Kato-San supervised to a degree, checking, for instance, when the supply of sodium hydroxide started disappearing for use as soap, and watching to ensure that the coil of a broadcast band radio wasn't wound to transform it to shortwave. But his office was at the other end of the building and separated by a door from the radio repair area. This left him ignorant of clandestine activity, or perhaps content not to know of any.[37]

In the radio repair area, Captain Zeigler had obtained permission to have a shop broadband radio, purportedly to listen to music, which led to Kato's inspecting the coil. In the meantime, Stanbrough created a replacement coil with shortwave capability. Under favorable circumstances (meaning rarely), they could receive war news in the shop.[38]

Yet it was Bunch, with his Dutch hat, who was the real hero. No one else was willing to smuggle parts from the workshop to maintain the radio hidden in the barracks' ceiling. Bunch risked detection while cannibalizing radio parts in the workshop (a Japanese radio "could be a nine-tube set but when it left the shop it would be a seven-tube set in working order," Feliz wise-cracked), but even more so when he carried the parts back to camp in the "double deck section" in the top of his hat.[39] Re-entering the camp after *work, each man underwent a pat-down search. "Amicitia vitam ornat," again Lindeijer might have thought. There were more ways than one to nurture a community; even a part of it.*

> Yasumi is from 9–9:15 a.m., after which we put our "bento" [lunch] on the stove. At 11:30, we await the lunch bell with warm bento on our lap and a spoon in hand. At 11:45, back to work again until 3:30 p.m. Officially, it's sweeping up time from 3:30 until 4, but in reality that is already done, [so] we take some yasumi again before we return to the camp.
>
> You see, the Denki is not bad; certainly not for me. Yasumi periods are short, but as result of the lax supervision, we manage to use much time "productively." Furthermore, there is a good electric water heater, which is very useful for washing your face in the morning, washing your clothes, and making tea (without sugar, oh misery!). I mend my socks there, and "borrow" paper, pencils, electric bulbs, soda, etc. I also hide my extra clothes there, which otherwise would be taken away from me during inspections in the camp.
>
> On arrival back "home" (± 4:30 p.m.), I immediately put my little eating pan at No. 23, on the table. A short time later the dinner bell sounds. After the meal there is still a fair amount of time for study, which not many know how to use. On bath day (once in three days) roll call is at 7:30 p.m. instead of 7 p.m., thus there is 1 hour's study for certain!
>
> … Oh Nel, how I would love to see how you manage and do things, perhaps in a camp. This morning the Japanese asked the addresses of all Hollanders who had not received any mail yet from the Indies. Things therefore seem to be moving in the right direction. The war goes slowly, doesn't it? Just keep courage!

That the Denki was "not bad" was an understatement. It was, as his entry made clear, a garden of security under the circumstances. That being said, it hardly eliminated the need to maintain one's balance in the face of external menace. Their liaison, above all, would have grasped this. With a family and home imperiled by bombing, as much or more than any of them, he stood in danger of losing everything.

> 25 December '44—<u>First Christmas Day</u>. Wishes, in thought, for a happy Christmas for my dear wife and children. How are you all? I hope there can be a lot of happiness and that for our children it will be a day with lovely memories. That will be the best reward for you too, Nel, will it not! Perhaps, also a Christmas tree. That is really the central event of Christmas day. Will you tell the story with it once more? The spiritual bread we need can be passed on in a simple way if it's but well meant.
>
> Here, the Christmas spirit is very good. There is even a large Christmas tree decorated with candles in the barracks, and another one in the hospital for the (fortunately) few sick. A further happy fact is that on our return home last night, we received an American Red Cross package. Delicious, with powdered milk, powdered coffee, chocolate, cheese, corned beef, prunes, jam, sugar, butter, raisins, cigarettes and soap. The cigarettes, I may sell to pay for books.

10. Ohashi, June 1944–April 1945

I've had a serious setback again: two books would have been sent, but the publishing company and bookstores were burned to cinders as a result of American bombing. Almost all bookstores in the capital are located in a particular region, and that had all burned down. Despite that I keep hoping. For one pack of cigarettes I can get at least 6 yen (say 3 guilders) and I have five packs.

In fact, three Red Cross packages per person have arrived, and they actually received them in the Kamaishi camp, too. However, our commander is not so honest, so we will be happy if we receive even one. On top of that, the other packages will only be distributed to those who've had not one single complaint regarding their work and attitude!

Beyond this, we don't have much to complain about. Thanks to my homemade clothes (which I hid the other day) and a Red Cross woolen pullover, I have enough to keep me warm. Only the battle against lice is more difficult. So I occasionally boil clothes in the "Denki."

We held a simple church service in the barracks this morning. Last night, the Catholics, for whom I turned two candle holders on my lathe, had their service.

This morning, I read all letters once again. Great! When will the first letter from Bandung arrive? A kiss from your loving Wim.

Lindeijer could hardly have said more about the devastation in Tokyo without raising the possibility that Iwashita reported it to him. Iwashita for his part kept his composure, before the day was out, taking the prisoners' photograph as they held their Christmas celebration. "Dutch, British, American, and Australian POWs forgot about what they used to think about each other and had fun all day long," he was to observe with satisfaction later.[40] *"They gathered around the stove and enjoyed chatting." His part was to loan his phonograph and records, and express pleasure at their "deep thanks."*[41]

28 Dec. '44

Today we may write 25 words home again, and I reported that the families in Holland were fine last year. Here, more snow and colder. Oh, that this might really be the last winter here!

Before daylight on December 29, the prisoners experienced a blackout. B-29s had reportedly flown west from Kamaishi. By the next day a prisoner returning from a hospital in Tokyo told of being threatened with death "if he told anything he saw or heard [there]." That same day, Reynolds reported witnessing emaciated Chinese prisoners. Some had to be "half carried by their friends," who were hit and pushed along by guards, as they returned to their barracks near the railway station. He had become "so damn mad just watching..." He'd remembered when he "had to walk and work just like these Chinks [sic] do now."[42]

1 January '45 The year that mother called the "Peace Year" in one of her letters has passed. Let us hope that other things have passed as well, such as our

disbelief, overestimation of self, pettiness, and spiritual cowardice; that we, in this new year, may see clearly the way of life which God prepared for us in our creation. Seeing the way ahead requires inner peace, courage, and confidence in our future, based on faith. We are not created for mental chaos and wilderness, into which we relapse so easily. Our spirit is created to develop and cultivate the possibilities and talents within us so that our lives become a harmoniously formed structure that may give joy and comfort to ourselves and our neighbors ...

Oh, God, be our Guide in happy and difficult times. That our household may walk along your road. That we may do that, in a reunited family life!

A matter of days later the camp was in the midst of a blinding blizzard. "The one thing is," Lindeijer's trading partner Reynolds had said, "the [Japanese] are as bad off as we are, only they don't have guards or live inside a wall."[43] *Lindeijer held to his hope that Iwashita would continue efforts to obtain the English-to-French dictionary for him. Producing a French grammar for the aspiring novelist was a project that held purpose and meaning.*

17 Jan. '45. Today I literally crept through the eye of a needle! I had two spools with me that I had made on my lathe for the sewing [clothes repair] party, when we returned from work. Nothing was found during the routine inspection, but once inside the barracks, a soldier came up behind me and said: "You have something on you." He searched me thoroughly but found nothing. That was a close call! You understand how very careful I will be for a while. To steady my nerves, I drank my last cup of Red Cross coffee, with milk and the last of my sugar.

On 30 January, Iwashita had stopped in. Despite a row about the French dictionary with the new commandant, Kawabe, he intended to try again to purchase it. Then perhaps with the new commandant still on his mind, he called on Captain Zeigler in the radio repair area, and elicited the latter's opinion of the previous commandant, Inaki: according to Zeigler, Inaki was "a good Japanese soldier."[44]

No sooner than the next day, Iwashita was as good as his word, producing the long-sought item. But Lindeijer's bit of good fortune was short-lived. Summoned to the camp office, he was ordered to return it. Afterward Reynolds remarked that "all of [the other prisoners] were surprised that he wasn't bashed." In the end, they considered it "Lindy's luck."[45]

Iwashita's judgment in confidence about the new commandant was that he didn't "think that [Kawabe] is respectable." All the more remarkable, then, his attempt to re-negotiate the dictionary with the man eight or nine days later.[46] *The effort was unsuccessful.*

20 Feb. '45 I would love to write to you every day: I long to such an extent for all of you. Oh, how very much a good "home" means to us! Thank God, the war is making rapid progress now. Yet who knows what misery the last few months

10. Ohashi, June 1944–April 1945

will bring us. My little lathe in the Denki still assures me of an independent place there, with a lot of pilfered time for Integral Calculus. These last months, I've put together a lot of interesting applications, viz. the calculation of lengths, surface areas, contents, points of gravity, and moments of inertia. Good exercises in elementary Integral Calculus. Now I've started again on the "Advanced Calculus" text of Hiashi-San [the Chinese student], because I fear that I won't be able to borrow it again if I wait too long. Otherwise, I've still been unable to get my hands on books.

We received our second Red Cross package on 8 Febr. [second in terms of what the prisoners received, out of four and a half, in total], with which I've begun to trade, in hopes of bringing some money home. My capital amounts to more than 43 guilders + 40 yen. I exchanged 40 yen with Captain Zeigler for 20 guilders, and hope to repeat that. Furthermore, through bartering I have added six tins of butter, one tin of coffee, one cheese, and one package of raisins to my supply. Delicious stuff.

My best comfort remains my "Calculus." Oh, Nel, how I long for my study books. I feel I've frittered my future away by hardly studying those seven years in Bandung!

Last night, I dreamed very clearly of Herman and Wimmie. That makes me both happy and sad. Wim is now nearly nine years old. May God grant that I return to you all, this year.

A good idea! Let us institute, Nel, when I return, that every Sunday one of the children may say which biscuits we'll have with the coffee in the morning, and one, what we will have for dinner. The next Sunday, the other two will have their turn. Let's try to help the children discover their own interests. Not only in taste, but in what they do and what they don't. He who has real interest in his work is a happy person, and certain of success in his work!

He was doing his best, once again, to cultivate a positive outlook. Apparently, so was Iwashita, who had stopped in for a chat on 9 February, and again on the nineteenth: despite what he termed the "increasingly serious situation" and Lindeijer's loss of the Larousse, he had "to go ahead with French."[47]

Impressed, Lindeijer had a further glimpse into his friend's character on 2 March. Offered all the cigarettes from Lindeijer's Red Cross packages as incentive for books, the liaison politely demurred. "I see what you mean, but I'm not a slave to material things."[48] *Clearly, he liked the POWs and was fascinated by their opinions; he even shared some of them. He also willingly did favors, and at times accepted gum or chocolate that was freely given. But his goodwill could not be bought.*

12 March '45. Yesterday evening, to our astonishment, we received our third Red Cross package (really, out of five and a half). True, a lot had been stolen from the boxes, and we had to divide four boxes over five men, but it could have been worse. My trade makes good progress: I now have over 165 guilders + 35 yen. Furthermore, there are rumors that Red Cross clothes and shoes for us have arrived in Kamaishi.

> Tonight we're allowed to write [home] again. For the first time, not a postcard, but a letter, even though it's just as limited. I am fine. I dream of you. My study is going well. I'm busy with the book of Hiashi-San again. When will I receive a letter from you, Nel? Who knows how many you have written already! A kiss from your <u>Wim</u>.

Receiving the Red Cross foodstuffs was an unexpected boon. On a given day, the Japanese in the workshops could be "nice as hell," in seamen's terminology; yet, just as likely, they could be angry over Japan's "taking a beating somewhere," or simply depressed. One, looking at his ragged clothes, could proclaim that "to be dead was better." Another, examining the pitiful contents of a lunch box, might throw it all away. Still another (as in the case of a certain Takahashi), might express cynicism about the war's leadership on all sides: "little men [want] to be friends but Number One [man] says fight so we must fight." A number gravitated toward communicating, mixing Japanese and English. "It's funny to hear us and the Nips [sic] talk ... part Nip, part English. But we understand each other," Reynolds remarked.[49]

> 31 March '45... This evening, 200 Canadians arrived in our camp. So the new barracks (built in November '43!) is finally being used. There seem to be quite a few sick among them.
> I work hard on Calculus! The boss of the Denki told me that I can have a new wood lathe made; thus, for the time being, at least, my job seems assured. Not bad, because I'm able to solve quite a lot of mathematical problems there!

The order not to talk to the newly arrived prisoners, placed under guard in their "new barracks," only aroused greater interest. The Americans vowed "Just wait."[50] *Iwashita, who would have been tantalized by the knowledge of French speakers among them, must have felt much the same.*

A short time later, the Canadians remained in their barracks, but four had been beaten "for talking to the Americans."[51] *The grapevine was "full of tales of bombing of Tokyo," according to Reynolds.*[52]

> <u>8 April '45</u>. Dear Wim and other celebrants!
> Today, a happy day for Wim: now nine years old. I try to imagine him as a big boy, but it is always that friendly little boy's face that comes to mind. I miss him terribly and celebrate this day with him in spirit. He will certainly appreciate something extra from you, Nel! I hope that he continues to attend school with pleasure and has good friends. And the boys, can they get along with each other? And with the little sister? The hemmed-in situation in the camp, where I suspect you are now, shouldn't decrease your companionship, should it?
> A few days ago, we were again surprised with nearly a half of a Red Cross package—in total, say 5.66 boxes (4+4/9 + 4/5 + 2/5 = 5 29/45, thus, 5 2/3 packages) now. This time with Red Cross shaving things, such as a razor, blades, cream, comb, soap, and toilet paper. The Japanese distributed the Red Cross clothes only to those who did not miss any of the working days over the last

three months. So, many did not get anything. It's a dirty trick. I received a pair of socks from the thieves!

The Canadians bring new life to the camp. They are very optimistic and think that we will return home this summer. I better stick to before Christmas. In Germany things develop fast now. Holland is in a festive mood, with our flag on top. [Liberation of the Western Netherlands, by Canadian troops, began on April 2, 1945.] Bye now, people, the work bell sounds. A kiss from your Wim.

Such a mood was not to last. On 15 April, Iwashita was transferred out of the camp. In the liaison's own opinion, this was "perhaps due to the fact that [he] had been too familiar with [the] POWs." Kawabe had reprimanded him in part for the "dictionary of [the] French language" that he purchased "by the request of [the] Dutch prisoner Ryndeyer [sic]."[53]

This was loss piled on top of loss. The majority of the camp had come to value the liaison's friendship and to respect the integrity of his "otherness." Iwashita had buffered the effects of the camp office and through his presence helped them keep balance. Now the prisoners might never see this remarkable man again.

11

Ohashi, April–August 1945— Edge of the Inferno

Concerned over the loss of Iwashita as their liaison, in late April 1945 Lindeijer and his colleagues monitored the moods of their captors as the war approached the Japanese mainland. Since the United States' capture of Iwo Jima on 26 March, the Japanese camp personnel had showed signs of moroseness and stress. A Japanese employee in one of the workshops had gone so far as to tell the prisoners that the Japanese planes were no longer armed. "They crash their victims." America needed to "hurry and end the war."[1] Despite their president's death, the American forces seemed to be doing just that—battering Okinawa with unprecedented force.[2] In response, Japan's defense of the last stepping stone to its homeland had been fierce. The modicum of good will that existed between the prisoners on the one hand, and their workshop bosses and the Honorable Men on the other, might not withstand the assault.

Critically, for captor and prisoner alike the memory of the firebombing of Tokyo on 9 and 10 March remained fresh. Smoke from some three hundred miles south had traveled all the way to their region. "An inferno," Stanbrough had called it; "a storm." It had "smelled like a fireplace burning pine wood…"[3] and obliterated the sun: an omen, perhaps, of the conflagration to come.

Lindeijer's entry on 30 April reflected his effort at a balanced perspective.

30 April. Birthday of Princess Juliana. My digestion has been troublesome again for a few days. My studies slacken. A while ago, I was surprised by the arrival of an English-to-English dictionary that I asked for almost a year ago.

Today we were given a new commander. This new one looks more trustworthy than the former hypocrite. Also, that nasty interpreter has left. Every day, we expect Germany to fall and big things to happen in this country. Our foreman (hancho) in the Denki has been laid off because he beat prisoners a few times [Sancha Fujii, a lower-level supervisor, usually of outside electrical work].[4] A good sign!

11. Ohashi, April–August 1945

The prisoners' diet was now primarily barley, in portions Reynolds described as "getting damn slim," though in nearly the same breath he acknowledged that "the Nips [sic] are not any better off."[5] Rumors that a Red Cross shipment was imminent stimulated the prisoners' hopes for improved sustenance. How much would the new man, Lieutenant Yoshida, give them of "what they had coming"? Some thought he looked "bad," but it was too early to tell—either about Yoshida or the latest change in camp jurisdiction, from Tokyo to Sendai.[6]

In the meantime, everyone was on edge waiting for the inevitable "big things." Not even the Denki was immune. Sancha Fujii had been disciplined for beating a Canadian who'd taken tape to hold up his socks. Captain Zeigler confronted Fujii about the beating, and other Japanese had backed the captain up. Fujii stopped back to apologize.[7] Civility could be fragile, but in this case had held.

All the more remarkable, then, the cooperation that could exist. Only yesterday, when Douglas Fyvie had left on the motorcycle with "Bird Legs" and Sasaki to bring back supplies from Morioka, Fyvie, alias "Paddy," had been outfitted for the occasion in full Japanese Army regalia—complete with bayonet and sergeant's insignia.[8]

<u>6 May '45</u> Today Holland is free. Oh, what happiness! And that right on the fourth birthday of our daughter. What joy there will be in Holland. Finally risen again! You will surely also hear it in the internment camps too. [Thus] A double celebration at home. How I would dearly love to give my daughter a birthday kiss. She'll surely look good enough to steal [away] in her beautiful little dress. But, I don't want a conceited girl, do you hear!

Germany's seizure of food going into Holland had resulted in deaths in the tens of thousands. Now, thanks to Canadian liberators, Dutch citizens would no longer fall dead in the streets from hunger. The Dutch "Hunger Winter" was over!

Regrettably, the Canadians in Ohashi—primarily French Canadian woodsmen—were no longer regarded so favorably. For Lindeijer, they brought "new life" to the camp; likewise for Reynolds, who was fast friends with one of them.[9] But for many the addition of two hundred men placed too great a strain on the camp's sanitary facilities. Resentment led to stereotyping, and the Canadians became the new "Other." Some from the original prisoner group characterized them as dirty, uncivilized, and disloyal—denouncing them as men without "loyalty to friends, to England, to anybody."[10]

Their detractors might have felt differently, had they only known that these newly arrived Canadian prisoners, members of the Canadian Royal Rifles and the Winnipeg Rifles, captured on Christmas Day 1941 during the *fall of Hong Kong, were the equivalent in heroism of their counterparts in Europe. Their senior officer, George MacDonnell, termed their "disloyalty" a strength—a means of keeping "their rural perspective" and poking fun at the army for "its bureaucracy, and its foibles." The same irreverence had made them "magnificent" during their imprisonment at Hong Kong's North Point and Shamshuipo camps, and more recently at the Nippon Kokan Yokohama Shipyard.*

Only a few other prisoners knew the reason for the Canadians' transfer to Ohashi. Their enlisted men had blown up the blueprint library and pattern warehouse at the Yokohama shipyard, and thereby shut down its shipbuilding completely. The shipyard's commander blamed the disaster on the firebombing rather than admit failed security. Not one of his prisoners had been punished.[11] They had merely been transferred to Ohashi.

> We are still fine here. Ready for the big bang. I expect Japan to surrender within three months of the invasion here. What will Russia do? We yearn for the end.
>
> Today, I hope to bring my new notebook and that English Dictionary in [to the camp office to get a stamp of authorization]. Food floods into Holland again. Thank God. Many letters arrive here, but nothing yet from Java for me. Bye; in spirit kisses for all of you! Your <u>Wim</u>.
>
> [Later:] It was a good day! I received the desired stamps on the notebook and dictionary. Furthermore, I received a neat new pair of summer trousers, which I needed badly.

Lindeijer's request for approval of a new "exercise book" for his mathematical and scientific work scarcely raised an eyebrow. Afterward, in seclusion, he removed the notebook's cover and placed it around the looseleaf body of letters and the precious photos. Above the protective stamp he inscribed it with a title: "Brieven" (or "Letters," in Dutch).[12]

> Finally, a good joke: our sergeant [Takahashi], nicknamed "the Tiger," was caught with four Red Cross packages by the "Kempé" (military police) on his way home for leave. He is held in Kamaishi. There will surely be follow-up on this, perhaps favorable for us. He was certainly not the greatest thief by a long shot.

Some momentary shift in perspective would have prompted this last thought. For the prisoners, Lindeijer included, their Red Cross packages were sacrosanct; taking them merited punishment. Yet Takahashi's taking the four packages home was a lesser misdeed in the overall scale of corruption. "Follow-up" could reveal trafficking in the packages more widely, and potentially at a higher level. This was, after all, the same Takahashi who expressed cynicism about his country's military rule, saying "little men [want] to be friends but Number One [man] says fight so we must fight."

11. Ohashi, April–August 1945

And of whom Reynolds had said "He treats us like men, not like POWs."[13]

New clothes and shoes are promptly distributed now. Furthermore, we could buy a little tea and a piece of soap. I'm healthy again and work full speed on Calculus. Our queen is back in Holland. What joy there will be!

<u>8 May '45</u>. As far as I know, the official day of Germany's capitulation. Finally, light, food, and joy in Holland again. We are anxiously awaiting coming events.

The prisoners found it difficult to contain their excitement. They gleefully moved on from a lottery on the date of Germany's surrender to another on the date of their next Red Cross packages.[14]

The looseleaf diary cover, originally the cover of an exercise notebook for Lindeijer's technical work. He received the Ohashi camp office authorization stamp on 6 May 1945, and he then recycled the exercise notebook cover as the letters' cover, inscribed with *Brieven* ("Letters") (Lindeijer Family Archive).

11 May '45. Today for the first time, we worked according to the new schedule, until five o'clock. So we now are busy for the Japanese from six o'clock in the morning until half past five, when we arrive home. This [the one and a half hours added] does not mean more work for me, but more study time at the Denki. At the moment, I'm reading "The Family that Overtook Christ [in English]," by Raymond.

Under the new schedule, experience outside the workshops was not so favorable. The economic situation that drove the change led to increased bashings.[15] *Lohrig from the* Houston *was set upon for not saluting, Frank Planton from the R.A.F. for failing to see a guard in time to bow, his compatriot Vernon for farting (now a nearly universal transgression), and the British Jimmy Garbutt "for not having his coat open during inspection."*

To make matters worse, on 21 May a potential new danger put the prisoners on edge. Bubonic Plague struck Ohashi ("our fair city," in Reynolds's *sardonic terms).*¹⁶ *British mine workers told of its existence at a nearby Chinese camp. Walking by on their way to work, they witnessed a crematorium that looked "like the mouth of a volcano." Japanese camp employees "were throwing in wood and dead bodies."*¹⁷ *Days later, as sickness—though not plague—struck their own camp, the Ohashi prisoners were dismayed to learn of their dependable Medical Sergeant Neko's transfer elsewhere.*¹⁸

7 June '45 I feel very weak, having had diarrhea for eight days now. There are no effective medicines. As a result of this I stayed inside today for the first time in nine months. While recuperating (I took salt this morning), I hope to spend the day well, studying Hiashi's book, which I can borrow until 11 June (from 1 June). I continue to work on an abstract of this book, which I hope to finish by the tenth. It is a great study, from which I may get quite a bit of use.

Oh Nel, my longing for you all can be so painful. Hundreds of letters reach this camp regularly, but nothing from you! What difficulties and dangers will the war yet bring you? Everything seems in preparation for the invasion here. Perhaps in the Indies too. We must wait and pray. This year, I did not receive any news from Holland either, but that is understandable.

9 June '45 My illness improves. Today is a free day and I can finish the abstract of the Calculus book. Yesterday, a half egg per man for "bento" [lunch]. By exchanging rice, I ate three and a half eggs! What a luxury; delicious! Rumors about Red Cross food, etc., on the way.

*The "luxury" and rumors helped offset bad news. Kato, the Denki and radio shop hancho, came back from Tokyo with tales of Japanese homes and whole sections of the city destroyed.*¹⁹ *As if in response, the cases of bad treatment continued. Lieutenant Yoshida counseled his ranks that their charges were weak and ill-nourished and should be treated as such. With the fighting in Okinawa in its final stages and Japan certain of defeat, some of the guards reacted angrily, however. One declared that the prisoners were treated too well. They should work harder. If they did not, they should be beaten; if they became sick, they should die.*²⁰ *Given the tense situation, Captain Zeigler "stopped the wheel": the code known to some for the radio.*²¹

19 June '45. Another diarrhea attack. This time, the doctor gave me two days off, during which I received porridge instead of barley. I feel much better now. Tomorrow, yet another official free day, yasumi. I feel as if I am having a long holiday. My calculus progresses nicely, as you can guess.

How much longer? Anxiety grips me over the possibility that we may have to stay here yet another winter. That would be terrible! Two boys are locked up in "iso" because they talked about the war with Koreans. Supervision is stricter again.

The same anxiety gripped his colleagues. Yet if the prisoners were weak and losing weight, so were the camp workers. And now disabled Japanese whom they liked were being called to the frontlines. Kuto stopped in with his new haircut to say goodbye (and actually left cigarettes); then Sirno. Now Monk, in his late thirties with children, had been called up. Reynolds spoke for the larger group: "Lots of Nips [sic] I'd rather see go than him."²²

Exhausted by illness, conflicting emotions, and air-raid alarms, the prisoners sought refuge in a musical program on the last night of June.²³ Three Canadians who were brothers and had managed, astonishingly, to keep their instruments with them performed.²⁴

Lindeijer's concerns were deeply personal the following day:

> 1 July '45 Our wedding day—now 10 years ago. My heart fills with sorrow and feelings of hate toward our enemies. And yet, I believe that God has a purpose with this torment of body and spirit. What else could it be other than putting us to the test and purifying our spirit? Was there not much that was foolish, bad, and unwise in our marriage? Much unnecessary sorrow, misunderstanding, and self-containment; lack of love and healthy understanding?
>
> Certainly for those who believe in God's guidance, there is reason enough to see this time as one of spiritual purification, in which God asks for our atonement and self-reflection.
>
> Will all now be better between us, Nel, and thus better and happier for our children? Oh, let's believe this. No one knows, but believing it may be worth a great deal: that is, to live toward it as if it were so. And who knows what God has in store for us ... Our life is full of deep possibilities.
>
> And how would I have wanted to celebrate this day? The best part of it would be togetherness in sincere happiness, the feeling we call joy. A joy that takes pleasure in both "giving" and "taking." The rest would come automatically and requires only a lively imagination to describe. A day of true celebration for our ten years of marriage: there are flowers and delights for the tongue, beautiful clothes, and cheerful children. All things that I miss so much here and hope to enjoy again in the future.
>
> Oh Nel, our children; what joy it will be to have them with us again, those boys with their tempers and affectionateness. How I love them! And our daughter will likely have surprises in store for me, may take me aback. Will our children have reason to be grateful for the guidance we have given them? We're quick to think so, but raising them requires character on our part.

His reflection took place against a backdrop of air-raid alarms; intermittent at first, now as many as three a night.²⁵ In the low mountain valley, with their radio turned off, the prisoners had no way of knowing how close the raids were coming.

> 3 July '45 Our Freddy, now 6! Already in the "big [primary] school." What clever children I'll find when I come home. Oh yes, next year, I'll be there to give you a birthday kiss. But who knows, your mother may have something in mind for you now! And then, not to forget your brothers and sister.
>
> I trust that you'll become a plucky boy who likes to do things on his own, and do them well, in order to please both yourself and others. Never force your help on someone, that's unworthy, but be ready to help where that's really

needed, regardless of whether help has been asked for. Also be sincere, so that people can trust you. When you are asked to do something, do it promptly and well. If it is difficult, persevere! A kiss from your Father

When alarms sounded on 6 July, the prisoners heard the camp loudspeakers roar out "Sendai," the location of their new jurisdiction's headquarters,[26] *several times. By the seventh and eighth, the warnings increased to five a day. Everyone's nerves were frayed: "Fleas eating us up. Air-raid alarms. Nips jittery and no smokes," Reynolds complained. They needed "more food just to scratch these infernal fleas," the men said. "Sure bad."*[27]

Yet events on the fourteenth eliminated such feeble attempts at humor. American planes flew overhead, and thunderous explosions sounded from the direction of Kamaishi. The American navy men listened to the timing. "That ain't bombs!" one said. "That's bombardment!"[28] *Prisoners returning from a wood gathering party high up on the mountain reported the sight of American warships outside Kamaishi harbor, shelling the city and "knocking down one after another the nine giant smokestacks of the main Kamaishi smelter."*[29]

Few besides Lindeijer could have known of the proximity of the Kamaishi camp to the blast furnaces. Fewer still could have conjured up mental images of its charred and devastated buildings. Yet what he could not know was the fate of his former associates. What would have befallen Dr. Pijma, whom he had assisted; or Becker, his former student from Java? What of those who helped carry the patients to the barracks on the day "big shots" inspected and a storm blew off half the hospital roof? And what of the patients themselves? In the midst of the shelling they would have had little chance to get out.

His Ohashi colleagues were gripped by their own sense of uncertainty. Everyone continued to go to work, though they all knew this was largely "for show." With Kamaishi's smelters shut down, their own mine complex was nearly idle.[30] *The camp's Japanese struggled with how to treat them. Most were quite civil, with the exception of certain of the office staff (unbeknownst to Yoshida) and the "punk kids"[schoolboys] who supervised those who still worked in the mines. "It makes them feel good," Reynolds said, "to beat a prisoner." Out of forty-two men on his twelve-hour shift, "only four or five missed getting beaten ..."*[31]

Nonetheless, the prisoners who were mistreated were hardly alone in their suffering. Outside the camp the bombardment had made an already bad time worse. Rain threatened the rice crop and U.S. planes again thundered overhead. Homeless people headed for the hills with little to eat and no real place to go.[32]

Under the circumstances, an encounter at the end of the month proved

11. Ohashi, April–August 1945

extremely dangerous. Feliz's version of the incident made the rounds: a Japanese civilian announced to an American naval ensign that Japan's military had taken San Francisco and was moving toward Salt Lake City. The ensign reacted in anger, blurting out (in Feliz's colorful language) "That's a lot of bullshit. You're getting your asses kicked out of the Philippines."[33] Word reached the commandant. On the morning of the thirty-first all working parties received orders to remain in camp; members of the dreaded kempeitai would conduct a search. Lined up on the parade ground, the men were directed to remove their clothing, to allow for its inspection. From inside the barracks came the sounds of their bunks being searched; then more ominously, of the ceiling boards being lifted. The inspection proceeded, board by board, from the back of the barracks toward the front, nearing the corner where Bunch and Stanbrough bunked.[34] Those aware of the radio's hiding place grew quiet. Too quiet, someone recognized. A whispered message passed through their ranks: "Talk, talk, talk!"[35] Miraculously—one board prior to the corner—the search stopped.

The last board straddled the barracks' front inner wall and must have seemed a dead end. Had the inspecting police only lifted it, they would have discovered a small space between the inner wall and the wall forming the barracks' exterior. Inside that space, they would have found the radio hanging from a nail. As it was, they missed not only the radio, but the purpose of the two nails with wash rags hanging on them at the back of Bunch and Stanbrough's bunks. These were "hot," used to charge the radio's battery. Touching them would have resulted in an electric shock.[36]

The prisoners' secret had survived. They began August with little cheer, nonetheless: they were weak, still eaten by fleas and collapsing from heat and stress.[37] Oddly enough, then, the sight of great numbers of U.S. aircraft on the ninth might have elated them more than it did. The planes dived toward Kamaishi against a backdrop of noise. The heavily damaged city was being bombarded a second time.[38]

Their camp administration took steps. Prisoners who might otherwise have opportunity to watch and identify the planes were confined all day in garages or other small buildings near the mine. Those assigned to the workshops remained in their barracks with the shades drawn, instructed not to look out. With the latter group Lindeijer lay on his bunk, at work on the calculus text to keep his mind off the attack. In need of more light, he made an ever-so-slight adjustment to the shade. This proved a mistake. From his office in the administration building, Sergeant Takahashi detected the movement and became enraged. Dashing over to the barracks and up the steps to the Dutch prisoner, he launched an attack: knocking Lindeijer's glasses off, throwing his books down, and dragging him to the office for a beating.

The sudden occurrence astounded the other prisoners as much as it did Lindeijer. Were Iwashita still with them, their "very bright" Dutch scientist[39] would not have been beaten, or bruised, as he was, about the face, back, and shoulders. Clearly Takahashi was not Iwashita, and yet neither, as Lindeijer had reflected earlier, was he a bad man. Under stress from the bombardment he had lashed out. With the war on their doorstep, even "Lindy's luck" could fail.[40]

Their mood was somber the next day as noise continued from the direction of Kamaishi. "…I guess the task force is polishing them off …" Reynolds commented darkly. Intelligence from a guard that Russia had entered the war against Japan seemed good news. The locals were suffering, they as prisoners were catching "hell" for the slightest offense, and food from their kitchen was going three times a day to the Kamaishi camp. "Let's get this over with quick," the U.S. Navy man said.[41]

Turning their radio back on, they learned what a "quick end" could mean. In broadcasts from Honolulu they heard something about a "big bomb," and "some huge bombing raids"—apparently "bigger than anything [...] ever seen" before.[42] Tens of thousands had been killed immediately by the explosion and subsequent firestorm produced by one such bomb on 6 August in Hiroshima; some tens of thousands more by another on 9 August in Nagasaki. The ending was coming with devastating vengeance, and in hellish fire.

15 August '45! We went to the tunnel entrance [to the mine] twice today. Later, it appeared that the Emperor capitulated at noon.[43]

Earlier that morning, Bunch had been summoned to town to keep a radio system operating during a speech by the emperor that the prisoners had assumed would announce Japan's surrender.[44] Being marched to the tunnel while this took place seemed ominous. In light of the recent bombardments and murderous new bombs, what could they expect from their camp guards?

Months earlier, they'd engaged in vague talk about "rushing whoever was at the guns" if an invasion prompted orders to shoot them. But no one had really believed that there were machine guns in camp,[45] and this morning to their relief they had learned that their removal was merely to prevent them from hearing the voice of the emperor.[46] Not even his own people, who considered him divine, had heard him speak before.

The prisoners marked the occasion quietly; Lindeijer, by collecting signatures for his diary.[47] By evening, however, even muted celebration ceased. Truckloads of horribly burned prisoners began arriving from Kamaishi. Those who had escaped injury came separately, by train.[48] For days Lindeijer had no time to write.

11. Ohashi, April–August 1945

Sunday, 19 Aug. '45 This morning came the important announcement that arms were laid down. In fact, this was so as of Noon 15 August. Since that day we have not worked outside any more. The Japanese guards remained nasty for a while, but [official] discipline slackened.

On the evening of 15 August, the entire Kamaishi camp, almost 400 hundred [sic, 350] men, was brought over here. Because of [American] naval bombardments, they suffered 4 deaths there on 14 July, and another 25 on 9 August! Very many with burns are now being treated in our hospital. We have given cloth and mosquito nets [for bandages]. The healthy guys are put up in a theater hall not far from our camp.

Those responsible for the shelling might not have known the camp was there. Relatively new, it was established in late 1943, mid-way through the war (initially under Hakodate's jurisdiction, as Hakodate Camp 3; later Tokyo 7; and ultimately, Sendai 5B).[49] *Its first prisoners, the Dutch with whom Lindeijer rubbed shoulders during his time with Dr. Pijma, had arrived from Java on November nineteenth of that year. When Lindeijer himself arrived, it was no more than a couple of weeks old.*

Men he might have known then were virtually unrecognizable now. Many had taken shelter in trenches, and when a shell hit a nearby building, the trenches caught fire. Their upper bodies and faces were badly burned; their hair, and in some cases parts of their ears, singed or gone. Dr. Pijma was among them. Unable to tend the victims himself, he had directed others to remove the dead skin from their wounds.[50] *He lay with them now in the Ohashi camp hospital, where doctors Tucker and Eppley struggled to provide treatment, even as bandages had run out. Lindeijer and his colleagues donated what linens or sheeting they had and washed the dead flesh off used bandages before boiling them to be used again.*[51] *Some braved the stench in the sick bay to feed an injured man, frequently learning soon after that the man had died.*[52] *Others scrambled to provide for the "healthy guys" crammed into the abandoned theater up the road.*

Yet with all this, something additional was troubling. Their former commandant Sublieutenant Inaki, now a first lieutenant, had been transferred to the Kamaishi camp and was in charge there during the bombardment. Inaki was the commandant the Ohashi prisoners had considered their best, who set up volleyball nets for them, made certain they received their Red Cross packages, and said none of them should be beaten by guards. Now, certain of the Kamaishi prisoners—Americans and British transferred in April from Yokohama—were accusing him of having refused to protect them from the bombardment. Their claims were dramatic: he had denied repeated requests from their senior American officer, Captain Frank Grady, to move the camp to a less vulnerable location; even after the first shelling, saying "This is the only place, Grady. We will not move. Sendai tells me what to do, not you." The refusal was cold in their view; Inaki "didn't care." Traumatized by the bombardment and distraught over their dead and wounded, they were determined to file affidavits against him after the war.[53]

For the Ohashi prisoners, the charge was bewildering. Inaki's tenure at their own camp had stood out for its honesty and responsiveness. The Dutch prisoners from Kamaishi had similar positive views. At least one—Van der Hoek, a navy man—planned to write to Inaki after the war.[54] *Lindeijer's algebra pupil Keith Edmonds gave voice to the Ohashi men's consternation. Inaki had been approachable "on any matter" and willing to "give a fair hearing." "If a request was reasonable he would put it into operation."*[55]

Sadly, an added cost of the bombardment might have been a loss of rationality on the part of those traumatized by the death and suffering. It wasn't clear that an alternative location for a camp of four hundred men even existed in northeast Honshu in the last months of the war. In any case, for the area commander to grant permission to move the camp would have been unimaginable: the townsfolk along the coast deserved equal protection. And Sendai itself had been bombed in July. Tragically, at the time, Inaki might have been right. Kamaishi was "the only place."

If Inaki had any flaw in the eyes of any of the Ohashi prisoners, it was no more than his inability to deviate from orders. Responsibility lay more directly with the highest-level Japanese officials. And what of Grady's countrymen who had carried out the bombardments—three weeks prior to the first atomic bomb, and on the same day as the second? Those sympathetic to Inaki had to hope for a just resolution in the postwar. Inaki "was a good guy," Stanbrough declared, certain that "they [won't] do anything to harm him after the war [is] over."[56]

For the present, Lindeijer and his fellows concentrated on ministering to the burned patients—while inwardly rejoicing over better food, and imminent freedom and reunion with their families.

> I can use many of these days for quiet study. I have just now finished the Calculus from Hiashi. Incredible, isn't that! And how fortunate that I wasn't transferred to Kamaishi [earlier]! It must have been predestined, Nel, that I've been spared for a new life with and in our family. How I long for it, to see you again. A short time only!

Lindeijer was once again experiencing gratitude for having been spared—and as a result, recognizing the need to acknowledge those things he might have done better. Acknowledging past wrong and committing to make things better in the future: surely these were the key steps to the reconciled new life he desired. Perhaps to all situations in which reconciliation was in order.

11. Ohashi, April–August 1945

Yesterday I received a telegram from Frits in Holland, dated the nineteenth of July '44 [his mother's birthday]. Mother was fine those days! However, the most difficult time for Holland was yet to come. That winter must have been terrible there.

In spirit, kisses for all of you from father, a free man again! Your <u>Wim</u>...

12

Ohashi, August–September 1945— The Slow Return

Though Japan had capitulated on 15 August 1945, Lindeijer and his fellow Ohashi camp prisoners were technically not yet free, having received Allied orders to remain in place under the authority of their own officers prior to the arrival of an American liberating force. Even as they waited, however, they felt the weight of their three and a half years' imprisonment begin to recede. They were "dreadfully weak," their stomachs able "to hold very little of what went into them" (as Ken Horne, Lindeijer's math pupil, observed).[1] Yet they were no longer under the control of the Japanese Army, rejoicing, along with Frank Planton, over "the feeling of freedom from roll calls, orders, searches, being guarded and watched at all times and [the imposition of] so many restrictions."[2] To return to their loved ones remained their greatest desire; yet during these first moments of freedom, they could only revel, with Horne, in "the intoxicating joy of being able to stroll, stop, stand or sit without being ordered," and with Planton, simply in being "alive once again," and asserting their rights to "each new tomorrow."

Ohashi

Wednesday 22 Aug. '45. Formally, we are still POWs, but under the command of our own officers. This was announced last night by a Japanese officer from headquarters, along with the information that, further, we would receive "plenty of food [in English]." Indeed, I can't finish my beans. Soup is still miserable, but we do get white rice.

The patients from Kamaishi badly need better medicines and bandages. My mosquito net has been torn up for bandage material. We anxiously await contact with the American Army! I have slept two nights under the open sky. Beautiful summer nights and no fleas!

If they as prisoners felt relief, the same could be said of a number of the camp's Japanese. In an incident that evening, Lindeijer's colleagues had broken two windows during a game of ball and were stunned at the response. Guards who would have reacted in anger had simply stood there

12. Ohashi, April–August 1945

and *"laughed like hell."*[3] *This gave cause to wonder: had some they'd considered taciturn actually been afraid to laugh earlier?*

Planton reported a similar occurrence. A group of the Americans had "decided to kill one of the pigs" that belonged to the Japanese, using knives that they'd kept hidden in case of an emergency. When the pig squealed, "a guard rushed out with a rifle at the ready and dashed round the back of the [barracks] to where the noise was coming from." The astonished man "stopped dead, surveying the scene, glancing at the dead pig, the knives the men were still holding dripping with blood," and merely said "'O.K.' and smiled." The thieves announced that the pig was tomorrow's dinner. "Another smile and [the guard] was gone."[4]

At times the turnabout was less than sincere, of course. Reynolds parodied those Japanese concerned about conviction for war crimes: they "now say please forget about your treatment in the past. Now you will be treated with care." Yet undeniably, a number whom the prisoners had previously reduced to no more than epithets were emerging as genuine. A case in point was the man they called "Hitler" as a result of his mustache. Not two days ago he had paid the barracks a friendly visit. Even the skeptic Reynolds had judged him "for real." "He likes me—shot the breeze, gave me a good cig [sic]." [I] "asked him about his little girl."[5]

With the relaxation of the rules, the lines between friend and foe became more ambiguous. In the past the prisoners had in some cases made hasty misjudgments as a result of the Japanese Army's repression, but in other cases, out of their own bias.

> Ohashi, Friday, 24 Aug. '45. Wonderful days, Nel! No work, except for some camp work [cleaning up and helping in the hospital]. How would you be doing? I long so much for some news from you.
>
> The letters P.O.W. are painted on the [barracks'] roof. The American Air Force may come this Sunday and drop medicine, etc. The patients need it badly. Three patients from the Kamaishi camp have already died of their burns here. In total, [there are] thirty-two dead now, from the bombardments. There are still approximately six seriously wounded and about fifteen other patients.
>
> Maybe, 31 August we'll be on board [an Allied ship] and <u>home</u> again for Herman's birthday!!

That morning, prisoners formerly assigned to the workshops were free to roam Ohashi village. Mingling with the inhabitants, they found them "all friendly as hell and begging for clothes."[6] *News of the Allied parachute drop had reached the villagers as well. Ken Horne confirmed the same relief the prisoners had noticed earlier: "Now that the Kempei Tai [sic] had disappeared along with the soldiers, the villagers were more relaxed and sociable."*[7]

Saturday, 24 [*sic*, 25] Aug. It was announced last night that American airplanes would fly over Japan "in large numbers" today or tomorrow. Above every POW camp "supplies" would be dropped (likely medicine and food). The Emperor himself had given the order to his army and citizens to hand over all articles dropped to the Allied commanders of the POW camps. This time the rascals will not dare to steal anything. Will today be the big day?

Ohashi, Sunday 25 [*sic*, 26] Aug. '45.

Indeed, approximately fifteen American fighter planes flew over our camp yesterday at $\pm$ 12 hours [Noon]. They circled our camp for a while, clearly with the intent to "spot" us. We were jubilant and waved with pieces of cloth. Some of the pilots rolled their planes in salute. Oh, what a joy! Freedom at last, Nel! Unbelievable, that I appreciated freedom so poorly in the past.

Two carrier planes had preceded the fighters. At the sound of their engines every prisoner had dropped what he was doing and run out to the parade ground. The pilots flew so low that their heads were visible, the men marveled. Each registered details that would remain with him forever. "My God, grown men looking up, waving and shouting with tears running down their cheeks," Reynolds exclaimed. He himself was "a big baby, but I'm proud and not ashamed."[8] *For Kenneth Horne, the planes represented "the way home."*[9] *Feliz remembered an indelible image: one of the packets dropped was anchored by a carton of a familiar brand of cigarettes. "They were Lucky Strikes, and I'll never forget that."*[10] *The packet contained a copy of the* Stars and Stripes *newspaper, with a headline announcing Japan's capitulation. A handwritten note—"Cheer up boys, only a few more days"—was signed by the pilot. Reynolds exulted. The airman deserved "a bottle of Scotch from each man here," and he was "going to deliver him one in person."*[11]

Ken Horne spoke for the majority of the British. "So at last we know. It's over." Then came the bombshell. A number of the prisoners had known for days: the Americans had a secret radio and had known "about Midway and Europe and all the rest ..."[12] *Captain Zeigler apologized. Had the whole camp been "too cheerful," the secret would have been compromised. "Fully understood," Horne's compatriot Planton allowed graciously. Asked whether he'd suspected the radio's existence, and whether the "rumors" it stimulated raised morale, he'd been emphatic: "Oh, always!"*[13]

During the next moments, the U.S. dive bombers had performed their air show. The camp's Japanese watched with their former prisoners, though more with awe than enthusiasm. "Old Hitler" was an exception, conversing excitedly with an Australian and one of the British. Lindeijer's colleagues took notice. "Old Hitler"—"Oti san," Reynolds added, seemed "as enthused as us": for the first time, linking the man's epithet to his real name.[14]

We expected the "supply" [in English] from the air today, but the cloud deck was too low, so they couldn't make it. It is already evening now. Twenty-eight patients [presumably, many of the burn victims] left for a military hospital in Morioka. Appley [sic, Eppley], Gribnau and Coffield are with them. There is a rumor that we'll pick them up later to board the boat in Marori [possibly, Marori Island, Indonesia].

The Japanese Army distributes everything now: tobacco, cigarettes, socks, underwear, soap, summer clothes, winter coats, shoes, blankets, toilet paper, and towels; all things that we needed so badly before. Now, the scoundrels try to offer "sweet bread." The officers were invited to the Japanese camp office and treated to baked chicken. I am happy to have my Leiden blanket back, which was taken from me a year ago—as a result of which, I suffered a lot of cold last winter.

Yesterday and today, the American Lieutenant Polak [sic, Naval Ensign Pollak][15] and I boiled pieces of whale to extract oil. The oil is heated with NaOH [sodium hydroxide, or lye] from the Denki, to make soap which foams and washes all right, but keeps smelling like whale oil.

Pollak was the "stupid ensign" whom a number of the prisoners had shunned after his rash words to a guard had threatened the radio, and thus, Bunch and Stanbrough. Whether the soap-making signaled Lindeijer's implicit forgiveness for the episode isn't clear. His entry was cut short, in any case, by an occurrence that sent a stir of excitement throughout the camp:

Iwashita was back!

Their liaison had been recalled by Lieutenant Yoshida to help with "matters required for [the prisoners'] repatriation," he said.[16] But his return (for the "first time in four months!")[17] was clearly much more than a bureaucratic assignment for Iwashita himself. Exhilarated, he roamed about visiting and taking photographs—and in a convivial moment, entered his name and Tokyo address in Lindeijer's diary in western script.

He was "a happy man," as one of the British observed[18]; war-worn to be sure and sober over Japan's surrender (the prisoners were "soldiers of the winning side," leaving him "lost for words"). Yet at the same time he was noticeably looser and freer in manner—excited over the lifting of censorship, his mind racing ahead. It was his intent to write a memoir about them, he said.[19]

Later that day he "held court," as a contingent of the prisoner nationalities visited him at the small house he inhabited while in camp. Their very diversity reflected the breadth of his influence on them. The Americans Dr. Tucker, Jess Stanbrough, and Wilburn Rockett; the British Percy Cooper, Norman Rothin, and Richard Peck; and the Indonesian Dutch Dias Dullois and Johan Camerik all came as one group to pay their respects.[20]

During the days that followed he was everything they remembered. His concern for his country was evident: while on a recent trip to his headquarters he'd walked through Tokyo's Ginza shopping district. "An ugly sight."[21] Yet even in this tumultuous period, his commitment as their liaison

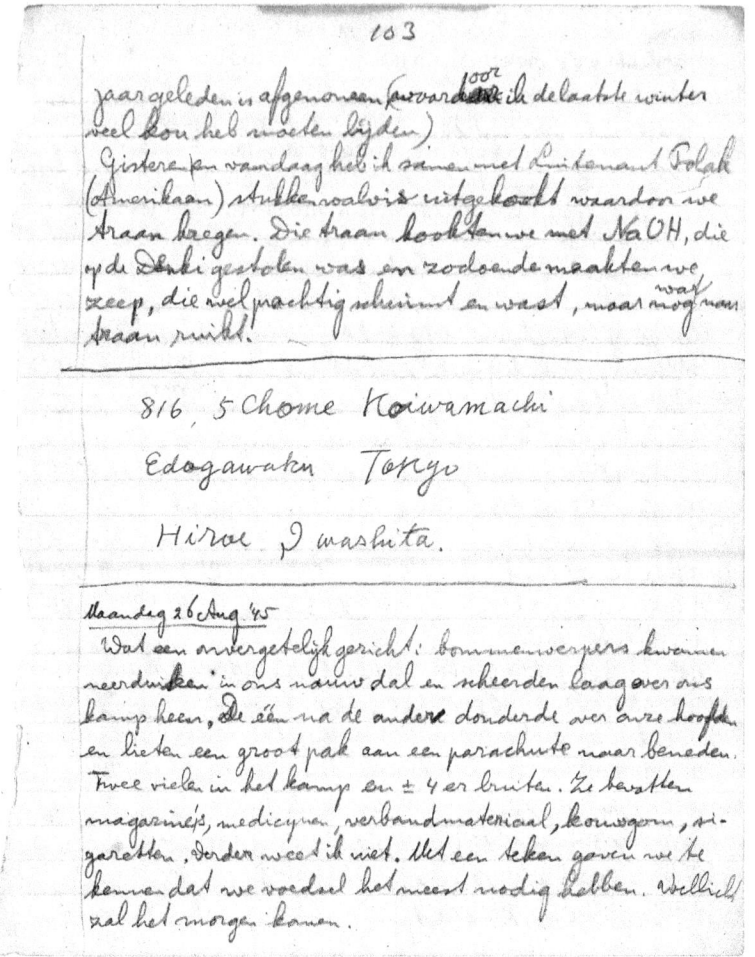

Letter entry on 26 August '45 [sic, 27 August], paused for Hiroe Iwashita to sign with his name and Tokyo address (Lindeijer Family Archive).

remained at the forefront. On the twenty-seventh he again brought his Victrola and records. Familiar tunes from his collection, hits from the 1930s, filled the camp. The selections could be endearingly touching: "Row, Row, Row," and "Last Night on the Back Porch I Loved You Most of All."[22] Their use of his epithet was affectionate. "Smitty the Spy" was back.

Monday, 26 [sic, 27] Aug. '45 An unforgettable sight: bomber planes came diving into our narrow valley and skimmed low over our camp. One after the other thundered overhead and parachuted a huge packet down. Two fell inside the camp and ± 4 outside. They contain magazines, medicine, bandage material, chewing gum, and cigarettes. Beyond this, we don't know. We signaled to them that above all we need more food. This may come tomorrow.

The packet dropped earlier had contained strips of colored cloth, with an explanation that these had been color-coded to represent needs they might have, such as medicine, food, or clothing. They were to lay out the colored strips indicating their most urgent needs on the parade ground.[23] *They had laid out every one, and then looked at the sky "until our necks became stiff," Feliz marveled afterward. Finally, one of the B-29 bombers they had heard so much about "opened up the bomb bays and sent out [its] precious cargo."*[24]

Tuesday, 27 [sic, 28] Aug. The Nippons [sic] work themselves to death. Last night a truck arrived with real rice and also butter and canned salmon. This morning one can of salmon and more than one pound of butter [per person] were distributed. Unfortunately, my stomach is completely upset. Also, ever more clothes: I received a good pair of Japanese short trousers.

Just now, the American planes flew over again and dropped down twelve bags with food stuffs, cigarettes, etc. Our boys would have loved to see this. Three bags without parachutes fell through the roof of the Japanese camp office. One Japanese was wounded by broken glass.

Evening: A four-engine bomber (B-29) dropped eighteen large boxes, all at the same time. It may have come from Okinawa. Most boxes did not have parachutes, so a large part of the canned food, such as soup, fruits, milk, cacao, and sugar, was spoiled. Further, excellent clothes, shoes, socks, etc. Finally, a message that they would return tomorrow! This afternoon, each of us received a half "breakfast box." But my stomach is still upset.

The drops became dangerous. The canned food was in forty-gallon barrels, many of which broke away from their parachutes, endangering the camp's inhabitants in what one of the prisoners called "the worst bombing raid that [he] had been in during the war. They came end-over end, right down on the camp..."[25] *Bill Stewart, hospitalized with a kidney infection, marveled that the medicine dropped, "particularly penicillin," couldn't have come at a better time; otherwise, he'd "have probably died." Yet when the planes neared, he was quick to obey the hospital attendant's admonition to "get your coat on and get out on the road and do whatever you can to stay away from here."*[26]

For others, danger or no, the reception of so much food produced near delirium. Feliz described how "the first pallet out got separated from the parachute and the food exploded when it hit the ground." It had contained his "very favorite fruit, cling peaches in heavy syrup." He made no bones about having dropped to his knees and "sucked up those peaches until they were all consumed"; even the juice, "which had partially penetrated the soil." It was difficult to explain his elation, Feliz said, but "nobody had ever had a more wonderful feast."[27]

28 [*sic* 29] Aug. No planes today.

No planes, but images of exploding cans of peaches and Spam were etched on the group psyche. Feliz came by to sign Lindeijer's diary: he was not going to forget the canned peaches for a long time. Ken Horne had "recollections of opening cans of corned beef and spam [sic], [and] smoking endless cigarettes," as well as "a vivid memory of opening a large can of peaches and plunging in a hand to pick the fruit out while the syrup ran all over the place." He was "transported," he said, and planned to sit up "late into the night talking, reading, and playing cards."[28]

Yet the high point of the day was something else.

Hiroe Iwashita, August 1945 (Lindeijer Family Archive).

Iwashita was taking photographs and jotting down orders for prints in a notebook he carried,[29] and giving away his card and a small photograph of himself. Autographed in some cases, his photograph was perhaps indicative of a desire to be remembered.

The small portrait was of a face that was war-weary and serious, yet kind. Tucked between the pages of his diary, Lindeijer's copy resided next to the photographs of his family.

30 Aug.[30] Two times a B-29 dropped her food load. Quite a job to salvage everything. A lot of chocolate, chewing gum, soup, fruits, and so on. The Japanese office personnel outdid themselves with the now superfluous distribution of Japanese Army shoes.

Numbers of the prisoners had gone to the mountains to locate more of the food that had dropped.[31] *They now had so much food that they "found it difficult to sleep between the boxes." They'd given the "good kids" from the workshops Spam, C-rations, and candy bars.*[32]

Lindeijer reveled with the others in the abundance, yet struggled to contain his emotions over the hoped-for reunion with his family; his letter to his wife on her birthday, a poignant cry.

31 Aug. '45.

This will certainly be a happy day for you, Nel [her birthday and that of Queen Wilhelmina]. Now, a free person! Free to go where you want to go, and to say what you want to say. And full of plans for the immediate future: no unrealistic ideas, but nothing less than happy ones. For God's sake, how would you and the children be doing?

We are most likely going to a camp near Manila, and there I hope to receive a message from you. Finally and at long last, the day approaches that we will see each other again. Almost fearsome: the happiness that can be built up there. God grant us the strength and the courage not to spoil it again, but to lead a free and happy life, as intended by Him.

I missed your letters painfully, Nel! Well, we all missed so much. You feel sick when you recall the horrible times that we now leave behind us. Time and again, I imagine the priceless moments that we'll have together. Once in a while a moment that is really and truly good; is that not enough to give lasting happiness? Happy is he who can also find joy in the fulfillment of his duties.

Our simple life as POWs is over. The confusing multiplicity of "normal" life slowly returns. It is already difficult to focus my thoughts on studying. Will I leave all efforts made during the last year to master more mathematics unutilized? Will I let this become lost? Nel, I feel myself a weak person! I cannot live alone anymore, like in the past. I long for home! A kiss from your Wim

[Postscript] Just now, four B-29s came over and each dropped quite a load. We now receive new clothes, shoes, etc. More food than we can eat, with 750 men.

The drops now were nearly lethal. Reynolds reported the latest delivery coming in "big fifty-five gallon drums": "one went through the Canadian barracks, two went through the galley [kitchen], one went in the toilet, one through the theater above the camp and four or five Nip [sic] houses across the street were wrecked."[33]

Kenneth Horne told the story of the drum that fell in the toilet: it had plunged into an empty stall and through the cement floor "into the cistern which by this time was almost full..." On "its journey" it had torn away the wall of the next stall "in which an unfortunate man was squatting to relieve himself." What Horne called "the ensuing tidal wave" covered the man in "the most unspeakable muck from which his rescuers hauled him in a catatonic state of shock." He was taken to a hospital where he was cleaned up and put to bed "for twenty-four hours before recovering power of speech." His first words upon recovery were "Oh shit!" Horne later said he had reason to "suspect that the story [was] apocryphal."[34]

Dark humor aside, in the midst of such chaos and the absence of camp rules, the range of prisoner behavior was extreme. To make matters worse, an American naval commander who had entered the camp along with the Canadians outranked Captain Zeigler, but refused to assert authority.[35] *Thus a certain ambiguity held sway. "I could write a book about today,"* Reynolds exclaimed. *"Some men stealing, some honest, fighting ... What a place."*[36]

Lindeijer ignored the disorder, continuing to collect signatures and addresses in his diary.[37] Iwashita likewise took it in stride, though evincing surprise at being shown the barracks' shortwave set. "Stanbrough had Iwashita san [sic] listening to the radio this afternoon. Quite funny," Reynolds commented.

Funny, perhaps. But by the next day, a loudspeaker in the barracks was connected to their set.[38]

> 2 Sept. '45. Yesterday, the roof of our kitchen was painted with the words "dangerous, no more" [in English] because the dropping of drums with foodstuffs, etc., about and inside the camp, is considered to be too dangerous by our American commander [E.V. Dockweiler, who in this case took action]. This morning, however, five B-29s dropped their "loads" again. Fortunately, all of it without accidents, except for a bruised Nippon arm. Enormous amounts came in, regardless of the fact that many a parachute broke off and half the load was lost.
>
> The official capitulation [formal surrender] of Japan took place at 10.30 hrs this morning: the papers were signed on board the battleship "Missouri" in the Bay of Tokyo. We heard it over our radio in the barracks.[39] A second group of patients (± 25) left for Morioka this morning. It's a pity that we'll have to wait for another four days or so.

The prisoners distracted themselves as best they could. On the third of September, their commander liberated the Chinese prisoners. ("Some of them were here messing around all day; we gave them lots of stuff.") When that interest subsided, they fraternized and traded with the locals. ("All these people are as happy to have the war over as we are.")[40] They were also daily gaining weight. Feliz had gained "eighteen pounds in fifteen days."[41] Reynolds said of himself that he didn't "look like Red Reynolds now. A mustache and a fat face."[42]

> 5 Sept. '45. A persistent rumor has it that we will leave with a transport ship from Kamaishi, tomorrow morning. The Japanese are now getting their rice with 70% beans, while we receive more rice than we can eat. The last two pigs were slaughtered yesterday. Our officers have a luxury car at their disposal.
>
> In this "prisoners camp," the American, British, and Dutch flags fly now! Indeed, the tables are turned. We buy eggs and chicken from the local people here. Everything is devoured, even sake!

Lindeijer's comments on the officers' luxury were restrained, whereas his colleagues' were not: "They are thinking of themselves and very little of

12. Ohashi, April–August 1945

us." They were "doing well for themselves" and "have automobiles, chauffeurs, servants, and so forth." The men "expected some of that," they said, "but they [their officers] are taking it too far."⁴³

6 Sept. '45. + 1 p.m. Apparently, a ship approaches Kamaishi, but it moves slowly, as mines have to be swept. I think we may board this ship tomorrow morning at the earliest. Our kitchen stopped cooking this morning. We received a K-ration for breakfast and just now for "dinner" two C-rations. Excellent and delicious food, that is! It seems that American occupation troops will be stationed here by the time we leave.

Despite the orders they had received to wait in place for the liberating force, a number of the prisoners were impatient. Their commander, Dockweiler, and Captain Zeigler had departed for Kamaishi and taken luggage with them, leaving their subordinates to wonder "if they are intending to come back or [are] they getting away from us."⁴⁴ Meanwhile, food at the camp was "playing out again."⁴⁵ A disgruntled group talked of leaving early.

Lindeijer again focused on collecting contact information from those of whom he'd grown fond, including his algebra pupil Kenneth Horne and the Indonesian Dutch Rijnders from the camp hospital.⁴⁶

<u>Saturday, 8 Sept.</u>

We continue to sit here. The army food is finished and some forty guys left for Tokyo yesterday. The officers were appalled, but it is their own fault. They did not care enough about food logistics and didn't know how to tackle desertion. It is good that no Hollanders [Dutch] left so far. It is against the orders of MacArthur!

Feliz and some others had decided that "enough was enough,"⁴⁷ and with a few belongings in backpacks, slipped out of the camp. "Luck to the boys," Reynolds said. "Two hundred seventy-five miles to Tokyo by air but railroad and highway may be twice as far." He later admitted that he would have gone too had he felt better. Disgusted with his superiors, the American army lieutenant Humble was "damn near ready to go, himself." The American naval ensign Pollak hurried off on the motorcycle to Kamaishi, where he reportedly found the commander and captain "in the leading hotel," with "plenty to eat and drink" and "entertainment and girls." The two came back "hot under the collar" at the insurrection, and telephoned ahead to threaten the reprobates into returning, with little success. A single older seaman had come back.⁴⁸

In Zeigler's case, the unfortunate behavior could be considered a lapse. As for the lackluster commander, whatever the true estimate of his character, more men were leaving. The damage was done.

Indeed, Lindeijer had acquired Ken Horne's contact information not a moment too soon. That very morning Horne, in a group of roughly a dozen British and a Canadian, had likewise "had enough" and left.⁴⁹

<u>9 Sept. Sunday</u>

A telegram from Tokyo today says that ships will leave from there tomorrow morning to pick up POWs from Sendai and Kamaishi. So, we! Hence, our ship will be here by tomorrow or the day after at the latest. Finally and at last, the light at the end of the tunnel of hope and waiting. Meanwhile, $\pm$ 40 men left already on their own, regardless of the resistance of their officers and the improvement of the food situation …

The next day, the Japanese military moved the healthy prisoners from the Kamaishi camp back to that city, and into the former barracks of a Japanese seacoast battery.[50]

13 Sept., Thursday, Ohashi

We are still waiting for the ship that may arrive in Kamaishi this afternoon. Although we lead a "life of luxury" compared to the past, you understand how we long for departure. Another B-29 came over yesterday and dropped $\pm$ 15 bags of food and materials. They came down close to and inside the camp on parachutes. So almost nothing was lost this time.

Some twelve of the Japanese who stole packages dropped on the ninth [of September] were handcuffed and brought into the camp. They must clean the camp—the benshos [sic, benjos—toilets], etc., and then spend some time in "iso."

I lose hope that I could be home for Herman's birthday. Honestly speaking, I am quite worried about you. I heard that the situation in the internment camps was not so good and that at the moment Australian planes are dropping medicine and food for them. We have not yet heard anything of an official capitulation [surrender] of the Japanese Army in Java!

Another B-29 came and dropped a good load of food relatively nearby, at approximately 1 hour before sunset this evening. As soon as everything was brought in it was divided, leaving us all in a festive Sinterklaas evening mood. How shall we celebrate a <u>real</u> one?

14 Sept. Ohashi, Friday

Australian photographers arrived here, today. They told us that we may go on board in Kamaishi tomorrow. We are not allowed to keep any of our clothes. Hence, we gave a lot away and sold a lot as well. In total, I earned 540 yen today. I am curious, though, what I can really do with all that money: more than 600 yen now. It may not be easy!

Sunday 16 Sept. '45, Hospital Ship, Kamaishi

Our greatest longings are being fulfilled now: we are on our way home, to the place where we hope to find and bring happiness! Is a happy family life not the deepest desire of every human being? Certainly it is mine. Yesterday was in fact the big day of our departure from Ohashi. So, exactly one month after the capitulation of Japan, 15 August, our last working day and the day on which the Emperor of Japan spoke to his people. It was too chaotic, then, to write about it.

12. Ohashi, April–August 1945

We packed in the morning, for as much as that had not been done weeks before. I fried myself an egg in bacon for breakfast. I used my course work on Latin to light the fire.[51] We left a lot behind for the Chinese POWs, who were to come to our camp as soon as we left.

The trip to the Ohashi station was a true tour of victory. Every group, Dutch, American, British, and Canadian, with their national flags up front, sang national anthems. At the train were the prominent citizens of Ohashi and a number of those who knew us through our work. But only those who knew that we appreciated them. Since we had more than we could use, we gave them clothes and food articles.

At last, there we went, with our national flags on the front of the locomotive. What a proud sight to see our tri-color banner fly again so freely!

A poignant note at the station was the presence of Iwashita. He'd shaken hands with Dr. Tucker. ("What a pity!" that he would never see him again; "bon voyage.") Also with Captain Zeigler and Lieutenant Humble.[52] Then in a grand gesture, he'd given the notebook in which he recorded orders for photographs to Richard Peck, one of the more gregarious among the British.[53] The notebook contained a representative selection of his prints, each mounted on a left-hand page, with the number of orders in Arabic numerals in the margin. Text handwritten in old Japanese, indecipherable to the prisoners, accompanied each photograph on a facing page. But what was clear at a glance was the fascination the prisoners had held for him.

In photograph after photograph, he'd recorded them—in groups in the workshops and mine, and in views highlighting individuals: among others, the Indonesian Dutch prisoners Bertsch, Samuels, Lens, and Van Eldick; the African Dutch Gutenberg; the British prisoner Kent and Chinese British Tan; the American prisoners Feliz and Stanbrough; and the European Dutch Lindeijer.[54] Their three Christmases at the camp had attracted his particular attention; the photographs from the consecutive years' celebrations grouped together chronologically and culminating with a view of the nationalities mingling at the most recent, in 1944.

The absence of a photograph of Commandant Kawabe was hardly a surprise; nor the inclusion of a close study of the good Medical Sergeant Neko. Only the prominent and seemingly flattering portrait of Lieutenant Naganuma, whom they considered "the Rat," was confounding. Did Iwashita have perspective on the man that they lacked? To the last, this civilian Japanese, whom they had learned to admire despite differences, was causing them at least to think twice.

Their experience with Kamaishi and its wartime suffering was likewise having its effect.

Kamaishi—bombed and burned—made such a desolate impression on us. The American marines had landed already and were everywhere, looking for souvenirs. A sense of bewonderment and jealousy came over me when I saw those well-fed and heavily armed fellows. The souvenirs popular with them were Japanese rifles, bayonets, money and samurai swords.

The bombardments had sparked kitchen fires across the small city and left it in ruins. Lindeijer's reference to the newly arrived American marines as "well-fed and healthy fellows" was subtly tongue in cheek. These were "new Americans," who in the eyes of the prisoners being liberated, were lacking in sensitivity to the local people, many of whom had lost everything. The American Jess Stanbrough had given voice directly to the indignation they were feeling at seeing these "new Americans chasing people and trying to take their swords away from them..." Their indignation extended to the newcomers' treatment of the local police, "because the police were really and truly law-and-order people and had never, ever bothered any of us..."[55]

Any one of the newly liberated might well have wondered, as Lindeijer had earlier: would the return to "normal life" erase from memory all that they, and perhaps the world, had learned from the war?

For the present, Lindeijer's Latin lesson, though burned, was likely fresh enough to provide encouragement. "Amicitia vitam ornat"—"Friendship adorns life"—would have taken on added significance with the appearance of Iwashita on the platform; and again, as he sighted fellow Dutch on the approaching ship that he was about to board—harbingers of home.

Landing sloops took us to the hospital ship "Rescue." From a distance, I thought I saw some American marines on board, but coming closer they called out happily to us in Dutch. They were ours and shipped here ahead of us. An hour later we walked around in the same dress [as the Dutch who had boarded earlier]: all clothes had to be left behind. A warm bath, disinfection and new clothes freed us from lice, fleas, and kitanai [dirty or filthy] dust, and cast our POW status into the past forever. What a delight. Then real bread, real jam, and milk. As much as we wanted!

We were lucky that we could not be transferred to a troop transport ship anymore that day. Hence, we slept in nice beds otherwise reserved for light patients. Everything spotlessly clean, practically arranged, and excellently organized. Yesterday I could send a telegram Nel! I may hear from you in Manila. Bye now; till I see you!

P.S. Also a letter to you and one to mother.

Monday, 17 Sept. Morning: We just arrived at Yokohama. The bay is packed with American and English war ships.

PART II

Traumatic Memory— Echoes from Past to Present

> "... I saw a high wall and as I had a premonition of an enigma, something that might be hidden behind the wall, I climbed over with some difficulty. However, on the other side I landed in a wilderness and had to cut my way through with a great effort until—by a circuitous route—I came to the open gate ..."—M.C. Escher, *The Regular Division of the Plane*

Between Borneo and Java, Winter 1945–46: Letters of Loss and Renewal

Lindeijer's focus was now entirely on his young family. Already, from the hospital ship he'd sent Nel a telegram. He followed this with a letter to her on 16 September, along with another to his mother, requesting that it be sent on to Nel's parents. Then again on 23 September, en route to Manila from Yokohama on the USS *Monitor*, he tried once more to reach out to his wife. His aerogram reflected both eagerness and anxiety:

What future awaited them? Could anything take the place of what had been torn away? And what would the boys really look like? He still could not picture Joke "in any other way than a random little girl's face on a printed photograph." Trying to remember was hopeless! How long he would have to stay in Manila he didn't know. There were rumors that his group would be going to Australia first. "You understand," he wrote, "that I would not be altogether happy with such a detour."

In Manila, he found that Nel and the children were on a Red Cross list of survivors. His happiness could not have been greater. Still, after three weeks in a camp there, he'd heard nothing from her, and news of violence in Java had him frantic with worry. On 17 August, two days after Japan's surrender, Sukarno and Mohammad Hatta had declared Indonesia's independence from the Netherlands. A revolutionary fervor gripped the country, yet the Allies were proving frustratingly slow to arrive. Sukarno and Hatta had urged restraint, but in spite of this, young independence fighters impatient to rid their country of European dominance were threatening the areas of the camps.

In Lindeijer's letter to family in Holland in mid-October, he expressed hope that he and others not yet released from the KNIL would be "sent to Java in one or two weeks under arms." Once there, he might manage to find and reunite with his wife and children. But as luck would have it, he was needed for the postwar cleanup elsewhere. In early November, he found himself stationed as an x-ray technician at a hospital in Balikpapan, Borneo. And there, on 23 November, in a message from his Dutch Naval chaplain brother Jan, the news had finally come: the Red Cross list had been wrong. His children were alive, but his beloved wife, Nel, had died in Muntilan on 25 July.

M.C. Escher's "Three Worlds" (© 2024 The M.C. Escher Company—The Netherlands. All rights reserved. *www.mcescher.com*).

The news was too much to bear. His entire world and hopes for the future fell apart. And what of his children; where were they, and were they safe?

Almost miraculously, on 25 November he received a letter from Adrie van der Baan, the young schoolteacher his family had befriended, along with her sister Riek, before the war. She was writing to let him know that his children were in her care. She didn't need to tell him how much it grieved her and Riek when they heard "that dear Nel had passed away," she said. They would "never forget what Nel had been for [them], not only during the prewar time, as an always welcoming and happy person, but also especially during the time in the camp, when [they] shared love and sorrow." They had helped Nel with the children while at their first camp, in Bandung, but had been unable to accompany her when she and the children were put on transport to a camp elsewhere.

However, now, after recovering from a period of illness herself, she was running an orphanage together with Riek in Batavia. And since yesterday, Wim, Herman, Freddy and Joke were there with them. "The children and we are very happy that they are here, especially since it was no longer so very nice in Semarang [the harbor city to which the four children had been liberated]."

She hoped that it would not be too long before he came their way, but in the interim she and Riek would care for his children as if they were their own. With dearest greetings and sympathy for his sorrow, she and Riek wished him strength.

He found himself cheered in a way that would not have seemed possible two days before. She had thought to have each of the older two children write a letter, and the younger two, draw a picture. In a letter carried by a certain Lieutenant Smit who was going to Batavia, he'd written back: "That scribbling is worth gold." "It makes me human again."

From that point, the letters flew. Adrie replied the next day, giving him news about the children's development to allay his concerns. She apparently sensed intuitively the worry he would have about relating to the little girl he hadn't seen since she was ten months old. Like her brother Herman, Joke did everything "with 100% concentration." He "should have seen [her] for example throwing rings around a stick. She also talks so funny. This to us was most remarkable because when they [Nel and the children] departed for Central Java, Joke still didn't find talking to be altogether such an essential condition of life. Her family understood her well enough with one or another incoherent sound. But now she already speaks altogether perfectly and has stories nineteen to the dozen which everyone greatly enjoys."

At the same time, Adrie had concerns of her own: The situation in Java was precarious. Should it "again become more dangerous, would [he] then be able to give [his] permission in the off chance for us to take [the children] to Europe?" They might "have to evacuate with the entire children's home for example."

She wrote again on December 8, chiding him: he had enclosed individual letters for each of the boys but not for the little girl whose personality eluded him: "Joke felt a little left out as she didn't get one, so don't forget your daughter next time. She exerted herself this afternoon writing to you. The result is traveling herewith and there are letters from the boys too."

In closing, she again expressed concern over the danger that threatened: the latest group of children who arrived from the camps had gunshot wounds. The orphanage had to be protected by guards. She and Riek would have liked to get a photograph taken of his children to send to him, but preferred "to keep them safely at home."

This time, he hadn't waited for a response. He had begun thinking of her. His letter of December 9 was in reply to hers of December first. He had tried twice to get leave to go to Java, he said, but without success, and he had no idea how long he would have to be in Borneo. Frustrated, he poured out his heart, and in doing so no doubt surprised even himself: In the first lines of the letter, he asked her to be his wife.

Then in a lengthy succession of paragraphs, he did his best to explain. It was not that he lacked "respect for the past [...] God knows how dearly I would have rebuilt our family anew with Nel, but He has not willed it." Neither was he asking her because he "felt unhappy" or because he had "a need of somebody for my children [...]" He asked because he was "eager to go into the future with [her]." She might find him "silly." But, he wrote, "All the old has been smashed to bits. Courage and inner contentment [were] needed to start anew." And he had admired these qualities in her even before the war. As for being in love, there would "come a time" when they would whisper their love to each other; and it was "in that confidence" that he dared ask her.

She took a week to write back. "I'm not angry, Wim, but why couldn't you have waited with this question?" Only yesterday she had met with Mrs. Marijnen, who had given her a letter for him from Nel. And besides this, after three years in a camp, she'd planned to travel and also to "enjoy in Holland all that lives and moves there and is being rebuilt and have my part in it there as well." She loved the children, but after corresponding for such a short while was really not "able to say whether [he was] the one with whom [she] would be able to discover the great miracle [of] love." Certainly, she could not say it before she had seen and spoken with him "and we have read it in each other's eyes."

He hardly needed to be motivated further. In mid-January, he managed to prevail on his captain to bend the rules. The officer granted him furlough and the only chance he might have to get to Java—in a military plane, lying flat on his stomach and looking out the bomb doors.

Days later, still in Batavia, he wrote to his older brother and sisters in Holland that the homecoming he'd feared might be strained had been "so delightfully spontaneous and happy." As he'd approached the orphanage, his children had been sitting out in front watching a transport of other children depart for the Netherlands. His eldest had spotted him immediately and jumped down from the porch and run toward him. The other three—even Joke who could not have recognized him—lost no time in following suit. Amid joyous cries of "Hi, Father!" his reunion had been achieved.

When the excitement died down, he spoke with his older two about their life in the camp where their mother had become so ill. Particularly Herman had told "so touchingly" of her final ordeal, he wrote to family members in Holland. A letter from Christien Slotemaker-de Bruine, the missionary who befriended Nel during the last weeks of her life, likewise provided him with an account. Yet "no letter from elders" could have given him as clear a picture of Nel's suffering as "this shaking little child's mouth." It was "deeply sad and yet such a relief, also to Herman himself, that he could talk it all out at last." His eldest "felt it really deeply," as well, "but had already digested it much more himself."

Learning of the dangers his children themselves had experienced, he was more relieved than ever to find them safe. After Nel's death they had been in two more camps in areas troubled by insurgents. Only in late November had the Allies reached them. At that point, they were taken by a truck convoy north toward Semarang, and attacked while en route, at a pass. Amid gunfire in Semarang harbor they were put aboard the ship that had finally brought them unharmed to Adrie and Riek in Batavia.

His meeting with Adrie took place later in quiet—and only after she had given him, unopened, the letter from Nel. Reading it, he was overcome by Nel's words granting him and the children the freedom they needed to move forward.

Wim, you should not continue to grieve for me. We have had our life together. Start a new life, with another wife. Only one thing, I beseech you: look for a good mother for the children. It would fulfill my deepest wish if it might be one of the Van der Baan girls; but, of course, I cannot look into your heart. Riek has such a rich inner life, but you know how I love Adrie too.

I hope that God will guide you in the choice of your new life.

In a last brave act, Nel had envisioned a future for her family. In his own way, Lindeijer had been attempting to do the same. Only now, reading her words, he could embrace that future freely and without guilt.

For him, and for Adrie when he shared the letter, the effect was seemingly providential. Adrie's previous indecision no longer existed. Nor did he feel the need for lengthy explanations. He had been able to look into her eyes and ask her to *want* to be his wife. Without qualms she accepted.

The realities of postwar Java dictated that their wedding take place quickly: Adrie and Riek needed to leave for the Netherlands with a transport of children. "It seems best to me that we first marry here," he wrote to siblings on 19 January. "That way Adrie carries not only the duties but also the [legal] rights of a mother over the children during the time that I am in Indië [Indonesia]." Adrie would also have a pension, should anything happen to him, he must have thought. They were married on 25 January in a civil ceremony in Batavia—and in a scene captured by a local artist, carried off in a rickshaw for a brief honeymoon. Following Lindeijer's release from military service, they were married again in a formal church ceremony in July in the Netherlands, with the four children they now shared as attendants. They truly did find "the miracle of love," and became the parents of four additional children.[1] This second group, three boys and a girl, arrived in the same order as those born before the war—and with them were always to speak of two mothers—Mother Adrie and Mother Nel.

"Just Arrived" in the Netherlands from Java, January 1946, the Lindeijer children with the "new mother" Nel promised them, Adrie Lindeijer-van der Baan. Row 1 L to R: Freddy (Frits), Joke, Herman; Row 2: Adrie and Wim Jr. (Lindeijer Family Archive).

13

Delft, 1992–95— A Son's Memory Work

Wim Lindeijer Jr., "Wim," as he was known to the family (the elder Lindeijer would forever be "Father"), grew to adulthood in the Netherlands, and by the early 1970s had become a civil engineer with a PhD, posted by development agencies and civil engineering companies to water and sanitation projects in third-world countries.[1] When his father died in 1981, after a distinguished tenure as director of the Technology Laboratory of the Dutch National Defense Research Organization, Wim inherited custody of his father's wartime diary. Busy at the time, however, with married life, career, and family, he'd let the diary and the events of his wartime childhood settle into the back of his mind.

Until 1992, that is, when he was sent home from a project based in Quetta, Pakistan, for treatment at the hospital for tropical diseases in Rotterdam. News traveled back of the ambush and killing of fourteen of his aid worker acquaintances at the Khyber Pass, causing him to suffer a breakdown. The report, received as he lay ill, was devastating enough in itself. Yet its deeper threat lay in the memory it awakened of attacks at a pass in another part of the world more than half a lifetime ago—when the Allied truck convoy liberating him and his siblings met the murderous fire of Indonesian independence fighters. The real subject of his disturbance was Central Java in 1945, not Pakistan in 1992.[2]

* * *

Seeking help, he embarked on a series of weekly sessions with a psychiatrist at the Sinai Center in Amersfoort, noted in the Netherlands for its groundbreaking work in treating anxiety arising from war experience. Disappointingly however, the sessions unfailingly covered the same ground, without yielding any progress. The psychiatrist ultimately released him with the sole suggestion that he reread his father's diary—an idea that Wim had brought up himself.

He had read it only once previously, at the age of thirteen. When his father had discovered what his eldest was doing, he had asked him to put it aside until he was older; then they would read it together. That had never happened, though his father had always answered Wim's questions about it, and both his father and his "second mother" Adrie encouraged talking through wartime anxieties during Saturday night family gatherings.

Reopening it as an adult might allow him to learn his father's coping strategies. It might also help in coming to terms with grief he'd carried with him since he was nine—and watched early one morning from a veranda at Muntilan as the sun climbed the Mount Merapi volcano and a small group of women carried the blanketed body of his mother out the gate on a stretcher, toward the cemetery up the hill.[3]

Taking his leave of the psychiatrist, he departed along the familiar hallway, turned left at the end, descended the narrow stair, and stepped outside the ring of buildings. He had work to do on his own. Yet interestingly, the small office with its yellowish walls, and particularly its black and white M.C. Escher print of a large fish staring up from under leaves that had fallen onto water, remained in his mind. He could not say why, possibly because of a family connection. Escher had been a friend of his wife's Aunt and Uncle Oosterhof, taking room and board with them when in Leiden and repaying them for his stay with drawings.[4]

At home in Delft, the family encouraged his project. He began putting the letters that made up the diary on an old secondhand computer that Joke had found for him. Yet invariably, the nightly disturbances in which he was pursued by monstrous figures continued. He would be asleep for a while, and within three to four hours the nightmare would build. He managed to train himself to wake up to stop it and then go back to sleep, though at times it resumed. His work with the diary at first offered little respite, triggering flashbacks in which he relived the events of his childhood: in the psychiatrist's terms, his *traumatic affect*, in which the initial numbing experience, never fully processed rationally, repeatedly and insistently comes back.[5]

He continued to believe that his task would assist in working through his experience and coming to terms with it, nonetheless. His father's accounts of the battle of Kalijati and the overseas transport described events at least as traumatic as those he himself had encountered. Serving as a medic during the battle, in the midst of gunfire and bombing, without air support, would have been terrifying; attempting to help the sick without medicines on the disease-ridden ship, even worse. Yet not two years later, when his captors required him to report on these experiences, his father had managed to do so in a voice that was rational and

13. Delft, 1992-95

controlled—to the extent that he communicated the inhumanity of the transport in a manner that they would understand.

Wim's disturbance brought on by news of the recent killings was proving resistant to such management. The news, in broad outline, was this:

> Three vehicles, each carrying five to seven of his aid worker acquaintances from a project to the north of his, had been traveling from Islamabad to Jalalabad, through the foothills to the Khyber Pass. At the pass, the vehicles were suddenly fired upon, most likely by elements from the drug trade intent on eliminating western influence. One person was killed immediately, and the others died moments later as the attackers came up to the vehicles and delivered each of them a neck shot.

As Wim heard the report, fourteen people were killed. Only one man, a Dr. van Rooij, the leader of the parallel project to the north, had survived. When the first shots were fired he had dropped out of the car he was riding in and run from boulder to boulder, back into the pass. At a certain point he had managed to jump onto the running board of a van that had succeeded in turning around from the shooting, and climbed inside.

Had it actually been fourteen who were killed or only four? A Dutch woman contact of Dr. van Rooij claimed the latter.[6]

For Wim Lindeijer, reminded so acutely of events in his childhood, exact numbers didn't matter. He'd been returned to the moment in late November 1945 when he stood with his siblings in a line of women and children to board trucks to which mattresses had been roped, each with two armed British Gurkhas on the roof. Under cover of Spitfire aircraft, their convoy of fifteen or so trucks had headed north from Central Java, toward the harbor at Semarang, where a rescue ship awaited. But in the pass, near Semarang, attackers had struck at dusk. Pushed out of the truck by their protectors, they lay in a furrow beside the road, the mattresses thrown on top of them. The shooting continued for a terrifying hour, with their air protection ineffective in the dark.

Afterward, moved for the night into a building still under construction, they lay on a concrete floor, the mattresses still covering them. In an opening between the mattresses he'd seen the light from tracer bullets that flew overhead.

At daylight, the Spitfire planes provided cover as they were loaded into the trucks to be taken to the harbor. Once there, they were rushed into a large hall to avoid snipers. But later as they ventured out and approached the torpedo boats that would take them to the larger rescue ship, the *Van Heutz*, shooting began behind the hall. Once again they fell to the ground, with mattresses thrown over them. The Spitfires and torpedo boats unleashed their guns, and for a second time they saw the Spitfire bullets through the openings between the mattresses. He and his siblings held on to each other. Freddy trembled unbelievably. Joke cried a lot. Herman was merely surprised, anxiously looking around. Wim himself remembered being afraid—and also fascinated by the little Spitfires going over before flying straight up and then making another round. Finally, they reached the torpedo boats. At the *Van Heutz*, they had to climb rope ladders to board, and then people had helped them in.

Reliving the incident had made him feel uncertain and caused trembling all over his body. Yet his father would have fought off similar disabling numbness, and had somehow developed a perspective that enabled him, even as a prisoner, to live largely within the present. Wim moved forward in the diary, determined to discover his father's secret.

An answer was not to come quickly. His father's letters written during the transport expressed concerns over his wife and children, activating Wim's memories of the same fraught period. "I do so hope that you can stay in our house," his father wrote on 4 November 1942—ironically, little more than a month before the family's forced departure for a camp in Bandung's Cihapit quarter. A Japanese general wielding a sword and accompanied by a cadre of troops had entered their home with the order.[7] Already shell-shocked by the invasion and traumatized by the loss of their father, the Lindeijer children "lost their feeling of safety," in the words of their mother. Freddy, the younger of his brothers, had been the most deeply affected. Joke had perhaps been too young to be aware, but Freddy was left "stiff with fear."[8]

The memory remained poignant for Wim even now. Yet examining it and others like it in light of his father's diary would surely help. He noted that his father had expressed his well-wishes for them while in the company of dying men, in the depths of a derelict ship. Perhaps he had held terror at arm's length by writing to them and attempting to visualize their situation. The very act of writing might have distanced him sufficiently from his surroundings to allow him to think more objectively and do what he could to improve things. The task that Wim set for himself—reading his father's letters, putting them on his computer, and printing out and sharing copies—might work in a similar way. He would confront his own experience, but within the larger perspective of his father's document, which might help with the distance and objectivity that he himself needed.[9]

He had little time to wonder whether this would be the case. Almost immediately the diary's factual approach stimulated him to begin searching for facts and dates of his own. Prompted by his father's remark of 4 November 1942, he began piecing together details that provided a clearer picture of the time than that dominated by the image of the Japanese general. These came from older adults and a letter his mother Nel had written to his father in February 1943 but had never been able to mail. A Sinterklaas festival had taken place at their house in early December. (He remembered! Seventy children had come—the number from his mother Nel's letter—and squealed with delight as Sinterklaas's helpers threw candy at them from behind his back.) The family Vemer had been living with them and paying rent since the first of April. And by this time people from Toon Lindeijer's family were living with them too.[10]

From one of these people he learned that the eighteenth or nineteenth of December had been the date of his own family's forced move. He recalled that their first "home" in the camp had been a house shared with an even greater number of others. They'd moved again shortly afterward to a garage, but were glad for a place to themselves. However, the camp had soon become overcrowded, meaning that their privacy was short-lived. His internment, at the age of six, had meant the end of a normal childhood. Herman had been four and a half; Freddy, three; and Joke, eighteen months.

Still, curiosity stimulated by the diary was overcoming his melancholy. He began attending the camp reunions that sprang up sometime during the 1980s in the Netherlands. Prior to this, former internees from the Indies had said little of their experience, inhibited by a public memory of the war that was focused on Europe. Dutch survivors of the "Hunger Winter" in the Netherlands had little interest in hearing about the suffering that took place in the Indies.[11] The reunions provided an opportunity that was otherwise missing for the former internees to compare notes and exchange information. Wim pored over the reunion exhibit tables full of diaries, maps, and photos, finding them strangely exciting.

He went most often to the reunion of the Cihapit camp. He had been interned there the longest, and as a result knew more of the attendees; they'd been children together. With friends such as Jan Tullner from the Dago Road in Bandung, he recounted making wagons using the wheels from old baby buggies, and then racing their "chariots" down the road. Cihapit had been better than the camps that came later, this helped him remember. The women at Cihapit had banded together. Adrie had run a clandestine school, and in addition to caring for boys who were orphaned or without their parents, she and Riek had helped his mother.

Things had changed greatly with their transport to Solo (more formally, Surakarta) on the Bengawan Solo River in Central Java. They had arrived in November of 1944, after two days and nights on a shuttered train that was packed with people and lacking in food and toilet facilities. They'd had to leave Adrie and Riek and the other single women behind, along with the boys over ten years of age—and even as children, understood that their mother had lost her support at a time when the concentration of internees into fewer camps made their very survival unpredictable. She had continued to do all she could for them, of course; pleased at one point that she found work for him helping a carpenter make wooden boxes. (He'd realized belatedly that these were coffins.) But her health steadily declined. When they were transported to Muntilan only six months later, she'd had to be carried aboard the train on a stretcher. He and his brothers and sister traveled the forty kilometers west without her, in the company of Mrs. Marijnen and her daughter, Tieneke.

Their next forced move had been on the twenty-sixth of July, the day after his mother died. This was to Ambarawa, an area of a dozen or so camps of Europeans, mostly women and children, roughly thirty kilometers north of Muntilan. Native independence fighters had damaged the railroads, so for the latter part of the trip they had to carry their luggage and walk with Mrs. Marijnen and Tieneke in a group of about 700 to Ambarawa Camp 8. Toward the end of their ordeal, women from the camp had come out to help them. But after one night, they had to pick up their bags again and set out for Banjobiru Camp 10, on Ambarawa's southern border.

He remembered that quite often at Banjobiru, particularly at night, they heard shooting, and at one point explosions. By September, the entire Ambarawa area had become volatile. In the absence of the Allies' arrival, radical young Indonesians (*Permuda* "freedom fighters") threatened the camps, anxious to rid their country of Westerners.[12]

Through all of this, more valuable than belongings, Wim and his siblings had brought with them their memories. One of particular importance was of family birthdays in August. Their mother would have them sit with her at a place on the grass near the communal kitchen at Cihapit and watch for shooting stars. At the moment of sighting, they silently touched her dress, counted to ten, and made a wish, trusting what she had told them, that their father was watching the same phenomenon. When forced to move on without her, they were heartened by her assurance that their father was alive and would reunite with them. She'd promised them further that they would eventually have a new mother.

Despite this, Wim, as her eldest, carried a burden distinct from that of the rest. Certain of her last words echoed in his head. Distraught over her final illness he had vowed that he would grow up and fight the Japanese for her. In a supreme effort, she had drawn herself up on her sickbed and gasped "No!"; that was the last thing he should do. Hatred was the cause of war. And with hatred in his heart he would never be able to love. Nonetheless, he had been unable to separate his grief over her loss from bitterness toward the Japanese—and bitterness toward himself. (What of his own part in it? If he had helped her more in the camps would she have lived?)

The same conflict held him captive as an adult. Looking for insight, he moved forward in the diary to his father's letter of 1 March 1943. To his astonishment, he found it only aggravating his dilemma. How could it be that in his father's description of a "single day" as a prisoner, he had positioned a visit from one of his captors—a Japanese camp liaison—prominently at the center? The 1 March letter suggested that his father had developed a close acquaintanceship with this man—no doubt the same whose photograph stored in the diary had perplexed his son as a young teenager. Wim ruminated now as he had then over its proximity to the photos of the family.

Yet respect for his father tempered Wim's reaction. The senior Lindeijer had taken obvious care with the letter, creating a "time capsule" in the form of a narrative. "At some future time, you may have difficulty imagining our life here; and because of the sheer number of impressions, my memory may be insufficient to provide a reliable picture," his father had written. He was sending an important message, and one that aroused Wim's curiosity and fascination. The "single day" would almost certainly have been a composite of many days, and by implication, many such visits. And the letter's characterization of the visitor as an aspiring writer of novels, with a passion for learning French (German "does not interest him at all"), indicated respect for him as an individual.

Analyzing the narrative closely, Wim noted a degree of playful discretion. His father's depiction of the visitor in the context of sly bedpan humor (Coughtry's "occupying his throne" and "various sounds" being produced) hardly granted him exalted status or the close ties of an "insider." Yet even in this, his father suggested someone regarded with relaxed good humor: the antithesis of a nightmarish, pursuing figure.

Bewildered by questions that yet had no answers, Wim took refuge in the birthday letter his father had written to him on 8 April 1943. It had affected him profoundly as a thirteen-year-old and influenced him decades later, after his return to Indonesia as manager of the country's "Six Cities" water supply project. His Indonesian driver had been wrongfully imprisoned in the case of an accident that killed a pedestrian. The driver at fault had sped away. Wim's driver had actually been helping the injured, but in the absence of another candidate to arrest the local police had settled on him. An innocent man and the sole support of his family, the driver was convicted and jailed.

"Be ready," the birthday letter had said, "to help others when they really need it, regardless of who it is or how much trouble it costs you." It had taken Wim months in pursuit of a court case to get the man out of jail. The distraction of the court case created tensions between Wim and the Dutch company that employed him, concerned about the impact this affair was having on its relationships with local authorities. There was likely to be backlash from a reversal of the court's decision as a result of testimony by a foreigner.

Wim testified even though doing so meant potential loss of his own employment. He'd received strong support from his wife. But support had come from an additional, wholly unexpected source, as well. Word of his commitment to help his driver had gotten around. Approaching the courthouse on the day of the appeal, he found the Indonesian workers from his project gathered on the steps outside, holding signs of appreciation and solidarity. Inside, the appeal had gone forward successfully. Afterward, Wim walked out of the courtroom, the words of his father's letter ringing in his head.[13]

But that had involved Indonesia, not Japan. He struggled with the lack of animosity toward the Japanese in either of his parents' documents, feeling a certain envy, and wondering how they had managed it. His father had made efforts to learn his captors' language. His mother, in her farewell letter, made no mention of bitterness, focusing on mitigating her family's trauma and facilitating their renewed life.

Further reading of the diary hardly resolved his quandary. He became increasingly convinced that his father had engaged in actual friendship with the man he called alternatively "Iwashita-San" and "that civil Japanese." The letters suggested relatively disinterested discussion of linguistic and other topics by the two men. And by the sixteenth of May 1944, his father had completed the unlikely task of producing a French grammar, undoubtedly for the liaison. Perhaps most indicative, on August 26, 1945, more than ten days after Japan's surrender, Hiroe Iwashita entered his full name and Tokyo address in the diary in western script.

Wim's long-held notion of the Japanese as the "Other" of his nightmares was being challenged.[14] Stimulated by the diary's references to Iwashita, he was struck by the memory of an additional case in which his father's charitable feelings had extended to his captors. As a teenager, he had asked about the diary's four missing pages repeatedly in his questioning—to the extent that his father had taken him aside one evening and described his experience during the corresponding time period.

Wim's youthful attention had centered on the more sensational aspects of what he heard: the focus of the nighttime visitor and the subsequent interviewers on the length of time needed by the Americans to make an atomic bomb; the arrival of the two scientists from Tokyo; and his father's success in convincing them, along with the detaining officers, that a good twenty-five years would be required. Yet he recalled now that his father's emphasis had been on the human communication that occurred. The officers had expressed authentic concern about the war. His father had responded with empathy, and to an extent dialogue had ensued.

13. Delft, 1992-95

Wim's perplexity grew; but likewise his fascination with the clearer, adult access he was acquiring to the events of his childhood. He continued attending the camp reunions, which by this time attracted media attention. The former internees were giving interviews, in an effort to integrate their experience more visibly into the Netherlands' public record. He listened to what others had to say and gave some interviews himself.[15] Yet he was uncertain what to make of the protest rallies conducted in The Hague, every second Tuesday of the month, in front of the Japanese Embassy. Supporters of the Foundation of Japanese Honor Debts sought an apology and reparations on behalf of all Dutch citizens who suffered under the Japanese during the war.[16]

Wim's uncertainty arose in part from the absence of animosity toward the Japanese in his parents' documents, but almost as surely from another source as well: a remarkable premonitory dream that he had at Cihapit as a child.

In the dream's strange sequence, he and his siblings had been guided by an unknown lady through a gate and into a courtyard of fountains and flowers. He had been troubled by its contradictory suggestions of an escape (the apparent security of the garden and the guiding female figure) and a trap (the ominous absence of his mother), and had told his mother about it. She had said not to worry; it was only a dream. But it had later proved to be more than that.

The dream's complete sequence was this:

They had come into a courtyard surrounded by a massive building that he had felt compelled to explore—an architectural wonder, built with its back against a slope, and with outdoor staircases interrupted by terraces on either side. Without a thought, he had scrambled up the staircases along the left side, to a third- or fourth-level terrace where he came upon a pool with goldfish and water lilies. Lying on his stomach, he stared, mesmerized by the swirling fish. Then continuing on, he had passed through a doorway into a garden, and via another door, through a wall. On the other side of the wall (and by this time, the other side of the building), he had been delighted to discover that he could jump down to a nearly dry stream bed and follow it back around to the gate he had entered originally, where he rejoined the others. At that moment, the dream faded, preventing him from seeing more.[17]

He had forgotten such things by late May 1945, when they were transported to Muntilan. His mother was already ill and had to be carried aboard the train on a stretcher. He and his brothers and sister traveled with Mrs. Marijnen and her daughter, and arrived at the camp ahead of her. The camp building was an enormous stone structure, a former Roman Catholic school and seminary, built against a lower slope of Mount Merapi.

Despite its overcrowded conditions, he had been struck as they entered the main gate by the existence of a garden—a stark contrast to their other camps—and had run, exhilarated, up a series of stairs in search of more such oases. At the fourth-level terrace, he came upon an old swimming pool and laid on his stomach watching orange carp swim under some sort of plant debris. And only when he heard the shouts of the guard pursuing him up the stairs did he recall—in the nick of time—that he needed to run to the right, through a doorway, into a garden, to another door through a wall ...[18]

Over the years, he had asked himself whether the synchronicity of dream and experience was no more than a bizarre set of coincidences. He was aware, too, of a certain fuzziness in his telling about it: a blurring of distinctions in some cases between the details of the dream and those of the actual events as they took place. (The unknown lady occasionally became Mrs. Marijnen.) Yet the dream had continued its hold on him, as evidenced by his having "returned to it" often during the family's postwar sharing, and innumerable occasions since. Though its meaning remained elusive, it was clearly a part of his traumatic affect, and as such, might hold a key to the dilemma that had haunted him since he was nine.

A Dutch military historian's groundbreaking account of events in Java around the time of his liberation was to prove crucial to his process of deciphering it. In January or February 1995, in spite of the slippery weather, he attended a meeting of women's camp survivors in Zwolle. Professor Petra Groen was delivering a speech about the Battle of Ambarawa. Wim was particularly interested in hearing it in hopes of developing a more accurate understanding of the chaotic period of the liberation of the camps—and his own experience as the truck convoy carrying him and his siblings headed for the harbor in Semarang, through the Gumbel (or in Dutch, *Goempel*) Pass.

What he was astonished to learn about from Groen's talk (and subsequently, her essay published as a pamphlet, entitled *Patience and Bluff*) was the remarkable heroism of a certain Japanese Major Kido Shinichirō[19]:

> From October 15 to 19, 1945, wholly on his own initiative, Major Kido had led his unit in five days of heavy fighting to put an end to the violent attacks on former civilian internees by Indonesian insurgents and regain control of Semarang and the area of the Ambarawa camps. The majority of the Japanese commanders had given over their arms to the Indonesians and put themselves out of the action. Kido had resisted pressure from his fellow officers and headquarters to do the same, using the rationale that he couldn't surrender arms bearing the chrysanthemum; this was the symbol of the emperor. The Allied British commanders who arrived after the fact couldn't say enough about "that

amazing Major Kido." His efforts, highly praised in their reports, had saved thousands of European civilians at the cost of more than 200 Japanese lives.

Learning this, Nel Lindeijer's eldest son was struck with the sudden realization that "hundreds of Japanese"—the same people that he had held responsible for her death—"had died fighting to protect me!"[20] His concept of the Japanese as the evil pursuing "other," first challenged by his father's friendship with Iwashita, was no longer tenable. Echoing in his head, as they had so often, were his mother's words when he had said that he would fight the Japanese for her. This time, the passionate response that he had never been able to understand met the moving edges of the narrative of Major Kido. He began entertaining thoughts that for a former internee at the time were unthinkable. By 1995 he had decided to go to Japan.

Yet even with this he had not thoroughly grasped the dream. A question raised by a friend upon hearing it once again helped with further deciphering it. Intrigued by a detail that seemed insignificant, but that Wim never failed to mention—the print that hung in the psychiatrist's office, of the single fish that stared up from under the surface of water on which leaves floated—the friend asked something that startled him. Had he seen any connection between the print (that he had identified as Escher's *Three Worlds*) and the fish of the camp and the dream? After a stunned moment, he answered that he had never consciously analyzed the print; yet the coincidence and possible subconscious associations left him speechless.

Escher had his own traumatic memories of the war in Europe, Wim knew. The artist's teacher, a Portuguese Jew, had been taken away by the Gestapo one night and never heard from again. "You can never forget such things," Escher told an interviewer twenty years later. "I cannot!"[21] Perhaps as a result, Escher himself had worked through the perceptual errors that accompany the binary concept of an "other" in the *Three Worlds* print. The psychiatrist had no doubt recognized as much when he selected it for his office. Its potential for stimulation of his patients at the Sinai Center for war trauma could only have been intentional—and likely productive at some level for a former internee of the Japanese nearly killed by Indonesian insurgents.

That the large fish with bulging, terrified eyes was somewhere in his awareness when he learned about Major Kido made sense to Wim. The fish surely represented one world, and the trees another, but what was the third? The fragile leaves floating on the water's surface—barely existent middle territory? In relation to the narrative of Major Kido, the three worlds might have been the Japanese, Wim himself, and the Ambarawa area where the major took risks in his behalf.

It was at this point that Wim began to consider whether Escher's treatment of perceptual problems might help shed light on the strange premonitory dream and the related events at Muntilan. Considering the stairways and terraces that he had navigated to circle the camp's stone structure, he was struck by their resemblance to the eerie architecture of Escher's *Ascending and Descending*.[22] In the print a succession of monks climbed up and down a series of staircases leading to terraces, from which additional staircases led to additional terraces, ad infinitum. He was struck with the thought that his own route both in the dream and in reality had consisted of the same continuous loop, or closed system, as that of the monks. Running from the guard had seemed to represent an escape, his subconscious hope, as a child, for a "happy ending." It had actually prevented him from coming to terms with his trauma and repeatedly brought him back to his own bitter hatred.

What the psychiatrist would likely have added, however, was that Wim's inclination from childhood to work through his trauma at the level of his subconscious might be assisting his attempts even now. His efforts to date had been characterized by openness to possibility and an imaginative use of resources—including the inner resources that he had sensed as early as the moment on the grass at Cihapit when he watched for shooting stars. And now, in an intuitive leap apparently made possible by his conscious and subconscious working through his childhood trauma, Wim realized that in the symbolic terms of the dream, he had to turn and face the pursuing "other." To find a true gate through the wall, he had to engage the Japanese.

14

Delft to Japan, 1995—
A Gate in the Wall

Wim's decision was made, yet he felt unease. "You were afraid to hear those voices again," he said, "speaking in a language so different that you couldn't understand..." Moreover, there was the question of fidelity to his mother. More than voices that raised the specter of the camps, he feared taking steps that might lead to forgetting, lessening his commitment to her memory. Even so, boarding his flight to Japan that October with Ada, and with his father's wartime diary in his hand luggage, he experienced a thrill. Symbolically, fifty years after the end of the war, his father was returning to Japan, and not as a POW.

His itinerary, under the auspices of a recently emergent Dutch group known as EKNJ ("Ex-Prisoners of the Japanese and Next of Kin"),[1] took him first to Mizumaki, a municipality on the southern island of Kyushu—1600 kilometers south of his primary destination of Kamaishi/Ohashi. There was a reason for this. He'd been impressed with the personal narrative of EKNJ's founder, Dolf Winkler, a former prisoner himself, who would lead the group's tour, and whose insight might be helpful. Winkler had revisited his Mizumaki camp in 1985 to overcome the war-induced nightmares he still suffered. He had been surprised to discover a makeshift monument to POWs who had died: a mound of earth with a cross on top, hastily erected at the war's end by officials who feared conviction for war crimes. He returned the next year, and with help from a local citizen, Hiroshi Kurokawa, pressed the town to construct a new and enlarged monument.[2] By 1987, Mizumaki's citizens had completed the new structure: a small house-like building of white-washed concrete, again with a cross on top, based on the assumption that most Westerners were Christian. Remarkably, however, they had added—with Dutch help—a bronze plate inscribed with the *names* of the fifty-three POWs who had died in Mizumaki. In a 1989 refurbishment, they had gone even further, adding the names of all Dutch prisoners who had died in camps in Japan, and acknowledging the motive behind the original makeshift mound.³

EKNJ's arrival, on 29 October 1995, was timed in coordination with Mizumaki's observance of a memorial ceremony at the monument that had developed into an annual tradition. Light rain fell this year on the monument's walls and glistened on the upright steles of the Buddhist cemetery on the hillside below. But Wim scarcely noticed his dampened clothes, stunned at having found the name of his father's fellow medic Jür Stenfert on one of the monument's brass plates, and overwhelmed by the day's events: speeches by Winkler and Dutch and Japanese dignitaries; laments sung by visiting choirs; and at the conclusion, the completely silent laying of flowers.⁴ One at a time, the 250 persons present ascended the small stairway built into the monument's right hand flanking wall and placed a flower at the base of the cross on the monument roof. Lost in reverie, Wim made the ascent and returned—caught on tape forgetting to leave his flower.⁵

Transported by the experience, within days he was ready to separate temporarily from Winkler's group and head north with Ada via train for Kamaishi/Ohashi.

The trip seemed to go by in a flash. Stepping onto the platform in Kamaishi, Wim suddenly realized how far he had come; at last he was here! A committee from the city, complete with reporters, stood ready to greet them. From Mizumaki, Shoji Kurokawa, Hiroshi's brother, and Shoji's wife, Chiai, had been busy with phone calls to Kamaishi city officials.⁶ Yet despite introductions and welcoming words, the atmosphere on the platform seemed formal and tense. Wim held tightly to the bag he was carrying containing his father's diary.

One of the reporters noticed his protectiveness and asked what was in the bag. Wim's moment of engagement had arrived. Almost without thought, he took a step forward and opened his bag to the reporter. From there it was merely a step further to open the black binder and reveal the pages of his father's Ohashi camp diary. He showed the reporter the photograph of Iwashita, and another that his father had acquired from Iwashita, of POWs in the Ohashi mine. By this time, more individuals had gathered closely around, and excited reactions ensued: "Oh!" "Hah!" "Ah!" Clearly at least some of those present had not been aware of the Ohashi and Kamaishi camps. The reporter asked whether he could borrow the photographs to copy them, and Wim decided to take the chance.

The next morning the photograph of Iwashita and a story indicating Wim's desire to locate him appeared in both the local paper and the local edition of the *Asahi Shimbun*, one of the largest national papers. It seemed to Wim that the journalist must have been working all night. The article in

14. Delft to Japan, 1995

the local paper included the photograph of the POWs in the mine, noting that it was valuable because it filled in a gap in knowledge about the POW camp.

The mayor saw the newspapers and asked to borrow the diary overnight to make a photocopy for the Historical Society. Meanwhile other officials had located two local people who remembered the Ohashi and Kamaishi camps and could provide Wim and his wife with a tour. In the company of a photographer, a reporter, and a translator, they set off to see the abandoned electrical workshop of the mine, the *Denki*; the entrance to the mine itself; and the former locations of the two camps. Wim was once again revisiting his father's experience, but this time, discussing it with Kamaishi citizens in the present.

All too soon, the next morning, he and Ada had to leave, to rejoin the EKNJ tour in Hiroshima. The mayor had kept his promise; the diary was now safely packed in Wim's bag. An article in the morning paper ("To Kamaishi: In the Image of his Father")[7] indicated the impression their visit had made. A contextual paragraph at the beginning of the article explained the existence of the nearly forgotten Kamaishi camp. Another at the end described the peace and reconciliation movement in Fukuoka Prefecture, Mizumaki village. Wim was happy. But his mission in Kamaishi was unfinished; he would need to return.

* * *

Following a moving visit with EKNJ to the Peace Museum in Hiroshima, Wim and Ada had returned with the organization to Mizumaki, where Wim found Shoji Kurokawa waiting for him with a group of local citizens who wanted to hear about Wim's father's wartime diary.

Wim was only too happy to sit down with them and take questions from Shoji through a translator, while another Kurokawa brother recorded the interview on video.[8] How, Shoji began, had Wim's father managed as a POW to write the diary? When did he do this? Wim replied that keeping a diary had been strictly prohibited. But his father had cared for the sick and was able to write as he watched over them at night, when guards were not around. Otherwise, he had kept the diary hidden. Even so, his father had written at every chance he had. He was writing the entries as letters to his family, and had even written some after the war ended: he hadn't known yet that his wife had died.

There were occasions, Wim said, when his father had written for the Japanese. Opening the diary to his father's report about the battle of Kalijati, Wim held it up. Several of the men came closer to examine it. Leafing further through the diary, Wim showed the family photograph of Nel with her children. Not only the men, but the women this time, crowded closely around to see it, in what must have seemed an epochal moment, more than fifty years after it elicited empathy in Ohashi. Then, almost as part of a natural pairing, Wim showed the photograph of Iwashita: "not a soldier," but a civilian liaison for the prisoners, who had done a great deal to help them. Wim wanted to meet him. As his listeners' questions delved into the prisoners' conditions under forced labor, Wim was amazed at their receptiveness and agreed to another meeting. He was to speak the next morning at a student program at Mizumaki Junior High School, but afterward could meet again.

Entering the school gymnasium with EKNJ the following day, he felt himself in a dramatically charged setting. Awaiting them, the school's 700 students sat on the floor in neat rows, in dark blue sailor suits. Overhead, the brightest lights had been dimmed and an upper tier of windows had the curtains drawn, the better to focus on the program space below, between the students and the rows of facing chairs for the Dutch visitors. But more than this riveted Wim's attention as he took his seat. Mounted on a mezzanine-level balcony that stretched across the back wall, in the almost liminal space between the darkness above and the light below, was an exceptionally well-produced piece of student art—a replica of the print he knew well as Escher's *Metamorphose III*.

He had seen an enlarged version of the original wood-cut print hanging in the Kerkplein Post Office in The Hague. Its graphical narrative consisted of an astounding progression of gradually transforming images: the interlocked black and white figures of reptiles became the hexagons of a honeycomb, then bees, and then black birds interlocked with oppositional white fishes. The continuing progression included boats interlocked with more fish, flying fish silhouetted against horses, oppositional black and white "flying envelopes" (complete with wings), and more birds silhouetted against other birds—which finally became cubes that turned into a town on the Amalfi coast! All of this, it was generally conceded, helped keep otherwise impatient lines of patrons at the Kerkplein Post Office amused.[9] The mural's use as a backdrop for the student program[10] was causing Wim to regard it much differently, however. Years later he would recount the effect of seeing it here.

In the dim lighting, his mind played with the mural's oppositional black and white figures. His own fear and anger had kept him locked in much the same opposition with the pursuing monsters of his nightmares. Continuing his partial absorption in the mural, he listened as five students came forward and in English gave a short but revealing overview of Japan's part in the war. Others sang a song that resonated with his experience at the Hiroshima Peace Museum.

As the students performed, he was noticing a change in the mural's black and white figures: in the progression from left to right, some were no longer defined merely by their external contour, but filled in with internal details. This had a curious effect. With the addition of detailed red characteristics, for instance, the white fish shapes that had been locked in opposition with black birds, stood out from their ground; individualized and somewhat *real*. Again, he made an association: it was openness to the particular characteristics and circumstances of "the other"—in Wim's case, those of Major Kido—that led to a view of him or her as an individualized human being. Knowing details made it possible to see similarities, find commonality, and begin to understand the other's perspective. By the same token, the fearsome rage that he had projected onto the monsters of his nightmares was a characteristic that resided in part in himself.

Just then, six of the students rose and each gave an unscripted peace declaration, after which they lifted and held up a long banner reading "We hope the relationship between the Netherlands and Japan will get closer."

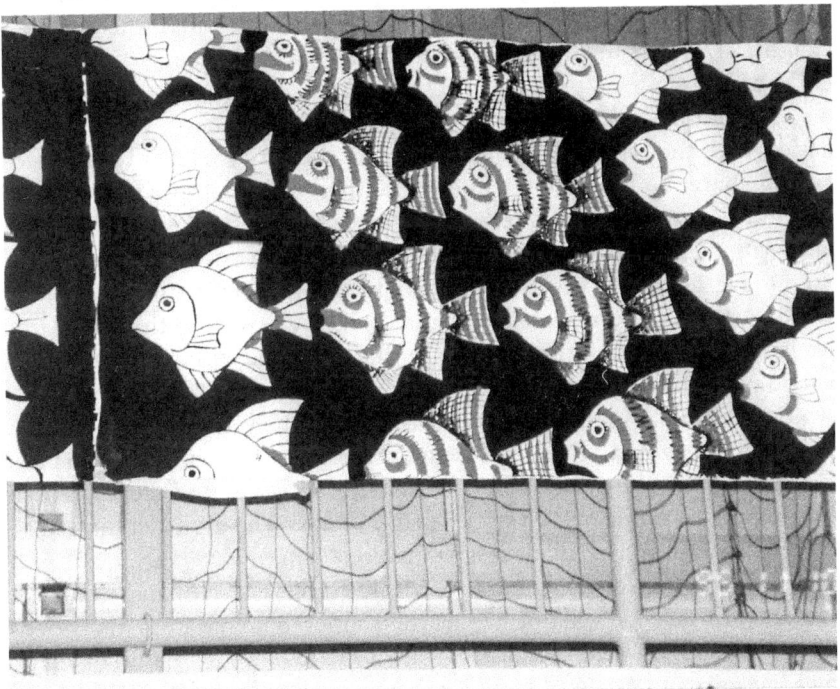

Detail of Escher-inspired student artwork hung across the entire balcony at the back of the auditorium during the Mizumaki Junior High School program for Dutch visitors (Photo courtesy of Principal Takayuki Shibata and Program Director Ms. Hiroko Uchida).

Associating them with the detailed birds at the far right of the mural, Wim felt a thrill of hope for the future.

It was time for him to speak. Stepping forward, he expressed elaborate and grateful thanks on behalf of EKNJ for the warm hospitality they had received. Then from the middle of the program space he felt suddenly motivated to make an emotional last-minute addition to his address: he had harbored extremely great anger and hatred for them since childhood, as a result of his mother's death, he said; he had *raged* against them. But now, his feelings had changed as a result of this trip. The students' genuine desire for peace made the last remnants of his resentment "melt away." He understood better than ever his dying mother's words about love. Like the students he was filled with hope.

Almost immediately afterward, Wim's interviewers sought him out. Struck by his words previously and in the gymnasium, they wanted to know "the whole story." "The whole story?" Flabbergasted, Wim followed them into one of the school rooms, where their questions continually dove deeper. Had his father thought that "these letters would be sent to his wife?" Why had his father been "arrested?" "How many people were caught?" Did this include women and children? How many women and children?

As his questioners' desire to know grew more intense, Wim's interaction with them grew proportionally more effective. He had a perspective to share: he had told them of his father's friendship with Iwashita and of the reports that his father had written at the request of the camp authorities. He told them now of the dialogue that Iwashita had engaged in with his father about the reports, and of Iwashita's returning them afterward. A buzz of conversation resulted. "Unbelievable!" the translator exclaimed. "For Iwashita to engage in this exchange with your father was very dangerous."

Wim took a further leap forward. During the war, he said, and even prior to that, in Japan there had been suppression of ideas. There had been one national ideology. Iwashita, Wim believed, "did not accept a closed ideology. He was one of the very few in those days who didn't let himself be completely crushed by an ideology of nationalism."

Whether consciously or not, during the interview Wim had been testing for the first time what he had learned about dialogue from his father's diary. Yet sadly, the next morning they were to leave for Bangkok. "Too bad," he wrote to Adrie. "I would rather go back to Kamaishi."[11] The journalist had found Iwashita's family. More urgently, Wim still needed to reconcile the steps he had taken with his commitment to his mother's memory.

Adrie Lindeijer-van der Baan and E.W. "Wim" Lindeijer, Jr., in front of the Ohashi Camp electrical workshop, "the Denki," during their 1996 trip to Japan, the trip in which Wim asked forgiveness of his former captors (Lindeijer Family Archive).

* * *

Not until the next year, in Kamaishi, was he to find the answer he looked for. With Adrie at his side this time, he confessed before an audience of Japanese students the hatred he had had for them as a result of his mother's death—and then asked their forgiveness. In a voice that drew on everything that he had absorbed and become, and in a rational manner that they could understand, he conveyed both his anguish over her loss and his desire to reach out. His grief for her would not be erased. The memory of severe loss didn't just disappear; he would never forget her.

But he could create a new personal story that included the loss and at the same time allowed him to move forward. To those in the Netherlands who were appalled at his asking forgiveness from students of his former enemies' society, he said that it was the most liberating thing that he had ever done.

15

The Unexpected Importance of the Once-Secret Diary in the Twenty-First Century

Wim's father's diary was attracting interest in Japan itself, and in the Netherlands, among Japanese in Delft, as a result of his and Adrie's 1996 trip. In Kyoto, Wim had met not with Iwashita—sadly, the camp liaison was deceased—but with his son, Fumio. A journalist from the Kyoto edition of *Yomiuri Shimbun*, Japan's largest national newspaper reported the striking outcome: the fathers of both men had included evidence of their friendship in their respective diaries.[1] In Kamaishi, Mrs. Naoko Kato, an English teacher and member of the school board, had invited Wim and Adrie to talk about the diary with her class and others, leading to interest in getting it translated. Mrs. Kato's daughter and another young woman committed to traveling to Delft in the near future to undertake the effort based on Wim's rendering of the diary in English.[2] In Delft, Japanese women in the city's International Neighbors Group asked Adrie about her trip and as a result learned about the diary and the camps. Word circulated that the family's testimony was "open and frank," yet distinctive in its absence of hatred and animosity. By 1999, upon hearing that the young women had completed their translation, members of the Japanese community in Delft convened a large meeting to consider what they could do to assist in getting it published.

One of the members who had a website carrying Japanese news posted a notice of the search for a publisher on the site's home page. The result was an almost instantaneous call from a Japanese professor of languages, Takamitsu Muraoka, of Leiden University, who had seen the notice and knew a publisher.[3] Not only this; he agreed to collate the young women's translation with the Dutch original, and in doing so make overall improvements.

Almost before they knew it, Wim and Adrie had signed a contract. In July 2000, Wim's father's prison diary, along with his mother's farewell letter, was published for the first time—and in Japanese.[4] The volume's jacket featured the photograph taken so long ago, after two prior attempts and with Adrie's help, in the garden behind the house on the Dago Road. Astonishingly, here it was now, emergent in Japan in the twenty-first century. From beneath a sensitive and moving title—in translation, *Kisses to Nel and the Children from a POW Camp in Japan*[5]—the gaze of Nel Lindeijer and her children engaged the Japanese reader.

The Japanese publication of the Lindeijer diary, titled *Kisses to Nel and the Children from a Prison Camp in Japan* (transliterated, in Japanese: *Neru to kodomotachi ni kisu o*), Tokyo: Misuzu Shobo Publishers, 2000.

15. The Unexpected Importance of the Once-Secret Diary

Overwhelmed, Wim threw himself into work with Adrie, Professor Muraoka, and others on the first of a series of annual Dutch–Japanese Dialogue conferences in the Netherlands.[6] Before a mixed conference audience that same month he spoke about the new publication, still amazed to be holding it in his hands.

In the meantime, Japanese media responded resoundingly. The *Kahoku Shinpo* cited the diary's description of "a cruel life with constant fatalities."[7] The *Kyoto Shimbun* placed it in context of "about 70,000 Dutch people interned in camps in Java alone," of whom "24,000 militaries and civilians died."[8]

Such characterizations were gratifying, as were the reviewers' findings of human dignity in adversity, and expressions of "care for family, intense desire and hope for a reunion." "Love rarely forms such a central and earnest theme in the literature against the background of war," the *Kyoto Shimbun* reviewer observed.

For Wim, reports of a television evening newscast from northeast Honshu brought the greatest thrill and surprise, however. He learned that a reporter had narrated as Mr. Sano, Wim's guide during his 1995 visit, toured the Ohashi mine and camp. At intervals the camera had moved between old camp photographs and related passages from the Japanese publication of the diary. An off-screen voice representing Wim's father had read the passages aloud, including one from a difficult winter. Wim checked the diary for the relevant entry: "It's a difficult time. There are now seven people dead, six of them of pneumonia. Right now we have 25 sick, 17 of whom have pneumonia. The last group has to be helped with everything…" For the senior Lindeijer's son, the knowledge that his father's diary had given voice to the prisoners' suffering over Iwate Prefecture television was deeply affecting. More than the reviews' statistics and generalized conclusions, they communicated human feeling. Viewers prompted to read the diary might experience a change in perspective. Wim had learned that at the program's conclusion, Mr. Sano revealed his own changed view. During the war he had been affected by the atmosphere of militarism and had thought little about the POWs. The passage of time and the experience of reading the diary had caused him to reflect on their conditions and loss of freedom.

Meanwhile, in Kamaishi, every bookshop had copies of the diary. Naoko Kato was engrossed in reading it. She had known little about the camps. The only war story she had known involved the second atomic bomb. Wim had been "the first person who made [her] think about the war." By the close of his 1996 talk, she understood that he had come to develop understanding of the war, in the interest of peace. She called together the members of her local "Friendship" association for a discussion with him and Adrie. Everyone had been "surprised to hear about an internment camp where two hundred prisoners were forced to work." They learned, she said, that "not only the United States, but *Japan* had done a terrible thing."[9] Now, reading the diary and Nel's letter, she was affected further. The family's story needed to be more widely known, to help prevent future wars and the reoccurrence of family suffering.

By 2004, she recognized an opportunity. A young social studies teacher at one of the city's junior high schools, Mr. Morimoto, was developing plans for a block of time in the curriculum that allowed each school to do something optional. Mrs. Kato met with him and spoke movingly about Wim's visits to Kamaishi. Mr. Morimoto had already come across the Lindeijer diary and was impressed by the family photo on the jacket. After hearing from Naoko Kato, he made up his mind: the project that he had conceived as a dramatic and choral commemoration of the sixtieth anniversary of the bombardments of Kamaishi would likewise commemorate the Lindeijer family and the Ohashi prisoners.

The production was such a success that Mr. Morimoto and his students decided to continue it for a second year. Their school was closing, and they wanted to mark the occasion with a dramatic ceremony: a complete reenactment of the Lindeijer diary.[10]

* * *

At the year's end, a video of this second production arrived in the Netherlands, in time for the 2005 Dialogue Conference. Watching with English subtitles, along with the rest of the audience, Wim was transfixed at the production's forthrightness.[11] A student acting as "Wim" introduced himself and spoke as though visiting the school as Wim had, during a trip in 2001. His father had documented his experience "while he was here in Kamaishi, from 1942 till 1945," he said, "in a camp as a prisoner of war." His father was a science teacher in the Dutch East Indies. "He kept the diary in order to survive, and to record his thoughts about his family."

The Wim character struck an empathetic note over his father's being taken prisoner: "In the few weeks of battle [sic], my father was part of the medical battalion. The Dutch surrendered Indonesia and he was taken as a prisoner of war." The scene shifted to documentary film footage of ragged and emaciated POWs disembarking, and an offstage voice read somberly from the diary, as subtitles paraphrased:

> It took two months to get to Ohashi. The voyage was horrible.
> Scarce food, poor quality rice. We were hungry all the time.
> Hundreds fell sick, no medicine. No disembarking for the sick men.
> No water for washing dishes or the wounded men. No hygiene.

15. *The Unexpected Importance of the Once-Secret Diary*

For Wim, in the audience watching, the effect was dumbfounding. The diary's absence of hatred no doubt encouraged frank exploration; yet this implied critique of Japan's wartime military was stunning. Nor was the portrayal of harsh treatment at the prison itself without daring. A scene of two prisoners being set upon by guards left the conference audience breathless:

> [One prisoner, despondent:] When is this war going to end?
> [Another, answering:] It won't last much longer. Japan is losing!
> [Guard:] YOU! You mentioned a defeat of Japan!

Acting enraged, student "guards" came out of nowhere to run at the prisoners. Knocking them down, they dragged them around a corner—presumably to be beaten.

In the audience, Wim was thrilled that such scenes enabled the students to empathize with the prisoners they represented, yet without losing sight of differences. The youth in the role of the mistreated Stenfert had written a letter to Stenfert's son, Wim knew. Likewise, the student who acted as Wim's father had sent a video message telling what he had learned of the war's effect on families. In one scene, he shared the photograph of Nel with her children: "Look! This is a photo of my family."

Wim could appreciate in addition that the production was far from one-sided. Through characterizations of Iwashita and the medical sergeant, Neko, the students highlighted good aspects of the prisoners' treatment. They also clarified the war's impact for participants on both sides, drawing attention to their own citizens' suffering during the bombardments. ("What's this noise; an air raid?" "No, a bombardment from warships.") And in unsettling tones, they spoke of the victims of the American atomic bombs:

> A new bomb killed 10,000 people. Ten thousand killed in one instant.
> Have they such a bomb? One day, that bomb might kill all of mankind.

Ultimately, their production drove home the war's tragedy for families. The plight of Japanese civilians after their nation's surrender recalled that of Wim's family at the war's beginning.

> Defeated! What will happen to us?
> Us? We must save our children.

In a final frame, the student acting as Wim spoke of his mother Nel's death and her message that resonated with the city.

> When my father came home, he was told about my mother's death.
> She died in a Japanese camp.
> I was nine then. I told her: "When I am grown, I'll beat the Japanese up."

> My mother said: "As long as you've hate in your heart, you won't be able to love anybody. Where hate ends [there] is room for peace."
> I've visited Japan and asked forgiveness for hating you. I received warmth and friendship.

Watching in the Netherlands, the Wim thus portrayed was stunned by the appearance of the well-traveled family photograph close to this conclusion.

Here was Nel—a woman stripped by internment of her family and her life—honored on a big screen by students in Kamaishi; her victimization acknowledged and dignity restored. Wim knew in this moment that he had never abandoned his commitment to her. But he realized, further, the larger significance of the students' efforts: by their public acknowledgment of the wrong done their society's victims, they made it possible not only for the victims' families, but their own city to move forward. Their sincere public performance—almost like mourning—overcame ghosts of the past and allowed for the creation of new stories; stories that honored the victims and freed their community to engage in healthy new life.

* * *

By the next year (2006), townspeople in Kamaishi had formed an association to continue the students' work, examining their history and engaging in dialogue with the Netherlands group.[12] What the long term would bring, Wim couldn't know. But he was inspired by a detail that cast new light on his experience in Mizumaki. He'd been influenced by the story of Dolf Winkler, who in 1985 revisited his former camp and pressed the town to rebuild the monument to the Dutch prisoners who died there. The rebuilding led to the annual ceremonies at the monument, and ultimately to Wim's transformative experience in the gymnasium. He'd asked forgiveness in Kamaishi the following year. What he knew now was that the entire chain of events leading to the ceremony at the monument had been set in motion decades before Dolf Winkler's return: when a single individual—a guard at the Mizumaki camp named Minoru Tamura—shared his lunch, and lightened the workload of a sick and weakened prisoner named Dolf Winkler. A primary motive for Winkler's return had been his desire to meet with his former guard.[13]

It was tempting to think, as a result, that as individuals, through empathy and enlarged perspective, took steps toward reconciliation, the circle could widen; whole towns or cross-cultural networks could join in the dialogue. Wim's vision was not wholly optimistic. He was well aware that revisionist attitudes toward Japan's role in the war still persisted among its politicians, to the dismay of its Asian neighbors. One only needed to think of the arguments over the "comfort women" during the

15. The Unexpected Importance of the Once-Secret Diary

war, the visits by officials to the Yasukuni Shrine, and the debates over content about the war in school textbooks. This was to say nothing of Dutch attitudes toward the Netherlands' relations with Indonesia. Much of the Dutch public remained blind to the injustice that marked its country's nearly 350-year rule over its former colony—and to the Dutch cruelties committed in the 1945–49 war the Netherlands fought trying to keep it (as James Huffman's foreword to this volume demonstrates).

Yet when considered in the light of human dialogue, the continuous cycles that figured in Wim's nightmares no longer disturbed him to the extent they once had. To theorize that the networks of dialogue would continue to expand might be a hope that was delicate and groundless. But in light of his experience with the young students in Mizumaki and Kamaishi, it was not one that he could rule out. Had he been asked to explain why, he could only have said that none of the individuals whose actions had led to the events in Kamaishi—certainly not his mother Nel, Minoru Tamura, or Iwashita himself—could have foreseen the results of the empathy they demonstrated.

Wim himself could hardly have foreseen that by June 2016 (less than three years after his death), the series of annual dialogue conferences initiated in 2000 would have Indonesian students in attendance, expanding under the name Dialogue Netherlands-Japan-Indonesia to include conversations about the dark side of colonialism.[14] Nor could he have anticipated the October 2016 impact of Swiss-Dutch historian Remy Limpach's book, *De brandende campongs van Generaal Spoor* (The burning villages of General Spoor), which cast glaring light on the atrocities committed by the Netherlands in the 1945–49 war. In a response that Wim could only have found striking, the Dutch government summoned a team of academics and researchers, including 12 Indonesians, to conduct a full inquiry (*Independence, decolonization, violence and war in Indonesia, 1945–50*), with research results presented in February 2022.[15]

Least of all could Wim have guessed that as early as May 26–27, 2022, the 23rd International Conference of the Dialogue NJI, "Forgotten Groups, A Chain of Voices," would have taken place within the very region where the three countries had brutally fought one another—at Airlangga University, in Surabaya, Java.[16] Talks by historians and researchers from the Dialogue's nationalities shed light on diverse perspectives too easily lost amid extremist either-or debates over wartime memory. The ghosts of mass violence still persisted, as backlash over a recent exhibition on the Indonesian Revolution at the Rijksmuseum in Amsterdam demonstrated. But in the conference breakout sessions, attendees who were once enemies worked toward reconciliation by acquiring mutual understanding of a shared past. In this effort Wim would have found great hope.

Chapter Notes

Foreword

1. Michael Bess, *Choices Under Fire: Moral Dimensions of World War II* (New York: Vintage Books, 2006), 311.
2. John Dower, *Embracing Defeat: Japan in the Wake of World War II* (New York: W. W. Norton & Company, 1999), 521.
3. It should be noted, for comparison's sake, that American intellectuals too have engaged in little reflection on their own war guilt, a fault Dower attributes to "racial thinking … on both sides"; see his *War Without Mercy: Race & Power in the Pacific War* (New York: Pantheon Books, 1986), 180. As he writes in *Cultures of War: Pearl Harbor, Hiroshima, 9–11, Iraq* (New York: W.W. Norton, 2010, 196), it was easy for postwar Americans to ignore their own "ruthless and barbaric" atrocities because "victors control the history books."
4. Ian Buruma, *The Wages of Guilt: Memories of War in Germany and Japan* (New York: New York Review Books, 1994), x.
5. Haruko Taya Cook and Theodore F. Cook, *Japan at War: An Oral History* (New York: The New Press, 1992), 159.
6. Saburō Ienaga, *The Pacific War* (English translation of *Taiheiyō sensō*) (New York: Pantheon Books, 1978), xi.
7. Hosokawa and Murayama were two of only three prime ministers after the 1950s who were not from the conservative Liberal Democratic Party. Hosokawa: in Yui Daizaburo, "Between Pearl Harbor and Hiroshima/Nagasaki: Nationalism and Memory in Japan and the United States," Laura Hein and Mark Selden, eds., *Living With the Bomb: American and Japanese Cultural Conflicts in the Nuclear Age* (Armonk, NY: M. E. Sharpe, 1997), 63. Murayama: https://en.wikipedia.org/wiki/List_of_war_apology_statements_issued_by_Japan#1990s; accessed February 11, 2019.
8. https://www.japantimes.co.jp/opinion/2015/01/10/commentary/japan-commentary/peoples-emperor-speaks-truth-power/#.XGHKR_ZFzcs; accessed February 11, 2019.
9. Norma Field, *In the Realm of a Dying Emperor: Japan at Century's End* (New York: Vintage Books, 1993): Motoshima's statement, 178; "you idiot," 196.
10. Laura Hillenbrand, *Unbroken: A World War II Story of Survival, Resilience, and Redemption* (New York: Random House, 2010); Eric Lomax, *The Railway Man: A POW's Searing Account of War, Brutality and Forgiveness* (New York: W. W. Norton, 1995).
11. Chapter 3, October 17, 1942.
12. Chapter 12, August 25, 1945.
13. Chapter 8, December 28, 1944.
14. Chapter 7, June 1, 1943.
15. Langdon Gilkey, *Shantung Compound: The Story of Men and Women Under Pressure* (New York: Harper & Row, 1966), 239.
16. Kobe Abe, *The Woman in the Dunes* (New York: Vintage International, 1991); compare 161, 239.
17. Chapter 5, January 24, 1943.
18. Elsbeth Locher-Scholten, "From Urn to Monument: Dutch Memories of World War II in the Pacific, 1945–1995," in Andrea L. Smith, ed., *Europe's Invisible Migrants* (Amsterdam University Press, 2003), 105–128, especially 125.
19. Steven Drakeley, *The History of*

Indonesia (Westport, CT: Greenwood Press, 2005), 48.

20. Cook and Cook, *Japan at War*, 106.

21. See "Debate," review of Remy Limpach, *De brandende campongs van Generaal Spoor* in special issue "New urban Middle Classes in Colonial Java," *Bijdragen to de Taal-, Land- en Volkenkunde*, vol. 173, no. 4 (2017), 567.

22. The inquiry is titled "Independence, Colonization, Violence and War in Indonesia, 1945-1950": https://www.ind45-50.org/en, accessed May 2, 2024.

23. Chapter 6, March 1, 1943.

24. Ernest Gordon, *Miracle on the River Kwai* (Glasgow: Collins Fontana Books, 1963), 162.

Preface

1. I have documented owner or owner-survivor permission for personal records or memoirs used, with one or two exceptions in which I have made a good-faith effort but could not find heirs.

Part I

1. Dr. Evert Willem "Wim" Lindeijer Jr. (EW Jr.), discussion with me over three weeks in Delft, November 2004; Herman Lindeyer, telephone conversation, February 11, 2005.

2. Films I viewed at the home of Adriana Lindeijer-van der Baan (hereafter, Adrie Lindeijer or Adrie), Zweith, Rotterdam, November 9, 2004. Married Dutch often keep their birth name, hyphenated following the spouse's name.

3. Nel's letter: Lindeijer Family Archive. Christien Slotemaker-de Bruine, a Protestant missionary interned with Nel, wrote in an accompanying letter dated 30 July 1945: "Alas, only in Muntilan [after transport from Surakarta] did we understand that the body was undermined to such a degree that recovery became doubtful. How fiercely we had to fight then, both physically and spiritually."

4. Adrie Lindeijer, in discussion with me, November 9, 2004.

5. Joke, pronounced "Yokə," is short for Johanna.

6. Red Cross document, 1 Feb. 1946, Batavia (Jakarta): "Petronella J. Lindeijer-Verhulst, Born 31/8/1906, Occupation: Teacher, Camp No: 22948, Death 25 July, buried in Muntilan, grave no. 27." Collection Eloy W. Lindeijer.

Chapter 1

1. The Japanese landed in four locations in the night of 28 February and on 1 March 1942. L. de Jong, *The Collapse of a Colonial Society: The Dutch in Indonesia during the Second World War* (Leiden: KITLV Press, 2002), 37.

2. L. de Jong, The Collapse of a Colonial Society, Introduction by Jeroen Kemperman, 32. "At the outbreak of war in the Pacific the strength of the regular KNIL was nearly 1,400 officers and slightly over 40,000 non-commissioned officers and men." More than two thirds were Indonesian. "In December 1941 some 32,000 conscripts (all Dutch or Dutch Eurasian) were mobilized."

3. Bogor, in today's Indonesia, a city in West Java, 60 kilometers south of Jakarta (then, Batavia).

4. The Japanese captured the Kalijati airfield on March 1. Its British and Dutch defenders either fled or were captured and killed. De Jong, *The Collapse of a Colonial Society*, 37–38.

5. A city in West Java, northwest of Bandung.

6. A city in West Java, northwest of Bandung and Cimahi.

7. Bandung was considered a resort city by the Dutch plantation owners.

8. Located in northern Bandung, in a hilly area of former tea plantations, this "institution" still exists today.

9. A city in the southeast portion of West Java, Purwakarta is the capital of Purwakarta Regency.

10. Colonel C.G. Toorop was ultimately held with high-ranking prisoners of the Japanese assembled as possible leverage in future peace negotiations. De Jong, *The Collapse of a Colonial Society*, 350.

11. I consider it noteworthy that when Lindeijer uses this term; nine times out of ten it is an abbreviation.

12. The Japanese invaded Malaya intent on reaching British-held Singapore. Malacca is a small Malaysian state on the southwest portion of the Malay Peninsula,

across the Straits of Malacca from Sumatra. The Dutch East Indies assisted the British with an air defense over Malacca in a failed attempt to stop the Japanese advance. Consequently, the Dutch had virtually no air defense left for the defense of the Indies.

13. On February 25, 1942, the Commander-in-Chief of the American-British-Dutch-Australian Command (ABDACOM), Sir Archibald Percival Wavell, resigned and subsequently evacuated from Java along with his staff. KNIL General Hein Ter Poorten, with poorly trained troops, took charge of Java's defense. "A garrison of 7,000 men, British, Australian, and American, under the command of British Major General H. D. W. Sitwell, was available to assist. The 3,500 British were predominantly anti-aircraft units. The 2,500 Australians were of Blackforce of Brigadier Arthur Blackburn. The 1,000 Americans were of the 2nd Battalion of the 131st Field Artillery, a Texas National Guard unit [that] was attached to Blackforce." World War II Database; Dutch East Indies Campaign, Java; "Battle of Java," C. Peter Chen, accessed January 27, 2019, http://www.ww2db.com/battle_spec.php?battle_id=23, accessed May 2, 2024.

14. The Dago Road runs north from Bandung to the mountain village of Dago.

15. After attempts to retake the Kalijati airfield failed, efforts focused on defense of the Bandung plateau. On 6 March 1942, fierce fighting took place at the south end of the Ciater Pass, on the road from Kalijati to Bandung. De Jong, *The Collapse of a Colonial Society*, 38. Lindeijer's nephew was an unarmed Red Cross soldier during this encounter, one of seventy-two Dutch military personnel who surrendered to the Japanese after finding their artillery position surrounded. When a Japanese reconnaissance plane dropped a cylinder containing orders for the Japanese commander to advance immediately toward Bandung, rather than leave prisoners guarded behind his lines, he ordered them lined up and shot. In one case, a survivor was rescued by Indonesian villagers. Known as the "*Ciaterstelling*-massacre," the incident is documented in Annie Bos's *Rode Aarde: A Story of the Forgotten War in Java* (de Prom, 2001).

16. A fishing village in West Java, located on the north coast.

17. UVA Miller Center, Presidential Speeches, Franklin D. Roosevelt Presidency, "February 23, 1942: Fireside Chat 20: On the Progress of the War," https://millercenter.org/the-presidency/presidential-speeches/february-23-1942-fireside-chat-20-progress-war, accessed May 2, 2024. The few American ground troops in Java took note: Jess Stanbrough, U.S. Army T/Sgt, 131st Field Artillery, Texas National Guard, Interviews by Dr. Ronald E. Marcello, Oral History Collection at North Texas State University, Denton, Texas (hereafter UNT), 0658, April 15, 1985, 69.

18. A town in West Java. Defense efforts here, by an Australian Army unit and members of the 131st Field Artillery, Texas National Guard, were perhaps the strongest during the Japanese invasion. De Jong, *The Collapse of a Colonial Society*, 37. For the view of the Japanese military, see Remmelink, Ed. *The Invasion of the Dutch East Indies, Compiled by the War History Office of the National Defense College of Japan* (Leiden: The Corts Foundation/Leiden University Press, 2015), 488–94.

19. On Saturday, 7 March 1942, the KNIL's line at Lembang was simultaneously stormed by a Japanese brigade on the ground and bombed from the air until it reached breaking point. The Lembang defeat marked the last gasp of the Dutch defense of Bandung, and Java itself. The Japanese had already entered Batavia two days before. De Jong, *The Collapse of a Colonial Society*, 38–39.

20. EW was one of 42,233 European troops in the Indies who became prisoners of war: "3,847 Dutch Naval personnel, 36,869 KNIL soldiers and 1,517 members of KNIL auxiliary corps." But for indigenous troops, "there are no accurate figures." De Jong, *The Collapse of a Colonial Society*, 283–84.

21. A portion of the Nineteenth Bombardment Group, U.S. Army Air Corps, escaped from the Philippines to fly combat missions in the Dutch East Indies. Members of the Second Battalion, 131st Field Artillery, Texas National Guard initially served as its ground support at Singosari, an air base near Malang, Java.

22. Per De Jong, *The Collapse of a*

Colonial Society, 36, "After the fall of Singapore, [British General Sir Archibald] Wavell concluded that Java could not be saved." Troops that had been en route to Java "were sent elsewhere."

Chapter 2

1. De Jong, *The Collapse of a Colonial Society*, 329–330.
2. *Ibid.*, 330, states only that the three "were caught some distance from the camp." EW Jr. believed based on information from his father that they had gone home for the night as previously allowed. In close juxtaposition De Jong documents a case in another camp in Bandung on the same day in which "the same punishment was meted out … to three KNIL soldiers who, as they had done more frequently, had left camp the previous evening …"
3. De Jong, *The Collapse of a Colonial Society*, 330–332, does not specify the 15th Battalion Camp, though it is clearly where this incident took place. He quotes Lt. Col. Poulus's eyewitness account, identifying him as "the senior officer in one of the largest camps in Bandung where initially about 12,000 prisoners were crowded together." Poulus was one of this camp's three leaders: Netherlands Center for War, Holocaust, and Genocide Studies (NIOD), https://www.indischekamparchieven.nl/en/search?mivast=963&mizig=276&miadt=968&miaet=14&micode=kampen&minr=1395568&milang=en&misort=unittitle%7Casc&miview=ika2, accessed May 2, 2024. And in a footnote, De Jong, 329, states that "Poulus became senior officer in the camp after Colonel C.G. Toorop was transferred to Batavia." Toorop was Lindeijer's commander during the defense of Java.
4. De Jong, *The Collapse of a Colonial Society*, 332, quoting Van West de Veer, NIOD IC, 81, 314.
5. De Jong, 330–333. By May 15, 1942, almost identical incidents had occurred at two more camps near Bandung, and at a third in Cimahi. In all, forty-three KNIL soldiers on Java were summarily executed for leaving camp.
6. EW Jr., discussion, November 2004.
7. The Gas School Hospital: A part of the Fifteenth Battalion camp. Lindeijer trained in countermeasures to chemical warfare prior to the invasion; however, the Dutch chemical weapons were never used. "Nevertheless, almost all major belligerents in WWII had prepared themselves for chemical warfare and kept vast stock-piles of chemical weapons close at hand." The Dutch war-history foundation, *kennispunt mei 1940*: http://www.waroverholland.nl/index.php?page=chemical-warfare, accessed May 2, 2024.
8. De Jong, *The Collapse of a Colonial Society*, 334.
9. The unorthodox beadle: My description is a paraphrase of De Jong, *The Collapse of a Colonial* Society, 335, who himself quotes the Indonesian Dutch writer Rob Nieuwenhuys.
10. De Jong, *The Collapse of a Colonial Society*, 334, quoting Poulus.
11. On 8 March 1942, the Japanese announced "a new era of peace and prosperity" and the closing of all banks and European schools. De Jong, *The Collapse of a Colonial Society*, 72,
12. Family details: EW Jr., discussion, November 2004. The neighbor was a Mrs. Tulner.
13. Burki was an accomplished artist, having studied architecture in Delft and art in Paris before working as an illustrator. He later survived the sinking of the ship that was transporting him to Japan. Once there, he was held at a forced labor camp in Nagasaki, where he survived the dropping of the second atomic bomb.
14. Retrieved after the war from a chest buried under a camp gateway, the majority of Burki's drawings hang in the *Museon* in The Hague. They exist in published form in his book, *Achter de Kawat: Charles Burki, Legernummer 9409 [Behind the Barbed Wire: Charles Burki, Army Number 9409]* (Amsterdam: Uitgeverij XTRA, 2010).
15. De Jong, *The Collapse of a Colonial Society*, 43.
16. De Jong, 72. De Jong, 71, also relates that "all Dutch or English signs on shops, cafes, restaurants and hotels disappeared in mid-1942 and were replaced by Japanese or Indonesian versions." In the same context, by early 1943, "the use in public of the Dutch or English language was also prohibited."
17. Burki, *Achter de Kawat*, 132–137.
18. De Jong, *The Collapse of a Colonial*

Society, 314, writes that collective punishments happened so frequently that "only one example need be given here." The one he chooses occurred "in early April 1942 in one of the barrack complexes in Bandung where about 10,000 prisoners were then being held." This may or may not have been the Fifteenth Battalion camp.

19. De Jong, *The Collapse of a Colonial Society*, 284.
20. The Department of Roads and Bridges.
21. De Jong, *The Collapse of a Colonial Society*, 335.
22. The Depot Battalion and Air Target Artillery areas were part of the large Fifteenth Battalion encampment.
23. De Jong, 335.
24. Toon Lindeijer, a distant cousin.
25. The Bandung Milk Center (or *Bandoengsche Melk Centrale*), with its Art Deco architecture, continues to be a popular gathering place and restaurant in Bandung today.
26. The primarily Christian Manadonese, from the northern Celebes, and Ambonese, from the island of Ambon in the Moluccas, "played a relatively large role in the KNIL." They were known for their fierce loyalty to the Dutch, and as a result, many received harsh treatment from the Japanese. De Jong, *The Collapse of a Colonial Society*, 70.
27. During the summer of 1942, POWs in West Java had their hair cropped. De Jong, *The Collapse of a Colonial Society*, 300.
28. De Jong, *The Collapse of a Colonial Society*, 89.
29. Ir. Wilhelmus George "Wim" Gribnau, during the war, KNIL soldier 2kl, Diary (Dutch), June 1942, Java—May 1943, Ohashi, Japan, copy given by Gribnau's children to the Lindeijer family, translation by Herman Lindeyer.
30. The camp guards' inability to fathom Dutch humor: Adrie Lindeijer, discussion, November 9, 2004; numerous sources.
31. Gribnau, Diary, 23 July 1942. The episode clearly pertains to 15 July 1942.
32. The series of deaths and the quotation: Gribnau, Diary, 23 July 1942.
33. Gribnau, Diary, entry on 10 August or later, talks about Dr. Smits' birthday "on 4/8 [European dating]."
34. De Jong, *The Collapse of a Colonial Society*, 87.
35. Gribnau, Diary, 8 August 1942.
36. Gribnau, Diary, 16 August 1942.
37. De Jong, p. 48.
38. Burki, *Achter de Kawat*, 118. Permission to use this drawing granted by the Museon, in The Hague, where it currently hangs.
39. Gribnau, Diary, 31 August 1942.
40. Gribnau, Diary, 6 September 1942.
41. Details of the departure to Cimahi: Gribnau, Diary, 1 October 1942.
42. The Dutch women laid siege: De Jong, *The Collapse of a Colonial Society*, 349.
43. "If only the Dutch women had been defending Java": Numerous accounts. I quote Stanbrough, UNT0648, 76: "We withdrew [from Buitenzorg, at the time of the Dutch capitulation] … One night we went through a little town called Sukabumi. In Sukabumi, I guess, at three o'clock in the morning, the little Dutch ladies were out serving us cookies and hot tea in the rain. It was really impressive. If the Dutch women had been put in uniform, the Japs [sic] would have had a hell of a lot harder time." Stanbrough's interviewer replies "I've heard that story before." Stanbrough continues, "Yes, well, it's true. They were right there, and they knew the Japs [sic] were right behind us there."
44. Circumstances at the minority Chinese school: Gribnau, Diary, recollections in a 23 October 1942 entry.
45. EW's message conveyed through his former student: EW Jr., in discussion with me, November 2004.
46. The order to be ready to leave with the group of five hundred: Gribnau, Diary, 10 October 1942.

Chapter 3

1. Excepting for the single hatch, the experience at Glodok prison and during removal to the dock and ship is recreated from the Gribnau Diary, entry recorded in Singapore on 25 October 1942. EW Jr. described the single hatch in discussion with me, November 2004. Multiple prisoner accounts agree.
2. De Jong, *The Collapse of a Colonial*

Notes—Chapter 3

Society, 348, identifies Captain P.C.F. Meys as the senior Dutch officer onboard the first transport of Dutch and Dutch Eurasians from Java to Japan. Meys' diary has his group embarking in Batavia's harbor on "De boot heet Tofuku Maru" on 16 October 1942 and reaching Singapore on 19 October. Captain P.C.F. Meys, Diary (Dutch), NIOD IC diaries, nrs., 216–17, 27 October 1942, passage translated for me by Jeroen Kemperman (NIOD). EW and his group of Dutch and Dutch Eurasians were clearly in this transport.

3. Dutch Marine Jürien Hendrick Stenfert, tag no. 170499.

4. Gribnau, Diary, 25 October 1942, recollects "red tapes around the arm in Batavia." Stanbrough, UNT0658, 133–34: Technical skill meant transport to Japan; others went to the Burma Railroad. Kenneth E. Horne, "The Spiral Staircase: The Autobiography of a Japanese Prisoner of War," unpublished manuscript, copyright 1992, 125. A "red ribbon" meant transport to Japan; a green one, the Burma Railroad.

5. Gregory Michno, *Death on the Hellships*, (Annapolis: Naval Institute Press, 2001), 87.

6. EW records re-embarking on 27 October on his itinerary. Captain Meys' later war crimes report gives this date also. Reserve Captain P.C.F. Meys, Report Concerning Transport of Allied Prisoners-of-War from Singapore to Japan in November 1942 (hereafter, Report), NACP, RG 331, SCAP Area Case Files, 1945–48, UD 1189, Box 985, TR-4, Miscellaneous, 1.

7. Meys, Report, 1.

8. The protesting officer was Major P.P. Andrews. Tofuku Maru Ship Case, NACP, RG 331, SCAP Area Case Files, 1945–48, UD 1189, Box 985, TR-4, Miscellaneous (hereafter, Tofuku Maru Ship Case), 6.

9. Meys, Report, 2.

10. De Jong, *The Collapse of a Colonial Society*, 348, tells of the selection of the Indonesian Dutch in this transport from a camp in Cimahi. They are clearly from the group that Lindeijer's train stopped to pick up there, en route to Batavia. A footnote on the same page completes the linkage, identifying Captain Meys with this transport.

11. The two after holds (the second, smaller), each with two levels (decks) plus a level below for cargo: Captain Meys' rough drawing, NIOD IC 80900. Per Meys' Report, twelve hundred prisoners were on board; 486 were Dutch. Per James E. Reynolds, Diary, Cruiser *Houston* Collection, University of Houston Libraries, 18: the Americans and Australians combined were less than one hundred; thus, the British numbered slightly over six hundred. The respective nationalities' berths come from the following sources, among others: Stanbrough, UNT OH0658,140; Horne, "The Spiral Staircase," 128–29; and Fred H. Miles, American Army, Deposition, NACP, RG 331, SCAP Area Case Files, 1945–48, UD 1189, Box 985, TR-4, Vol. 1, 1.

12. The hatch, its uses, and permission: Testimony of Chief Gunner R.L. O'Brien, U.S.S. *Houston*, Tofuku Maru Ship Case, 4; Jack Martin Feliz, U.S.S. *Houston*, 2cl.Pet.Ofr., UNT OH1373, 102.

13. Main deck area and permission: Reynolds, Diary, 18. Horne, "The Spiral Staircase," 135. Meys, Report, 2.

14. The *Tofuku Maru*, *Honan Maru*, *Singapore Maru*, and *Dai-Nichi Maru* departed Singapore for Moji on 30 October 1942. All but the *Tofuku Maru* reached Moji on 24 November '42. The latter did not arrive until 30 November 1942, as a result of its stop for repairs in Saigon. NACP, RG 331, SCAP Area Case Files, 1945–48, UD 1189, Box 985, TR-4, Vol. 1

15. Reynolds, Diary, November 4, 1942. Horne, "The Spiral Staircase," 135.

16. Kenneth Horne (RAAF), Keith Edmonds (RAAF, email message to me, February 7, 2008), and Ross Drabble (RAAF, Tofuku Maru Ship Case, 5), were on the *Tofuku Maru*, with respective compatriots.

17. Water ration and secret collection from taps on the winches: Meys, Report, 2; others.

18. Gribnau, Diary, recollection on 21 December 1942, in Ohashi, Japan.

19. The first cases occurred on November 3, 1942. Meys, Report, 2.

20. "I am sorry, but let him die": Gribnau, Diary, recollection on December 21, 1942. Meys, evidence given in the Tofuku Maru Ship Case, 4: "Requests to put PoW [sic] sick ashore at Saigon and Takao were met with 'I am sorry but let them die.'"

21. The addresses, which are signed

Notes—Chapter 3

upside down in relation to EW's entry, are both in Sumatra.

22. EW Jr., discussion, November 2004. Gribnau, Diary, multiple entries.

23. James Garbutt: RAF medical orderly (2cl.act.). NACP, RG 389, OPMG, 460A, Box 2131, American POW Information Bureau Records Branch, General Subject File, 1942–46, Camps: Japan—Sendai Group, Folder "Sendai POW Camp Name List, 1 of 2," File "Name List Sendai P.O.W. Camp-4B (hereafter, Name List Sendai POW Camp 4-B). EW's schedule for care of the sick lists "Garbitt" [sic].

24. Gribnau, Diary, 21 December 1942, recollects the watches and the rapid increase in cases of dysentery. Meys, Report, 1, identifies Van Slooten as the second Dutch doctor.

25. Gribnau, Diary, 21 December 1942, recollects the two doctors bringing "some medicines and bandage material from Singapore." Meys' Report, 3: Prior to Takao, medicine was running out.

26. Meys, Report, 1.

27. EW's experience on the night of November 7: Adrie Lindeijer, telephone conversation with me, June 8, 2008.

28. Tofuku Maru Ship Case, 2, and numerous other accounts.

29. Meys, Report, 1.

30. NACP, RG 331, SCAP Area Case Files, 1945–48, UD 1189, Box 985: Tr 4, Miscellaneous, contains the translated Japanese "Certificate of Death and Burial" for Royal Air Force 521623 Corporal Samuel Allan, deceased on board the TOFUKU Maru, on 9 Nov. 42. Gribnau and others mention Allan's death. Gribnau says "Allen."

31. The bad news: Reynolds, Diary, November 10, 12, and 14, 1942; the reduction in speed is on November 15.

32. The Dutch death: Reynolds, Diary, November 13, 1942. The method of sea burial and the ship's continuing at full speed: Meys, Report, 2.

33. Reynolds, Diary, November 9 and 12–16, 1942.

34. Itinerary: EW's insertion, "Dai Nichi Maru," as the ship that transported him from Java to Singapore, was clearly done after the fact in the only remaining space, and in error, as Meys' details show. Other nationalities imprisoned with him in Japan had traveled from Java to Singapore on the *Tofuku Maru* and must have influenced his thinking.

35. Reynolds, Diary, November 16, 1942.

36. Tofuku Maru Ship Case, 4; George C. Craig (Australian), Statement, NACP, RG 331, SCAP Area Case Files, 1945–48, UD 1189, Box 985, Tr-4, Vol. 1, 1.

37. Ben Kenneth Kelley, U.S. Army Sgt., 131st Field Artillery, UNT OH0565, 96.

38. Gribnau, Diary, recollection on 21 December 1942. Adrie Lindeijer learned after the war of the difficulties the medics had carrying the wooden casks up the ladder to empty them: telephone conversation with me, 15 June 2008.

39. The convoy and its becoming scattered: Reynolds, Diary, November 20–21, 1942.

40. Ill prisoners lying on the hatches: William J. Stewart, Seaman First Class, USS *Houston*, telephone conversation with me, April 2, 2010. A small hole was left so that prisoners who were able to do so could still make the climb to the top deck. Jack Feliz, in discussion with me, Palm Springs, February 18–19, 2007 told of additional sick laid out on the main deck.

41. Meys, Report, 2. Reynolds, Diary, November 22, 1942, documents diphtheria on the ship, as does S.C. Smith, R.A.F., Affidavit, September 12, 1945, NACP, RG 331, SCAP Area Case Files, 1945–48, UD 1189, Box 985, Tr-4, Vol. 1, 1.

42. Reynolds, Diary, November 22–24, 1942.

43. The seven Japanese deaths and the cases of Irish stew, Reynolds, Diary, November 23 and 24, 1942.

44. Tracing the ship's commandant proved impossible; thus, only the captain and the commander of the guards could be charged, per The Tofuku Maru Ship Case summary page. The ship's captain at his war crimes trial testified to the responsibility of "the Anchorage Command Singapore." U.C. Berkeley War Crimes Studies Center, Singapore Cases, http://istsocrates.berkeley.edu/~warcrime/Japan/singapore/Trials/Otsu.htm, accessed August 16, 2011 (site discontinued prior to this volume's publication).

45. The twenty-seven Allied deaths by nationality: Thirteen were Dutch (Meys, Report, 3); two, Australian officers, from diphtheria, per Stanley Chapman, R.A.F.,

affidavit for the Australian War Crimes Commission, NACP, RG 331, SCAP Area Case Files, 1945–48, UD 1189, Box 985, Tr-4, Vol. 1; one, American; and eleven, British.

46. Accounts of prisoners who disembarked at Moji differ on how they traveled across the strait. Conditions on the date of arrival, or even expediency, may have dictated more than one method of transport.

47. Meys, Diary, NIOD collection nr. 401, diary nr. 216.

48. Reynolds, Diary, 21, tells of this train, which took them eastward from Morioka to Kamaishi, as well as a small local train, which then took them to their final destination, "Ohasi, a small town and mining camp," in northeast Honshu.

49. After the war, Lindeijer, Gribnau, and Stenfert were recognized for exceptional service during the voyage and awarded the Dutch East Asian Star.

50. EW wrote this report on both sides of a form supplied by the camp administration. His report on the Japanese invasion of Java, submitted at the same time, was written single-sided, on eight sheets of paper.

51. The Tofuku Maru Ship Case concluded that "… there was no active brutality and quite possibly no malice on the part of the accused [the ship's captain and the commander of the guards]. And yet the suffering of the victims was considerable and deaths were many. All this clearly resulted from the prevailing attitude of all, or nearly all, Japanese towards prisoners of war . . . that to transport PoW [sic] like cattle . . . was not a normal and proper procedure." Ultimately, the sergeant major was acquitted and the ship's captain given a light sentence, because of insufficient evidence of intentional negligence. U.C. Berkeley War Crimes Studies Center, Singapore Cases, accessed August 16, 2011, http://ist-socrates.berkeley.edu/~warcrime/Japan/singapore/Trials/Otsu.htm (site discontinued prior to publication).

Chapter 4

1. Reynolds, Diary, November 30, 1942.
2. Reserve 1st Lieutenant J. M. van Well Groeneveld, Report about the Prisoner of War Camp Ohasi (Hakodate II) covering the period from 30th November 1942 to 20th February 1944, NACP, RG 331, SCAP Area Case Files, 1945–48, UD 1189, Box 959, Folder SE-5, Vol. 4, Miscellaneous (Ohashi No. 4 Investigative Reports, Sendai 4-B); (hereafter, Groeneveld, Report).

3. Kelley, UNT OH0565, 100; Stewart, UNT OH0544, 89.

4. EW, Gribnau, and Groeneveld all agree on a total of ninety-one Dutch. In addition to EW, Gribnau, and Stenfert, one of the three Dutch lieutenants present may have been European Dutch. NIOD records do not clarify this.

5. Groeneveld, Report, 2. Feliz, UNT OH1373, 116.

6. The prisoners were hired out to the Nittetsu Mining Industry, Ltd., Kamaishi Works. Kamaishi Mine POW Camp Report. Kamaishi Historical Museum, Trans. Takamitsu Muraoka, Professor Emeritus, Leiden University, 1.

7. Captain L. L. Zeigler, 2nd Battalion, 131st Field Artillery, Texas National Guard.

8. The rooms and allocation by nationalities: Reynolds, Diary, November 30, 1942.

9. Feliz, UNT OH1373, 116.

10. December 2 details: Stewart, UNT OH0544, 90. Per Reynolds, Diary, December 2, 1942, "I kept my notebooks [diary] in my bosom so they didn't see them. Sure hope I can hang on to this stuff throughout this war."

11. Meys, Diary, 27 November 1942: In Moji Dr. Lutter was assigned to a group of British prisoners. Lack of mention of Van Slooten suggests he may have remained under Meys' command.

12. The sick bays, EW and Stenfert ailing, and Gribnau aid to the Japanese doctor: Gribnau, Diary, 7 December 1942.

13. The stoves and the quotation: Groeneveld, Report, 4, and Stewart, UNT OH0544, 98, respectively.

14. Wetters as "a Hollander": He may or may not be one of the four European Dutch indicated by EW's tally on 6 December. Over generations the racial identities of Dutch families residing in the Indies could become blurred.

15. Sendai 4-B List of Deceased POWs, NACP, RG 331, SCAP Area Case Files, 1945–48, UD 1189, Box 959, Folder Se-5,

Vol. 4 Miscellaneous (Ohasi No. 4 Investigation Reports, Sendai 4-B), hereafter, List of Deceased POWs.

16. The weather and the prisoners' afflictions: Reynolds, Diary, December 6, 1942.

17. EW's poetic caricature of Gribnau: a Dutch *Sinterklaas* holiday tradition.

18. The three medics' activities, and the Japanese medical sergeant's appreciation: Gribnau, Diary, 7 December 1942. The medical sergeant is Sergeant Major M.D. Z. Neko (or Nikko).

19. Groeneveld, Report, 6.

20. The deaths: KNIL Private Rudolph Albert Ogilie [Ogilvie], age 48; KNIL Private Gustauf Adolff Pfaff, age 34; RAF Private Thomas Howard Rees; and RAF Private Austin Black Noble. List of Deceased POWs.

21. Cremation duty, the funeral, and Reynolds' remarks: U.S. Navy Seaman 1st Class James E. Reynolds, Diary, December 7-9, 1942. Prisoners considered to have succumbed to infectious diseases were cremated prior to burial.

22. U.S. Navy privates Alfred Glenn Seidel and Gene Fanghor. List of Deceased POWs.

23. Stewart, telephone conversation with me, April 2, 2010Feliz, UNT OH1373, 118. Others tell of the same episode.

24. KNIL Private Anrooij Benjamin van Hijmans. List of Deceased POWs.

25. Stenfert's struggle, and Gribnau's exclamation: Gribnau, Diary, 21-22 December 1942.

26. Gribnau, Diary, apparent 22 December 1942 entry. The official cause: List of Deceased POWs.

27. Reserve 1st Lieutenant J. M. van Well Groeneveld letter to Dutch officials, October 26, 1945, praising the service of all three Dutch medics during the transport. English translation in my possession.

28. The dazed medics, and the inadequate outdoor clothing: Gribnau, Diary, apparent 22 December 1942 entry, and Groeneveld, Report, 5, respectively.

29. Gribnau, Diary, apparent 22 December 1942 entry.

30. The Christmas day weather and iced-over toilet and bath house: Reynolds, December 27, 1942, implies that the weather has been similar for a number of days.

31. Gribnau, Diary, 25 December 1942.

32. De Jong, *The Collapse of a Colonial Society*, 472, documents reports of packages sent by the South African Red Cross to help internees in Java in late 1942. I can only speculate that the rumor arose from this or something similar.

33. Division of the watch, the diagnosis, and the denial. Gribnau, Diary, 26 December 1942.

34. KNIL Lt. Frederick Johan Van Leent.

35. Gribnau, Diary, December 23, 1942.

36. De Jong, *The Collapse of a Colonial Society*, 348, quoting Meys.

37. The katakana is the less commonly used of the two Japanese scripts, the other being the cursive "hiragana." Stewart, UNT OH0544, 117, discusses the katakana strokes, which he and a very few others made the effort to learn.

38. The rumor may have sprung from Japan's losses at Guadalcanal. The three-day Battle of Guadalcanal took place in November 1942, but conflict continued during December.

39. KNIL reservist Second Lieutenant F.J. van Leent.

40. A hotel from the 1890s renovated in the late 1920s by the Dutch architect C.P. Wolff Schoemaker, with the assistance of a young architect named Sukarno, the future president of Indonesia. It remains a functioning hotel to this day, in the heart of Bandung, close to the business and financial district."

Chapter 5

1. Reynolds, Diary, January 1, 13, and 16, 1943.

2. The quotations and ethnicities: Reynolds, Diary, January 4 and 10, 1943.

3. Reynolds, Diary, January 1, 1943.

4. Nightly inspections: Feliz, UNT OH1373, 167; fights prevented: Reynolds, Diary, January 1 and 10, 1943.

5. Reynolds, Diary, January 5, 1943.

6. Reynolds, Diary, January 5, 1943, "Was a good long, clean fight. Draw." Water bucket incident: January 7, 1943.

7. Stewart, UNT OH0544, 107; Kelley, UNT OH0565, 101.

8. The future work assignments and

Feliz's election: Reynolds, Diary, January 7 and 8, 1943, respectively.
    9. Feliz, UNT OH 1373, 11. The exact quotation is from my discussion with him in Palm Springs, February 2007.
    10. Groeneveld, Report, 2 and 3.
    11. Stewart, UNT OH0544, 93.
    12. Groeneveld, Report, 3.
    13. Selling used tobacco for wherewithal: Reynolds, Diary, January 9, 1943.
    14. Kelley, UNT OH0565, 131. "We had patch on patch, so our shirts and pants got pretty thick."
    15. Lt. Naganuma's threat and events of 11 January: Reynolds, Diary, January 10–11, 1943.
    16. Reynolds, Diary, January 12, 1943.
    17. No ink was available at the camp. The addition was made after the war. EW Jr., discussion, November 2004.
    18. Reynolds, Diary, January 13, 1943.
    19. Groeneveld, Report, 2.
    20. Feliz, UNT OH1373, 162.
    21. Stewart, UNT OH0544, 94–95. Horne, 2011 telephone conversation with me, recalled Stewart's problem.
    22. Reynolds, Diary, January 13, 1943.
    23. The derivation, from the Sinhalese word "beri," indicates "weakness"; the "reduplication," intensifying this. *The Compact Oxford English Dictionary, New Edition*. (Oxford: Clarendon Press, 1996), 128.
    24. Japan occupied Chinese Manchuria in 1931 and created the puppet state of Manchukuo in 1932—an act condemned by the League of Nations in 1933. Japanese military expansion nonetheless continued into China, and eventually into French Indochina, resulting in the American embargo in July 1941.
    25. The daily trek, honey buckets, the quotation and kindnesses: Reynolds, Diary, January 9–11 and 13–16, 1943.
    26. "broken Nippon lingo": Reynolds, Diary, January 15, 1943. Stewart, UNT OH0544, 118. Kelley, UNT OH0565, 110, and Feliz, UNT OH1373, 129, express similar sentiments.
    27. Feliz, UNT OH1373, 145. Elaborated in discussion, Palm Springs, February 18–19, 2007.
    28. Feliz, *The Saga of Sailor Jack* (Lincoln, Nebraska: iUniverse, 2001), 1. Frank Planton, RAF, email message to me, December 14, 2009: Feliz reminded him of "one of the bandit Mexicans I had seen in the cowboy films."
    29. EW's visits: Reynolds, Diary, January 19 and 22, 1943. Reynolds' ills and anger: Diary, January 18 and 26, 1943.
    30. Horne, *The Spiral Staircase*, 270–71, recounts learning at the war's end of the clandestine knowledge, which included Midway.
    31. The secret radio: The parts of a broadband radio that the Americans had converted in stealth to shortwave in Java survived the transport and could be reassembled in Ohashi; plus, one or more radios were built there, as Chapter Ten reveals. The distribution of news: Feliz, discussion, Palm Springs, February 18–19, 2007. Others confirm.
    32. Corporal Howard Curtis Hovis, of the Texas National Guard.
    33. The ungodly wind, snowfall, and "mashing": Reynolds, Diary, January 25, 1943, and February 4, 5, respectively.
    34. Earthquake, "all get out," and bleeding hands: Reynolds, Diary, February 21, 22, and 27, 1943, respectively.
    35. EW's visit with coffee, and "leveling off ground": Reynolds, Diary, January 27, 1943. "Stir crazy" is on the 28th.

Chapter 6

    1. James D. Hornfischer, *Ship of Ghosts: The Story of the U.S.S. Houston, F.D.R.'s Lost Cruiser, and the Epic Saga of Her Survivors* (New York: Bantam Books, 2006), 179: The entire *Houston* crew was relegated to an MIA list.
    2. Kelley, UNT OH0565, 120. "… we [the Second Battalion, 131st Field Artillery] were called the 'Lost Battalion.'"
    3. Reynolds, Stewart, Horne, and others consistently refer to EW as "Lindy." Feliz, during my 2007 interview with him, did not remember "Lindeijer," but immediately recalled "Lindy," who "helped sew my foot up once."
    4. The Western ordering of Iwashita's name. In Japanese practice, the surname would come first ("Iwashita Hiroë").
    5. "Jan's": Possessive form of a familiar name for the Dutch Army. Also, per *The New Routledge Dutch Dictionary* (New York: Routledge, 2003), 179, "the (ordinary) man in the street."

6. Those in this paragraph not previously identified: RAF member Alfred Coughtry, U.S. Army Private First Class George Joseph Zerbis, and KNIL soldier Hendrick Rijnders.

7. "brown soja lobak soup": Malay for tofu, or soybean and vegetable.

8. The Japanese prison guards were rotated on a quarterly basis to prevent black market trading or other fraternization with the prisoners. Lindeijer Jr., in discussion with me, November 2004. Others confirm.

9. A white cloth that could be placed under Iwashita's cap to hang over his shoulders as protection from sun or dust from the mine, in typical Japanese fashion at the time.

10. An epithet referenced with growing respect, as time passed; e.g., Stanbrough, UNT OH0658, 206. In one anecdote, Iwashita says his surname is the equivalent of "Smith" in Japanese. Frank Planton, http://hyaku-san-juu-ni.blogspot.com/2011/07/20-honourable-men-and-rice-cakes-part-2.html; accessed May 2, 2024.

11. Personal History of Iwashita, Hiroe, Records of Iwashita, Hiroe, NACP, RG 331, SCAP Area Case Files, 1945–48, UD 1189, Box 959, Folder Se-5, Vol. 4 Miscellaneous (Ohasi No. 4 Investigation Reports, Sendai 4-B) (hereafter, Personal History of Iwashita, Hiroe).

12. In fact, the eleventh century *Tale of Genji* is often called the world's first novel. The Japanese author Saikaku wrote novels in the seventeenth to eighteenth centuries, and modern novels have flourished since the late 1800s.

13. Hiroe Iwashita, "To Gribnau," 22 February 1943 (in English), 1, and Personal History of Iwashita, Hiroe, 1.

14. Black market trading with prisoners was forbidden—an indication that Iwashita did not follow the "party line."

15. EW recorded the quotations in this paragraph in English.

16. A reference to the rough bunch of Indonesian Dutch selected from the camp in Cimahi for the first transport to Japan. Yet notably, in this entry and elsewhere EW highlights some of them who stand out for their contributions.

17. Bertsch is KNIL Corporal Cornelis Bertsch.

18. *Chihaya*: a clever method by which Japanese women tie back the sleeves of a kimono to make it a practical garment in which to work; thus, an appropriate name for a newspaper intended to encourage women while their men are at war.

19. KNIL soldiers N. Ludwig Riedé and Alexavith Mulder help keep watch over Alfred Coughtry, RAF, and KNIL soldier Hendrick Van der Veen (or Ven).

20. Feliz, discussion, February 18–19, 2007. Multiple others.

21. Praise for Neko is unanimous in the former prisoners' accounts. His and his wife's purchase of medicines on the black market: Feliz, *The Saga of Sailor Jack*, 57, and Stanbrough, UNT OH0658, 163.

22. Reynolds, Diary, March 4, 1943. Rich is U.S. Army Private First Class John Edward Rich.

23. "Exceptions" not identified earlier are KNIL soldiers Jonan Thurner and Jan N. Nierath.

24. Reynolds, Diary, March 16, '43, the same date that EW completed his 1 March '43 "Single Day" entry.

25. This news appears to come in part from the secret radio, and in part from a Japanese newspaper. When papers were made available to the prisoners in English, they were typically laced with propaganda but could nonetheless hold clues. The language of this paper is unknown, but the news of the Germans being pushed back is accurate.

26. EW addressed his letter to the house on the Dago Road, but by this time his family was interned. EW Jr., discussion, November 2004."

Chapter 7

1. Reynolds, Diary, March 29, 1943.

2. Reynolds, Diary, March 20 and 22, 1943, respectively.

3. Reynolds, Diary, March 18, 1943, and numerous others.

4. The two quotations: Reynolds, Diary, April 14, 1943, and Kelley, UNT OH0565, respectively.

5. Personal History of Iwashita, Hiroe, 2.

6. Groeneveld, Report, 2. Stewart, telephone conversation with me, April 2, 2010; Frank Planton, RAF, discussion with me,

Notes—Chapter 7

King's Lynn, Norfolk, U.K., October 22, 2010.

7. Multiple trips and cleaning up: Reynolds, Diary, April 1, 1943, and Stanbrough, UNT OH0658, 157, respectively.

8. Gribnau, Diary, 2 May 1943, states "[Jimmy Garbutt lives here [in the hospital] also."

9. The quotations: Reynolds, Diary, April 1 and 5, 1943. Planton and others confirm widespread use of "the hut."

10. Barracks' description: Records of Reynolds, Groeneveld, Kelley, and Stewart.

11. Camp layout and description: Records of Groeneveld, Kelley, Gribnau, and U.S. Army Captain MC Edwin W. Tucker. Conversations with Planton (King's Lynn, Norfolk, UK, October 22, 2010) and Stewart (April 2, 2010).

12. Assessment of work assignments: Numerous prisoner accounts.

13. Kelley, UNT OH0565, 111, ff.; Reynolds, April 19, 1943.

14. Mine location and four levels: Reynolds, April 19, 1943; Stewart, UNT OH 0544, 113, and telephone conversation, April 2, 2010; and Planton, discussion, October 22, 2010.

15. Nature of the mine work: Reynolds, April 18–30, 1943; Kelley, UNT OH0565, 111, ff.; Feliz, UNT OH1373, 125–126, 143.

16. Military strictness: Reynolds, April 6 and 11, 1943. The hot bath and new shoes: April 11 and 16, respectively.

17. Details in this paragraph, including Reynolds' associated remarks, the Australian captain's preparation of a protest, and Reynolds' help for the abused Indonesian Dutch prisoner: Reynolds, April 22, 1943.

18. "The miserable food": Groeneveld, Report, 2. The cooks were now drawn from the prisoners' own ranks, but could only use the meager supplies they were given.

19. Feliz, *The Saga of Sailor Jack*, 64.

20. Reynolds, Diary, April 7, 1943.

21. Unfortunately, this was true, though it involved not Japanese POWs but civilian Japanese American citizens, who under FDR's "Executive Order 9066," February 19, 1942, were forced to move into converted stables and animal pens. John Dower, *War without Mercy: Race and Power in the Pacific War* (New York: Pantheon Books. 1986), 84.

22. The officers' protest, Naganuma's refusal, and the response from Hakodate: Reynolds, April 23, 1943.

23. Feliz, UNT OH1373, 143.

24. Dutch property of strategic value in Indonesia was destroyed by the unit to which Wim Swaan belonged—action the Japanese punished by execution. EW Jr., discussion, November 2004.

25. The first in a series of Mr. Moto novels by John P. Marquand, about an inscrutable Japanese detective.

26. Reynolds, May 2, 1943.

27. Feliz, Testimony, NACP, RG 331, SCAP Area Case Files, 1945–48, UD 1189, Box 959, Folder SE-5, Vol. 1, A-F. Reynolds uses the same terminology, June 26, 1943, indicating it was customary.

28. Likely, Purwoasri, today; a village in East Java, five km. south of Kertosono.

29. Reynolds, May 11, 1943, records 30 departing: "9 Americans, 3 Aussies, 3 English, 1 Chinese, and 14 Dutch." Groeneveld, Report, 1, records only the number of Dutch who departed, as "13 Netherlanders." If he is correct, Lindeijer's total of 29 is likely correct as well.

30. Planton describes his group on arrival. "We must have looked a bedraggled sight to them, we had come from a camp where there had been no let up. We had been starved, brutally beaten and overworked continuously, our strength and spirits had been drained, stretched beyond the limits of endurance at a camp run by an evil, sadistic Commandant. We were covered with sores, disheveled clothes hanging on our spare frames." http://hyaku-san-juu-ni.blogspot.com/2011_05_01_archive.html, accessed May 2, 2024.

31. Reynolds, May 17, 1943.

32. Hakodate conditions (quotations): Planton, email message to me, November 8, 2009.

33. Planes that the Dutch East Indies had purchased for its defense, which because of the rapid Japanese advance, were diverted to British India. EW Jr., discussion, November 2004.

34. The U.S. regained control of the Aleutians in April 1943. It's not clear what led to EW's reference to Americans doing "excellent work in China"; perhaps a garbled rumor.

35. *yasumi* day: The standard English transliteration for the Japanese word for rest.

36. Reynolds, Diary, May 16–17, 1943. Stranks is Leslie Richard Stranks, R.A.F. NACP, RG 331, SCAP Area Case Files, UD 1189, Sendai 4-B List of Liberated POWs (hereafter List of Liberated POWs), Box 959. American POWs Ben Kelley, Earl May, and Jack Feliz describe his beating, NACP, RG 331, SCAP Area Case Files, 1945–48, UD 1189, Box 959, Folder SE-5, Vol. 2, American Affidavits, E-N, 1–2.

37. Reynolds, Diary, May 25–26, 1943.

38. Roll call on the thirteenth, including quotations: Reynolds, Diary, June 13, 1943.

39. Iwashita's duties: Personal History of Iwashita, Hiroe, 2–3. His influence: Feliz, discussion, February 18–19, 2007; multiple prisoner documents. Loyalty: Hiroe Iwashita, "To Gribnau," 22 February 1943, 1–2.

40. Prime Minister Tojo's speech and the beating of the kindly supervisor: Reynolds, Diary, June 18 and 26, 1943.

41. Nel did indeed write messages that never arrived. EW Jr., discussion, November 2004.

42. Reynolds, Diary, May 4—July 1, 1943. Horne, email message to me, July 14, 2011, recalled Reynolds' "terrible case of Beri-beri [sic] ... He literally sloshed around when he turned over in bed. I think he thought, with good reason, that he was dying."

43. Herman Lindeyer, email message to me, December 2009, tells of EW's doing this. It likely stimulated the prisoners' collecting and trading of recipes that began to perk up Reynolds, Diary, August 7 and 14, 1943.

44. "British L/Cpl Leslie Merralls, R.A.F. (V.R.) 84 Sqdn, age 33," died on 13 July '43, of "colitis and acute perforation peritonitis." List of Deceased POWs.

45. Reynolds, Diary, July 13, 1943. Price is Seaman First Class Fred D. Price. List of Liberated POWs.

46. The "Honorable Men": Reynolds, Diary, July 9, 1943; Groeneveld, Report, 3; Kelley, UNT OH0565, 104–106.

47. Reynolds, Diary, July 24, 1943, documents sharing his diary with others in the hospital. Its later use in war crimes trials is evidenced by an unclassified telegraphic message from the War Crimes Branch (J J O'Keefe) ajs 6651 3 October 46. NACP, RG 153, JAG War Crimes Case Files, A1 143, Box 747, Case 35–878, Vol. I.

48. Ross Drabble's beating: sworn affidavits, NACP, RG 331, SCAP Area Case Files, 1945–48, UD 1189, Box 959, Folder SE-5, Vol. 1, A-F; additional affidavits, NACP, RG 153, JAG War Crimes Case Files, A1 143, Box 747, Case 35–878, Vol. 1.

49. Reynolds, Diary, July 18, 1943.

50. Feliz, UNT OH1373, 120.

51. "Italy capitulated": EW is incorrect, perhaps influenced by rumors about the Allied invasion of Sicily, in full swing by July 12, 1943.

52. EW's Silver Cross training [Red Cross equivalent] was cut short by the outbreak of war; thus, he received no Red Cross certification. EW, Diary, September 30, 1942.

53. Reynolds, Diary, entries on August 5, 7, 8, and 10–13, 1943.

54. Reynolds, Diary, August 8, 1943.

55. Groeneveld, Report, 1: "On 9th August 1943 an American doctor arrived from the Camp "Zentsuji." Reynolds, Diary, August 10, 1943: Eppley arrived at "about midnite" [sic] on the ninth.

56. Jackson's death on "1943/8/9," of "colitis and malnutrition": List of Deceased POWs.

57. Curtis visiting Reynolds: Reynolds, Diary, July 30, 1943.

58. Reynolds, Diary, August 10, 1943.

59. Groeneveld, Report, 7; Reynolds, Diary, August 14, 1943; Feliz, discussion, February 18–19, 2007.

60. Reynolds, Diary, August 26, 1943.

61. The negotiated truce and subsequent studious avoidance: Reynolds, Diary, August 25 and 29, 1943, respectively.

Chapter 8

1. Blanket weather, speculation, "plagues," and Elvy: Reynolds, Diary, August 30–31,1943. Also on Elvy: Testimony, Kelley, NACP, RG 153, JAG War Crimes Case Files, A1 143, Box 747, Case 35–878, Vol. 1; and Kamaishi Mine Camp Report, 1, which states that "first-class private of the RAF (Elvy Stanley) at the dawn of 30.8.43. Jumped over the fence, but was recaptured about 1600 hrs same day."

2. Reynolds, Diary, August 31, 1943.

3. Hakodate's strategic value: Planton, discussion, October 22, 2010, based on his forced work at Hakodate's docks.

4. EW Jr., discussion, November 2004. Adrie Lindeijer, telephone conversation with me, October 22, 2009.

5. Reynolds, Diary, October 10, 1943: Elvy was removed from the Ohashi camp on this date. The Kamaishi Mine POW Camp Report regarding Elvy: "Sentenced on 30.10.1943 to a 15 years' imprisonment at a military court. Deceased on 23.3.1944 of acute pneumonia while serving the term in Hakodate Prison."

6. Quotation: Groeneveld, Report, 6. More exactly, the new doctor "knew how to exert influence on the Jap. camp staff..." Added details, Reynolds, Diary, August 17 and 19, 1943.

7. Reynolds, Diary, September 3, 1945, alludes to new intelligence. Numerous prior hints of a radio source. Feliz, discussion with me, February 18–19, 2007. Feliz, *The Saga of Sailor Jack*, 59–61; Feliz, UNT OH1373, 85 ff.

8. Feenstra later dies in Tokyo. Private (or SLD.2KL) Klaas Feenstra, age twenty-two, died on January 18, 1945, of sarcoma of the kidney. List of Deceased POWs.

9. I surmise that the 6 September entry is likely innocuous, but breaks off as result of EW's having removed an entry for 12 September and at least one additional entry, likely from late November, from the diary's double-sided pages. The closing lines of the latter entry remain ("... writing, just like I did when I began these letters..."). He described the officer's night visit to Adrie Lindeijer and EW Jr. on separate occasions after the war.

10. Reynolds, Diary, September 9, 1943. EW's 3 August 1943 entry reports erroneously that "Italy capitulated."

11. Reynolds places high-ranking officers in the camp late on September 12, 1943.

12. Adrie Lindeijer, email message to me, including precise dissertation title, May 24, 2010.

13. In July 1943, Japan's Army (not its scientists), sought export of German uranium to Japan. Joseph Mark Scalia. *Germany's Last Mission to Japan: The Failed Voyage of U-234* (Annapolis: Naval Institute Press, 2000), 186.

14. Reynolds last notes EW's presence in the Ohashi camp on 9 September 1943; however, his record of high-ranking officers present on the night of the twelfth suggests that EW was not removed until sometime after that.

15. The Kamaishi camp was not established until 10 Nov. 1943. Its first group of prisoner inhabitants from Java did not arrive until 19 Nov. (NACP, Record Group 407, A1 1063, POW General Correspondence Files, Box 12). Reynolds, who traded food for cigarettes with "Lindy," does not mention him at all between 9 Sept. 1943 and mid-Jan. 1944, underscoring EW's absence for roughly three months. If he was not in Ohashi, and the Kamaishi camp did not yet exist, he had to be somewhere else—likely not far from the place where he was ultimately dropped off.

16. Much later Technical Director of the Dutch Laboratory for National Defense, EW may have experienced concern that any discussion of his with Japanese military or scientists on nuclear topics could be mischaracterized.

17. EW Jr., discussion, 2004. Further, EW, in postwar letters to Holland from Manilla, October 16 and December 1945, reports his wartime access to the radio's intelligence.

18. Details of EW's interview, including the human contact with the officers: EW Jr., discussion, November 2004.

19. The pre-war legal status of mixed-blood citizens of the Dutch East Indies: De Jong, p. 47.

20. The two scientists who came from Tokyo: In work unknown to EW Jr. when he related this episode, the American historian John Dower makes clear the conviction of Japan's scientific establishment (but not its Army) of the impossibility of building a nuclear weapon prior to the war's end. Japan's top nuclear scientist, Dr. Yoshio Nishina, assigned two much younger and less experienced scientists, Takeuchi Tadashi and Kigoshi Kunihiko, to the Army-subsidized NI-project for isolating the U-235 uranium isotope, at the Riken, in Tokyo. From roughly June 1943 until March 1944 (note the time frame), the two were largely responsible for the NI-project. Takeuchi expressed "puzzlement concerning his designated lot." J.W. Dower, "Science, Society, and the Japanese Atomic-Bomb Project During World War Two," *Bulletin of Concerned Asian Scholars*, Volume Ten, Number Two, 1978, 41–54.

21. "Dutch camp": Dutch POWs from Java. See "Sendai POW Camp #5-B, Kamaishi," http://mansell.com/pow_resources/camplists/sendai/Sendai_5_Kamaishi/sendai_5_main.html, accessed May 2, 2024.
22. *Ibid*. POWs at this camp provided labor for the same steel blast furnaces that the Ohashi camp supplied with iron ore. "Nippon Steel, known today as Shin-Nittetsu Sumikin (Nippon Steel and Sumitomo Metal)" ran the operation.
23. "… the assurances of one officer in particular": EW Jr., discussion, November 2004.
24. Dutch First Lieutenant (MC) George Pijma (or Pyma, in camp records).
25. Dutch Sergeant Hugo Mathieu Henri de Vogel. List of Liberated POWs.
26. The wind, Bolt's beating, and the shuffling of personnel: Reynolds, Diary, January 4, 1944, and December 18 and November 29, 1943, respectively. The exact numbers of those "shuffled": Kamaishi Mine POW Camp Report.
27. Private Jacobus H. Hilling died on January 7, 1944, of acute pneumonia. List of Deceased POWs.
28. Reynolds, Diary, December 18, 1943: "The Nips [sic] have tried to work in a spy on us. No. 549 in the new bunch is it … He's a Dutchman but he was run in on this bunch … He don't [sic] even know anything about Java."
29. Quotations regarding "Wingy's" gift: Kelley, UNT0565, 119, and Reynolds, Diary, December 24, 1943.
30. Reynolds, Diary, January 2, 1944.

Chapter 9

1. Reynolds, Diary, January 26, 1944. Grant is Larry Sherman Grant, U.S. Navy Petty Officer, 3cl. I've found no other Ohashi POW accounts that mention the directive. Highly unusual, it was issued in at least some camps under Hakodate's jurisdiction in January 1944 (as the Ohashi camp was). Captain P.C.F. Meys, in a camp on Hokkaido, January 31, 1944, documents a request to write about experiences during the war prior to being taken prisoner: "My impression is that [the request for] these stories came [. . .] from an order from higher hands." NIOD collection no. 401, diary no. 216, Trans. Niels Lindeijer.
2. Gribnau, Dialogue, December 16, 1942. Copy, collection of Eloy W. Lindeijer. Trans. Herman Lindeyer.
3. "Your impression of this War" vs. "The impression of this War": the discrepancy occurs in the English translation that I received from the Lindeijer family, I maintain it in support of their belief that it reflects the manner in which Gribnau and his friend Lindeijer understood the assigned topics.
4. EW's reports, on the battle of Bandung and the transport, are included herein, in Chapters 1 and 3, respectively.
5. Reynolds, Diary, January 26, 1944.
6. The original copy of EW's submission, collection of Eloy W. Lindeijer, shows the annotations.
7. A copy of Iwashita's original letter and Gribnau's English response, given to EW Jr. by Gribnau's family, is in my possession. Interestingly, per EW, 1 March '43, "German doesn't interest [Iwashita] at all." The liaison might have been versed in German, and thus able to translate Gribnau's submission, despite not wishing to pursue the language further. It's perhaps more likely that in the interval between 16 December and 22 February '43, he found someone to translate it for him.
8. The American Jess Stanbrough reports a statement by Iwashita underscoring the latter's independent thought. "If they [Japanese military authorities] could read my thoughts, I would be executed." Stanbrough, UNT OH0658, 207.
9. Reynolds, Diary, February 29, January 21, 1944, and March 2, respectively.
10. Departures (on 20 February 1944): Groeneveld, Report, 1; Reynolds, Diary, February 20, 1944. EW forgets to count U.S. Naval officer Dr. Eppley (Jr. Ltn. NMC), who remains at the Ohashi camp. List of Liberated POWs.
11. Groeneveld, Report, 4.
12. Reynolds, Diary, January 7, 1944.
13. Iwashita's letter, "To Gribnau," dated 22 February 1943.
14. Gribnau's response is undated, but presumably followed in short order.
15. A bibliographical reference on 10 February 1944 indicates EW's awareness, at a minimum, of the subject matter of this volume and possible reading of it.

16. De Jong, *The Collapse of a Colonial Society*, 348, documents the origins of this particular group.

17. Reynolds, Diary, March 5 and 8, 1944.

18. Reynolds, Diary, March 12, 1944.

19. Tojo's speech and "holding Nippon up": Reynolds, Diary, March 13 and January 17, 1944, respectively.

20. Frank Desmond Planton, RAF Leading Aircraftman. Planton, discussion with me, October 22, 2010.

21. "Made in Japan," "These people," and "My God": Reynolds, Diary, March 3, January 24, and March 13, 1944, respectively.

22. Planton, email message to me, December 14, 2009. The few armed soldiers not yet drafted conducted the inspections.

23. Planton, email message to me, December 14, 2009.

24. Reynolds, Diary, March 24 and 25, 1944.

25. Reynolds, Diary, March 27, 1944.

26. Reynolds, Diary, March 31, 1944.

27. Kamaishi Mine POW Camp Report, 1. Reynolds, Diary, April 22, 1944.

28. Reynolds, Diary, April 23 and 28, and May 2, 1944. KNIL Cpl. Dullois Dias. KNIL Sdt.lkl Johannes Fredrik Van Room. Becker is either KNIL Sdt.lkl Frederick Napoleon Becker or Gustaaf Adolf Becker.

29. Reynolds, Diary, 29 April 1944.

30. EW, Diary, 30 September 1942.

31. Gribnau *Overzicht* (Overview), 4. Copy, Collection of Eloy W. Lindeijer, Trans. Herman Lindeyer.

32. Stewart, letter to me, 30 June 2007: "We had three jugs of acid there [in the electric repair shop]. I knew they were hydrochloric, nitric, and sulphuric but the jugs were not labeled. I asked Lindy how to identify [them]."

33. "ashita testo": The transliteration of the Japanese should be "ashita tesuto."

34. Feliz (discussion, 2007) and Stewart (telephone conversation with me, April 2, 2010) place the Americans on the end of the barracks nearest the camp's front gates. They place Americans Jerry Bunch and Jess Stanbrough on the top tier of the row of bunks nearest the parade ground, next to the wall facing the front gates. Reynolds, Diary, January 2, 1945, has "Lindy" only "three bunks other side of me," and on September 3, 1945, locates himself (and Lindy) near "Stanbrough and Jerry's radio about 5 foot away."

35. Location of groups in the barracks: Stewart, telephone conversation, April 2, 2010; Planton, discussion, October 22, 2010; Planton, email message to me, February 13, 2011. Total number of prisoners by nationality: Kamaishi Mine POW Camp Report (original number of prisoners, and transfers in and out by date); Name List Sendai P.O.W. Camp 4-B; Sendai 4-B List of POWs Transferred (by name and nationality), NACP, RG 331, SCAP Area Case Files, 1945–48, UD 1189, Box 959, Folder SE-5, Vol. 4, Miscellaneous; Groeneveld, Report.

36. The "black Dutch": Stanbrough, UNT OH0658, 173, 190. Concern about informers: Stewart, UNT OH0544, 92. Gribnau's translation of fifth column material: Note entitled *Voorval* (Occurrence). Copy, Collection of Eloy W. Lindeijer, Trans. Herman Lindeyer. Gribnau, Overview, 4.

37. Stewart, telephone conversation, April 2, 2010.

38. Fifteen more months, new area commander, and Iwashita quotation: Reynolds, Diary, May 6, 10, and 16, 1944.

39. Hans Fallada's novel wraps the history and politics of Germany between the world wars around the story of a young couple trying to raise a family and survive the Depression, providing insight into how Hitler gained power.

40. Planton, discussion, October 22, 2010.

41. Reynolds, Diary, May 22, 1943.

42. Reynolds, Diary, May 19, 1944, records leaving the hospital.

43. The references to an "American end" of the barracks near the camp's front gate, along with a total of forty-seven in the "American group," suggest that twelve members of this group were accommodated on the top tier of bunks on the side of the barracks farthest from the parade ground, and twelve more immediately below them. Per Bill Stewart, eleven members of the American group (including Jerry Bunch, Jess Stanbrough, Reynolds, Stewart, and seven others) were accommodated on the top tier of bunks on the side nearest to the parade ground, with EW as the twelfth man, positioned between them

Notes—Chapter 10

and the Dutch middle section. Below the American top tier on this side, there would have been a dozen more of the "American group," making a total of forty-seven in all.

44. Stewart, UNT OH0544, 113, reports four mine levels, at 350, 500, 550, and 800 meters.

45. Kent is Arnold Watson Kent, RAF, 1cl.Act. List of Liberated POWs.

46. Reynolds, Diary, May 24, 1944.

47. Letter, Nel to EW, dated February 1943. Collection of Eloy W. Lindeijer, Trans. Herman Lindeyer.

48. Planton, discussion, October 22, 2010.

49. Feliz, discussion, February 18-19, 2007.

Chapter 10

1. Stanbrough, UNT OH0658, 156; Feliz, discussion, February 18-19, 2007.

2. Jerry Judson Bunch, Jr., U.S. Navy 2cl.Pet.Ofr. Both Bunch and Jess Stanbrough, U.S. Army T/Sgt, had extensive radio expertise. Per Feliz, *The Saga of Sailor Jack*, 60: It was Bunch who took responsibility for maintenance of the set in the barracks and the risky role of smuggling in parts from the radio area of the camp's electrical workshop. Stewart, UNT0544, 141, calls Bunch "our radio man."

3. Feliz, discussion, February 18-19, 2007; multiple other eyewitness accounts.

4. Stewart, telephone conversation with me, April 8, 2014.

5. The dissemination of news: Feliz, discussion, February 18-19, 2007.

6. Reynolds, Diary, June 8 and 10, 1944.

7. Obvious from the original page for this entry in the diary.

8. Reynolds records concerns about his diary being found on May 10, 13, and 22, 1944.

9. John T. Correll, "The Matterhorn Missions," *Air Force Magazine*. March 2009, 62-65, http://www.airforcemag.com/MagazineArchive/Pages/2009/March%202009/0309matterhorn.aspx, accessed May 2, 2024. While the missions were not highly successful, that of June 15, 1944, resulted in a direct hit on the Imperial Iron and Steel Works at Yawata on Kyushu.

10. Reynolds, Diary, June 17, 1944.

11. Stanbrough, UNT OH0658, 164-165.

12. Stanbrough, UNT OH 0658, 164. Feliz, discussion, February 18-19, 2007.

13. Reynolds, Diary, June 2, 1944.

14. Feliz, discussion, February 18-19, 2007. Reynolds, Diary, May 1 and June 20, 1944.

15. Reynolds, Diary, May 30, 1944.

16. Stewart, UNT OH0544, 136-137.

17. Reynolds, Diary, July 12, 1944.

18. Reynolds, Diary, August 2, 1944

19. Kelley, UNT OH0565, 108. The story may be apocryphal, based on an incident in which the battery was removed from the radio and brought under the motorcycle seat to the electrical workshop for refurbishing, then returned to the barracks in the same manner. Stanbrough, UNT OH0658, 156.

20. Stanbrough, UNT OH0658, 168.

21. EW's new hiding place for the letter-diary confounded me until Stewart (telephone conversation, 4 July 2012), told of this area that was not concrete.

22. Stewart, UNT OH0544, 119.

23. Sublieutenant Kawabe Osayasu, Ohashi camp commandant, 28 July 1944-27 April 1945. Kamaishi Mine POW Camp Report, 1.

24. Reynolds, Diary, July 28, 1944.

25. Reynolds, Diary, August 11, 1944, the bashing; August 10 and 18, 1944, searches.

26. Reynolds, Diary, September 10 and 21, 1944.

27. Operation Market Garden, September 17-25, 1944.

28. Per the Lindeijer family: In Dutch, pejorative for Germans, popularly understood as an abbreviation for *Menschen ohne Freunde*, or "people without friends," in context of German World War II occupation of the Netherlands.

29. Stewart, letter to me, June 30, 2007. Unlike the diary, EW's great body of technical work was not prohibited so long as it did not interfere with camp duties, and thus did not need to be concealed.

30. Horne, July 8, 2011, email; Edmonds, January 18, 2008 email; EW Jr., discussion, 2004.

31. Stewart, letter to me, June 30, 2007.

32. Roughly three lines of the 9 November '44 entry (Diary, page 81) were removed,

perhaps after the war, for personal reasons. The material remaining on the reverse (page 82), is an innocuous segment about firewood from the 11 December '44 entry. A large X has been struck through it, as though EW thought of removing it then changed his mind, likely because it is part of his record of a single day in the *Denki*, which continues on page 83.

33. Personal History of Iwashita, Hiroe, 3. Iwashita, diary entries, 8 and 9 February 1945.
34. Stanbrough, UNT OH0658, 164. Feliz, discussion, February 18–19, 2007.
35. Stanbrough, UNT OH0658, 207. Donald Keene, in *So Lovely a Country Will Never Perish* (New York: Columbia University Press, 2010), provides examples of World War II Japanese diarists who feared that liberal views they recorded would come to the attention of the military police.
36. Iwashita diary entries, 1 January '45, and 8 and 9 February '45. I have copies of thirteen of Iwashita's entries for the first four months of 1945. Merely from these, five indicate conversation at the *Denki*, some detailed.
37. William J. Stewart, telephone conversation with me, July 4, 2012, provided details for this paragraph.
38. *Ibid.*
39. Feliz, *The Saga of Sailor Jack*, 59–61.
40. Iwashita Camp Notebook, Collection of Australian citizen David Peck, son of British POW in Ohashi, RAF Pcl. Act. Richard Edgar Francis Peck. Trans. Yoshiko Tamura, POW Research Network Japan, copy in my possession.
41. Personal History of Iwashita, Hiroe, 3.
42. December 29, 1944 details in this paragraph: Reynolds' entry on this date.
43. Reynolds, Diary, January 6, 1945.
44. Iwashita, Diary, 30 January 1945.
45. Reynolds, Diary, January 31, 1945.
46. Iwashita, Diary, 30 January '45 and 8 February '45, respectively.
47. Iwashita, Diary, 9 and 19 February 1945. Later on the ninth, Iwashita had the Larousse dictionary returned to him, but not for Lindeijer's use.
48. Iwashita, Diary, 2 March '45.
49. Attitudes of Japanese in this paragraph: Reynolds, Diary, February 19 and 22; March 3, 7, and 9, 1945.
50. Reynolds, Diary, March 31, 1945.
51. Statement, James D. Early, Chief Water Tender, U.S. Navy, NACP, RG 153, JAG War Crimes Branch Case Files, 1944–49, A1 143, Box 603, Trial 33–164, 3.
52. Reynolds, Diary, April 1, 1945. The massive March 9–10, 1945 firebombings of Tokyo, which killed 100,000 people, with good reason would have greatly disturbed Japanese camp personnel.
53. Personal History of Iwashita, Hiroe, 3. While the latter document lists 15 April as the date of transfer, Iwashita's diary records this as 17 April 1945.

Chapter 11

1. Reynolds, Diary, March 27, 1945.
2. The Battle of Okinawa began on April 1, 1945.
3. Stanbrough, UNT OH0658, 155.
4. Stewart, telephone conversation, January 24, 2013.
5. Reynolds, Diary, "damn slim" and primarily barley: April 28 and 30, 1945, respectively.
6. Lieutenant Yoshida Zenkichi became commandant on 28 April '45. The Ohashi camp became Sendai Camp 4B on 8 April '45. Kamaishi Mine POW Camp Report, 1. Early concerns about Yoshida: Reynolds, Diary, April 30, 1945.
7. Reynolds, Diary, April 24, 1945.
8. Reynolds, Diary, April 29, 1945. Fyvie, a Scot, was nonetheless known by the Irish-sounding sobriquet "Paddy," in the camp. Reynolds refers to Fyvie as "Patty [*sic*]," in recording this episode.
9. Reynolds, Diary, May 4, 1945.
10. Stewart, UNT OH0544, 127. The quotation is from Stanbrough, UNT OH0658, 174.
11. George S. MacDonell, retired Deputy Minister in the government of Ontario, in discussion with me, Canadian Veterans' Day, November 2007. Also, George S. MacDonnell, *One Soldier's Story, 1939–1945: From the Fall of Hong Kong to the Defeat of Japan* (Toronto: The Dundurn Group, 2002), 44–45 ("magnificence" of his men), 115–117 (his enlisted men's sabotage act).
12. EW Jr., discussion, November 2004.
13. Reynolds, Diary, March 8, 1945.
14. Reynolds, Diary, May 10, 1945.

Notes—Chapter 11

15. The bashings: U.S. Navy Fireman First Class Charles W. Lohrig and British Army Gunner Amos Vernon, per Reynolds, Diary, May 11, 1945; Frank Desmond Planton, former RAF Leading Aircraftman, per discussion with me, October 22, 2010; Jimmy Garbutt, per Reynolds, Diary, May 12, 1945.
16. Reynolds, Diary, May 21, 1945.
17. Planton, discussion, 22 October 2010, Norfolk, UK.
18. Reynolds, Diary, May 24, 1945.
19. Reynolds, Diary, June 1, 1945.
20. Yoshida's counsel vs. the angry guards: Reynolds, Diary, June 10, 1945.
21. Reynolds, June 12, 1945. The word "radio" has been added in ink over the word "wheel."
22. Kuto stopping in; Sirno and Monk called up: Reynolds, Diary, June 21 and 23, 1945, respectively.
23. Air raid alarms, "a big fire," and the music program: Reynolds, Diary, June 27, 29, and 30, 1945, respectively.
24. Likely, Canadian Army Privates James Elmer McKnight, Gerald Ernest McKnight, and Melville G. McKnight. List of Liberated POWs. Reynolds first mentions the three Canadian brothers and their instruments (coronet, saxophone, "and something else") on April 30, 1945.
25. Reynolds, Diary, July 2, 1945.
26. The Ohashi camp's jurisdiction and nomenclature: initially Hakodate 2, then Tokyo 6, and by now Sendai 4B.
27. Details for July 6–12: Reynolds' entries during those dates. Quotations about fleas, his July 1, 1945 entry.
28. Kelley, UNT OH0565, 126 ff.
29. MacDonnell, *One Soldier's Story*, 120
30. EW, December 1945 letter to his brothers and sisters in Holland, trans. Herman Lindeyer.
31. Reynolds, Diary July 22 and 28, 1945.
32. Reynolds, Diary, July 16 ("Homeless people all over the roads."), July 22 (the rice crop), and July 28 (U.S. planes and homeless people), 1945.
33. Feliz, *The Saga of Sailor Jack*, 61.
34. Feliz, *The Saga of Sailor Jack*, 61–62. The search that Reynolds records on 31 July '45 is almost certainly the one Feliz writes about, and that Lindeijer reported to family after the war. It lasted from 7:30 a.m. until 12:15 p.m.
35. Adrie Lindeijer, discussion, 2005: reported by EW after the war.
36. Stanbrough, UNT OH0658, 156.
37. Reynolds, Diary, entries for August 1–8.
38. This second U.S. bombardment was on the same date as the dropping of the second atomic bomb, on Nagasaki.
39. Stanbrough, UNT OH0658, 164. "We had a Dutchman across the way ... he was very, very bright."
40. Steps taken by the camp administration and details of Lindeijer's beating: Perpetuation of Testimony, Basil Bunyard, U.S. Navy, 9 December 1946, NACP, RG 331, SCAP Area Case Files, 1945–48, UD 1189, Box 959, Folder SE-5, Vol. 1 A-F, 4. Reynolds, Diary, August 9, 1945: "The Tiger came rushing up my ladder [to the second tier of bunks] this afternoon, grabbed Lindy, bashed him. Then took him to the office and worked him over."
41. August 10, 1945, details, including quotations: Reynolds' entry on that date.
42. Stanbrough, UNT OH0658, 197.
43. Japan's capitulation took place at 12 Noon Tokyo time on August 15, 1945. The date was August 14, 1945, in the West. Japan's formal surrender ceremony was on September 2, 1945 (as EW notes on that date).
44. Stewart, UNT OH0544, 141.
45. Stewart, UNT OH0544, 142. Kelley, UNT OH0565, 127..
46. Stanbrough, UNT OH0658, 197.
47. Signatures on 15 August: Americans John E. Rich, Jesse W. Stanbrough, and R.L. Coffield; Australian, Albert F. Parker. On 19 August: Australians Lasslett, Hindes, Drabble, and Ward; Indonesian Dutch C. J. Bos.
48. Reynolds, Diary, August 15, 1945.
49. NACP, RG 407, Box 12.
50. Details concerning the victims, including Pijma: Frank J. Grady and Rebecca Dickson, *Surviving the Day: An American POW in Japan* (Annapolis: Naval Institute Press, 1997), 231, 233.
51. Reynolds, August 17, 1945.
52. Frank Planton, RAF, had this experience: http://hyaku-san-juu-ni.blogspot.com/2011/08/23-horror-of-sick-bay-and-end-of-war.html, accessed May 2, 2024.
53. Grady, *Surviving the Day*, claims vs.

Inaki and quotations, 220; postwar affidavit filed, 258.

54. Copies of Van der Hoek's letters are in my possession, provided by the granddaughter of Lieutenant Inaki, Ms. Satoko Kogure, a journalist for *Newsweek* magazine, during a visit to my home, November 2013.

55. Statement, William Keith Edmonds, RAAF Boiler Maker's Assistant, NACP, RG 331, SCAP Area Case Files, 1945–48, U.S. 1189, Box 959, Folder SE-5, Vol. 1, A-F, 3.

56. Stanbrough, UNT OH0658, 189. Grady, *Surviving the Day*, 258, ultimately distanced himself from his accusations: "…Inaki was a man with some good traits … who "was tyrannical because of the chaos of war, not because of genuine evil in him." The Yokohama War Crimes Tribunal found Lt. Inaki innocent of failing to protect the prisoners or to aid them during the bombardment. Yet in what might be seen as "victors' justice," he served eight years' imprisonment for other charges based on affidavits rather than testimony from live witnesses who could be cross-examined. Positive views of the Ohashi POWs or the Dutch POWs in Kamaishi were likely not considered.

Chapter 12

1. Horne quotations in this paragraph: "The Spiral Staircase," 272.
2. Planton quotations in this paragraph: http://hyaku-san-juu-ni.blogspot.com/2011/09/24-supplies-from-skies-and-freedom_09.html, accessed May 2, 2024.
3. Reynolds, August 23, 1945.
4. Planton, http://hyaku-san-juu-ni.blogspot.com/2011/09/24-supplies-from-skies-and-freedom_09.html, accessed May 2, 2024.
5. Quotations in this paragraph: Reynolds, Diary, August 22 and August 20, 1945, respectively.
6. Reynolds, Diary, August 24, 1945.
7. Horne, "The Spiral Staircase," 276.
8. Reynolds, Diary, August 25, 1945.
9. Horne, "The Spiral Staircase," 270.
10. Feliz, UNT OH1373, 177.
11. Reynolds, Diary, August 25, 1945.
12. Horne, "The Spiral Staircase," 270–71.
13. Planton, Email, Oct. 11, 2009, and discussion, October 22, 2010.
14. Reynolds, Diary, August 25, 1945.
15. U.S. Naval Ensign Edward George Pollak. Name List Sendai P.O.W. Camp 4-B.
16. Personal History of Iwashita, Hiroe, 3.
17. Iwashita, Diary, 26.8 [1945].
18. Planton, discussion, October 22, 2010.
19. Iwashita, Diary, 26.8 [1945].
20. *Ibid*. Visiting Americans: Edwin W. Tucker, 1st Lt., MC; Jesse Hedrick Stanbrough, Jr., T/Sgt., 131st FA; and Wesley Wilburn Rockett, Sgt., 131st FA. Visiting British RAF personnel: Percy George Cooper, A.C.2; Norman Rothin, A.C.2; and Richard Edgar Francis Peck, A.C.2. Visiting Indonesian Dutch KNIL personnel: Dullois Napoleon Alijons Petes, CPL; and Johan Edward Wilhel Camerik, SDT2Kl.
21. Iwashita, Diary, 17.8 [1945].
22. Reynolds, Diary, August 27, 1945.
23. MacDonell, *One Soldier's Story*, 139. Feliz, UNT OH1373, 177.
24. Feliz, *The Saga of Sailor Jack*, 68.
25. Kelley, UNT OH0565, 142.
26. Stewart, UNT OH0544, 138.
27. Feliz, *The Saga of Sailor Jack*, 68.
28. Horne, "The Spiral Staircase," 276.
29. Iwashita taking photos: Feliz, discussion, February 18–19, 2007; Reynolds, Diary, August 29, 1945; Stanbrough, UNT OH0658, 207, and Iwashita's Personal History, 3. Iwashita's notebook, copy in my possession, clearly records the number of orders beside each photo.
30. The 30 August entry is squeezed to the right of Jack Feliz's name and address.
31. Reynolds, Diary, August 29, 1945.
32. Quotations: Feliz, *The Saga of Sailor Jack*, 69.
33. Reynolds, Diary, August 31, 1945.
34. Horne, "The Spiral Staircase," 274–75.
35. Lt. Commander Edward V. Dockweiler. Lack of leadership: Reynolds, September 6–9, 1945. MacDonnell, *One Soldier's Story, 117–119*, doesn't name the officer who shuns involvement, though it's clear to whom he refers.
36. Reynolds, Diary, August 31, 1945.
37. Signatures of Americans 1st Lt. Maxwell Humble and Cpl. Millard Ellsworth Godfrey, both of the 131st FA.

Notes—Part II, Chapter 13

38. Reynolds, August 31 and September 1, 1945, respectively.

39. Connection of the radio to a loudspeaker in the barracks: EW, letter from Manila to Holland, 16 October '45. Reynolds, Diary, September 1, 1945. Whether Iwashita arranged this, or the prisoners did it themselves isn't clear.

40. The prisoners' distractions: Reynolds, Diary, September 3 and 4, 1945.

41. Feliz, UNT OH1373, 155.

42. Reynolds, Diary, September 4, 1945.

43. Quotations about the officers: Reynolds, Diary, September 5, 1945.

44. *Ibid.*

45. Reynolds, Diary, September 6, 1945.

46. These and additional names and addresses appear between EW's 6 and 8 September 1945 entries.

47. "enough was enough": My way of expressing Feliz's attitude about leaving camp early, UNT OH1373, 149, 179.

48. The quotations and details regarding the early departures: Reynolds, Diary, September 7, 1945.

49. Horne, "The Spiral Staircase," 280ff, records departing with thirteen British. Reynolds, Diary, September 8, 1945, records a Canadian departing with this group.

50. Reynolds' date for the move is September 10, 1945; Grady's memoir, *Surviving the Day*, 248, places it on "8 September [1945]"; and the "Report of Investigation, Sendai No. 5 Internment Camp Situated at Kamaishi," NACP RG 407, Box 12, at least by 13 September 1945. I have used Reynold's date.

51. Burning the Latin lesson: Per EW Jr., the former POWs had been instructed to take so little when leaving the camp that his father had feared even losing his diary.

52. Iwashita details and quotation: Iwashita, Diary, 15. 9 [1945].

53. Iwashita, Camp Notebook, Trans. Yoshiko Tamura. Iwashita could have given it to Richard Peck during the 26 August '45 group visit. Yet Reynolds records Iwashita's taking photographs and orders on 28 August '45. Informed deduction thus suggests its presentation at the station as a gesture of farewell.

54. KNIL Corporal Cornelis Bertsch, KNIL Sdt.Sk1 Emile Samuels, KNIL Sergeant Hugo Lens, Dutch Navy Mtrs. Gustaaf Adolf Van Eldik, KNIL Sergeant William Jacobus Otto Gutenberg, RAF 1.cl.Act Arnold Watson Kent, and RAF 2cl.Act Khay Joo Tan. Name List Sendai P.O.W. Camp 4-B.

55. Stanbrough, UNT OH0658, 202.

Part II

I'm indebted to Herman Lindeyer for his Dutch-to-English translation of the seven letters of his father and four of his Mother Adrie that provide the basis of *Letters of Loss and Renewal*. I've closely paraphrased from these letters and also quoted from them for impact and immediacy.

1. EW ultimately became Director of both the Technology Laboratory of the Dutch National Defense Research Organization and the Applied Scientific Research Organization, joint positions he held until his 1973 retirement. In April 1972, he became an Officer of the Order of Orange-Nassau (i.e., was awarded Knighthood) in recognition of work with the sick as a POW. He died in 1981 of lung cancer from exposure to asbestos. Adrie raised the eight children, served on a Montessori schoolboard, occasionally taught, helped found the International Neighbors Group Delft, and met annually with "her boys," for whom she was housemother in a boys' camp in Java. She too became an Officer of the Order of Orange-Nassau and passed away in 2011 at 94. EW Jr. became a civil engineer; Herman, a landscape architect in Australia; Freddy (Frits), an engineer; and Joke, an employee in traffic safety.

Chapter 13

Unless otherwise indicated, material in the Epilogue is drawn from phone conversations with EW Jr. in 2005 and 2006, and from discussions with him in Hilversum, 2003; Delft, 2004; Northern Virginia, 2005; and Delft, 2006.

1. Wim's pension ultimately came from work on projects in Pakistan, Indonesia, Africa, Jamaica, and India.

2. In 2006, Professor Petra Groen, Netherlands Institute of Military History, helped Wim and me identify the location of the 1945 attacks as the Gumbel (in Dutch, *Goempel*) Pass, south of Semarang, Java.

3. EW Jr., discussions; Herman Lindeyer, telephone call with me, February 11, 2005.
4. EW Jr., discussions; Ada Lindeijer, telephone call, June 7, 2014.
5. Wim's "traumatic affect": Cathy Caruth describes this "sometimes delayed" response to trauma, as "repeated, intrusive hallucinations, dreams, thoughts or behaviors stemming from the event, along with numbing." Cathy Caruth, ed. *Trauma: Explorations in Memory* (Baltimore: The Johns Hopkins University Press, 1995), 4.
6. The doctor himself was unreachable, having moved on to a U.N. project in Africa. Regarding the number killed, Wim's wife, Ada, has said to me firmly, "Well, the point is that this is what the incident was for Wim."
7. The Japanese general wielding a sword; EW Jr., discussion and conversation with multiple other family members.
8. Nel Lindeijer, letter to her husband that she was unable to mail, February 1943. Trans. Herman Lindeyer.
9. My treatment of Wim's story is informed by LaCapra: "When the past becomes accessible to recall in memory, and when language functions to provide some measure of conscious control, critical distance, and perspective, one has begun the arduous process of working over and through trauma." Dominick LaCapra, *Writing History, Writing Trauma* (Baltimore: The Johns Hopkins Press, 2001), 90.
10. Nel's February 1943 letter and EW Jr., discussion.
11. EW Jr., discussion; numerous accounts of the period.
12. EW Jr., discussion; Adrie Lindeijer, discussion with me, November 9, 2004, October 2005.
13. The incident during Wim's management of the Six Cities' Water Supply: EW Jr., discussion with me and others, recorded on video by Hans Lindeijer, November 2006.
14. Growing belief in his father's friendship with Iwashita: E. Wim Lindeijer Jr., "Ohashi Souvenirs," *Representing the Japanese Occupation of Indonesia*, Ed. Remco Raben (Zwolle: Waanders Publishers, and Amsterdam: Netherlands Institute for War Documentation, 1999), 179–180.

15. Informal prior to 1995. Reggy Moltzer, "Interview with Wim Lindeijer," *Society for Children of the Japanese Occupation and the Bersiap 1941–1949*, Kawatberichten, 1997, 11–14, trans. Dutch to English, Dame Elisabeth H. Foppen. Michael Henderson, "Forgiveness Out of Suffering," *For a Change*, Vol. 16, No. 1. February 1, 2003.
16. *Stichting Japanse Ereschulden* (JES), a non-governmental organization organized in 1990, whose protests began in 1992 (late partly as a result of delayed recognition in the Netherlands of the suffering of Dutch in the Indies). The U.S. had persuaded the Netherlands to sign the 1951 Treaty of Peace, which eliminated most reparations, clouding the issue of Japanese responsibility. https://www.nytimes.com/2001/09/04/opinion/recovering-japan-s-wartime-past-and-ours.html, accessed July 26, 2020, also https://www.awf.or.jp/e3/netherlands-00.html, accessed May 2, 2024.
17. EW Jr. described the dream, to my (then) embarrassment, during a meeting in Amsterdam with eminent Dutch-East Asian scholar Professor J.L. Blussé van Oud Alblas, in November 2004. By 2006 I recognized the insight it offered into his traumatic affect.
18. EW Jr., telephone conversation with me, June 9, 2006, with simultaneous reference to the map of Muntilan camp. See *Japanse Burger Kampen* (Japanese Civilian Camps), "Moentilan, Central Java," https://www.japanseburgerkampen.nl/Plattegrond%20Moentilan.htm, accessed February 4, 2019. Also see https://files.archieven.nl/963/f/kampen/hjlegemaatemoentilan01.jpg, accessed May 2, 2024.
19. "Patience and Bluff: de bevrijding van de Nederlandse burgergeïnterneerden op Midden-Java (augustus-december 1945)," *Mededelingen van de Sectie Militaire Geschiedenis van de Landmachtstaf ns 8 (1985)*: 91–154; in English, "Patience and Bluff, the liberation of the Dutch civilian internees in Central Java (August-December 1945)." *Announcements Military History Section, VII (1985)*. The events in Groen's account are commented upon in English, in Siong, Han Bing. "The Secret of Major Kido: The Battle of Semarang, 15–19 October 1945." *Bijdragen tot*

de taal-, land- en volkenkunde. Leiden: KITLV Press. ISSN: 0006-2294. Issue: No.3 vol 152 1996. Volume number: 152. 382–428. Siong resided in Semarang when these events took place.

20. EW Jr., discussion, Hilversum, 2003. Tears streamed down Wim's face as he told me of his recognition.

21. Doris Schattschneider, *M.C. Escher: Visions of Symmetry* (New York: Abrams, 2004), quoting Escher, 15.

22. Escher's *Ascending and Descending*: https://en.wikipedia.org/wiki/Ascending_and_Descending, accessed May 2, 2024.

Chapter 14

1. In Dutch, *Ex-Krijgsgevangenen en Nabestaanden Japan*.

2. Asami Nagai, *Daily Yomiuri* Staff Writer, "Making peace with the past," Copyright *Yomiuri Shimbun* 2000, http://www.mansell.com/pow_resources/camplists/fukuoka/fuk_01_fukuoka/fukuoka_01/DY000729.htm, accessed February 5, 2019 and May 2, 2024.

3. Kurokawa efforts, addition of names and acknowledgment: "Mizumaki Town Social Section—Timeline of EKNJ, memorial visits, etc.," document via email from Ralph Schriock, American city employee, July 18, 2014.

4. Ceremony and weather: EW Jr., letter to Adrie Lindeijer-van der Baan, 30 October 1995. For monument photo, see https://www.nl.emb-japan.go.jp/e/relation/peace_exchange.html, accessed May 2, 2024.

5. Video of the 1995 ceremony, Shoji and Chiai Kurokawa. Copy in my possession.

6. Ralph Schriock, discussion with me in Mizumaki, April 12, 2012.

7. The newspaper name is not included in the copy I have. The date is 6 November 1995.

8. That the video survived, Shoji terms "a miracle." When by accident the cassettes became wet and moldy, he ruefully put them in the trash. Providentially, his wife, Chiai, rescued them and put them in a drawer to dry. Once dry, they proved intact and viable for lending to me at the close of the evening I spent at their home in April 2012.

9. Description based on the reproduction in Schattschneider, *M.C. Escher: Visions of Symmetry*, 258–262.

10. Event photos courtesy of Ms. Hiroko Uchida, a teacher at the school and the event coordinator, during discussion with her and the school's principal, Mr. Takayuki Shibata, 12 April 2012. The mural was out on loan.

11. EW Jr., letter to Adrie, 10 November 1995 (a paragraph he added to Ada's letter to Adrie on that date).

Chapter 15

1. "A Dutch Prisoner and a Staff Member: The Survivors' Heartfelt Meeting," *Yomiuri Shimbun/Kyoto Edition*, 5 November 1996.

2. Ms. Noriko Kato, of Kamaishi, Wim's translator during his 1995 visit, and her friend, Ms. Yukari Abi, of Sendai, had frequent assistance via telephone from Ms. Kato's mother, Mrs. Naoko Kato. Wim's English translation had received significant polish from his revered high school teacher, Dame Elisabeth Foppen.

3. Professor Muraoka had first met with Wim in the late 1990s. Appalled at hearing Wim's story and learning of the wartime suffering that Japan inflicted, he thenceforth embarked on doing whatever he could to spread awareness among its citizens and apologize to its victims. See Takamitsu Muraoka, *My Via Dolorosa: Along the Trails of the Japanese Imperialism in Asia* (Bloomington: Author House, 2016).

4. Misuzu Shobo Publishing Company, Tokyo.

5. Transliterated, in Japanese: *Neru to kodomotachi ni kisu o*.

6. Dialoog Nederland-Japan, now Stichting Dialoog Nederland-Japan-Indonesië (Netherlands-Japan-Indonesia Dialogue Foundation), https://www.dialoognji.org/en/our-organization/, accessed May 2, 2024.

7. *Kahoku Shinpo* (*The Kahoku News*), a major newspaper of the Kamaishi area, 8 July 2000.

8. *Kyoto Shimbun*, 20 August 2000.

9. Mrs. Naoko Kato's description of the impact of Wim's story is from my discussion with her on 22 April 2012.

10. Mr. Morimoto's description of the two-year project and its rationale: in discussion with me, Kamaishi, 22 April 2012. Student classes from three different years were involved, with each student group focused on a slightly different area of research, including the Lindeijer diary and the bombardments of Kamaishi.

11. Play Title: *Furusato o mitsumete* (*Looking at Our Hometown: Step by Step toward a Peaceful* Future), developed by Kamaishi Municiple Second Junior High School students, with the school's Japanese language teacher as playwright. Based on the diary of E.W. Lindeijer Sr., and the U.S. bombardment of Kamaishi. Directed by Mr. Morimoto Shinya. Performance by Yosuke Nasu as Wim Lindeijer Jr., with numerous other student actors. Performed at the school's assembly hall, 23 October 2005, 2 p.m. Footage transferred to a service provider for creation of the video sent to the Netherlands with English subtitles.

12. The Kamaishi International Exchange Association, chaired at the time by Mrs. Naoko Kato, with assistance from Mrs. Takemi Wada.

13. Asami Nagai, *Daily Yomiuri* Staff Writer, "Making peace with the past," copyright *Yomiuri Shimbun* 2000, http://www.mansell.com/pow_resources/camplists/fukuoka/fuk_01_fukuoka/fukuoka_01/DY000729.htm, accessed May 21, 2016 and May 2, 2024.

14. Dialogue NJI Conference 19: See https://www.dialoognji.org/nl/thuis/, "Conferences"; accessed May 2, 2024.

15. A joint research program of the Royal Netherlands Institute of Southeast Asian and Carribean Studies (KITLV), the Netherlands Institute for Military History (NIMH), and the NIOD Institute for War, Holocaust, and Genocide Studies. https://www.niod.nl/en/projects/independence-decolonization-violence-and-war-indonesia-1945-1950

16. Dialogue NJI 23 rd International Conference and Dialogue on Japanese Occupation and Indonesian Revolution, "Forgotten Groups: A Chain of Voices," https://www.dialoognji.org/nl/2022/05/26/23th-international-conference-and-dialogue-sejarah-unairdan-nji-may-2022/, accessed May 2, 2024.

Bibliography

Abbreviations

CHC: Cruiser *Houston* Collection, Special Collections and Archives, University of Houston Libraries, Houston, Texas.
JAG: Judge Advocate General
KITLV: *Koninklijk Instituut voor Taal-, Land- en Volkenkunde* (Royal Netherlands Institute of Southeast Asian and Caribbean Studies), Leiden
KNIL: *Koninklijk Nederlands-Indisch Leger* (Royal Army of the Dutch East Indies)
NACP: National Archives at College Park, Maryland
NIOD: *Nederlands Instituut voor Oorlogs-, Holocaust- en Genocide Studies* (Netherlands Institute for War, Holocaust, and Genocide Studies)
OPMG: Office of the Provost Marshall General, American POW Information Records Branch
RG: Record Group
SCAP: Supreme Commander for the Allied Powers
UNT: Interviews conducted by Dr. Ronald E. Marcello for the Oral History Collection at North Texas State University, Denton, Texas

Official Reports

Investigation Report: Sendai #4 Branch Camp Situated at Ohashi, NACP, RG 407 (A1) 1064, Box 112.
"Kamaishi Mine POW Camp: Its Outline History," Kamaishi Historical Museum, obtained by Lindeijer, Jr., 1995, translated from Japanese into English by Takamitsu Muroaka, Professor Emeritus, Leiden University.
Report about the Prisoner of War Camp Ohasi (Hakodate II) covering the period from 30th November 1942 to 20th February 1944, by Reserve 1st Lieutenant J. M. van Well Groeneveld, NACP, RG 331,
Report Concerning Transport of Allied Prisoners-of-war from Singapore to Japan in November 1942, by Reserve Captain P.C.F. Meys, NACP, RG 331, SCAP Area Case Files, 1945–48, UD 1189, Box 985, Tr-4, Miscellaneous; NIOD IC 1095–1089.
Report of Investigation: Sendai No. 5 Internment Camp Situated at Kamaishi, by Captain R. Todhunter and 2nd Lieutenant John N. Kocher, NACP, RG 407 (A1) 1064, Box 112.
SCAP Area Case Files, 1945–48, UD 1189, Box 959, Folder SE-5, Vol. 4, Miscellaneous (Ohashi No.4 Investigative Reports, Sendai 4-B).
Sendai 4-B List of Deceased POWs, NACP, RG 331, SCAP Area Case Files, 1945–48, UD 1189, Box 959, Folder Se-5, Vol. 4 Miscellaneous (Ohasi No. 4 Investigation Reports, Sendai 4-B).
Sendai 4-B List of Liberated POWs, NACP, RG 331, SCAP Area Case Files, UD 1189, Box 959.
Sendai 4-B Name List, NACP, RG 389, OPMG, A1 460A, Box 2131, American POW

Information Bureau Records Branch, General Subject File, 1942–46, Camps: Japan—Sendai Group, Folder "Sendai POW Camp Name List, 1 of 2."
Tofuku Maru Ship Case, NACP, RG 331, SCAP Area Case Files, 1945–48, UD 1189, Box 985, Tr-4, Miscellaneous.

Unpublished Eyewitness Accounts

Feliz, Jack Martin, UNT OH1373.
Gribnau, Ir. Wilhelmus George "Wim." Dialogue (questions posed in German by camp administration and Gribnau's answers in English), 16 December 1941, copy given by Gribnau's children to the Lindeijer family.
———. Diary (Dutch), June 1942, Java—May 1943, Ohashi, Japan, copy given by Gribnau's children to the Lindeijer family, translated into English by Herman Lindeyer.
Horne, Kenneth E. "The Spiral Staircase: The Autobiography of a Japanese Prisoner of War," copyright 1992, Kenneth E. Horne, copy in author's possession.
Iwashita, Hiroe, Camp Notebook. Trans. Yoshiko Tamura. Collection of Australian citizen David Peck, copy in my possession.
———. Diary (selected excerpts, January '42—September '45).
———. Personal History of Iwashita, Hiroe, NACP, RG 331, SCAP Area Case Files, 1945–48, UD 1189, Box 959, Folder Se-5, Vol. 4 Miscellaneous (Ohasi No. 4 Investigation Reports, Sendai 4-B).
———. "To Gribnau," letter handwritten in English, 22 February 1943, copy given by Gribnau's children to the Lindeijer family.
Kelley, Ben, UNT OH0565.
Lindeijer, Evert Willem, Sr., Diary. Trans. Herman Lindeijer and Dame Elisabeth Foppen, Order of Orange Nassau. Ed. Melinda Barnhardt. 15 May 1942–17 September 1945. Collection Eloy W. Lindeijer.
Meys, Captain P.C.F., Diary (Dutch), NIOD IC diaries, nrs. 216–217.
Meys, Captain P.C.F., Drawing (*Tofuku Maru* ship holds), NIOD IC 80900.
Reynolds, Red (James E.), Diary, March 1, 1942—September 15, 1945. CHC, Special Collections and Archives, University of Houston Libraries, Houston, Texas.
Stanbrough, Jess, UNT OH0658.
Stewart, William J., UNT OH0544.

Books

Burki, Charles. *Achter De Kawat: Legernummer 9409 (Behind the Wire: Charles Burki, Prisoner Number 9409)*. Amsterdam: Uitgeverij XTRA, 2010.
Caruth, Cathy, ed. *Trauma: Explorations in Memory*. Baltimore: Johns Hopkins University Press, 1995.
Dower, John. *War Without Mercy: Race and Power in the Pacific War*. New York: Pantheon Books, 1986.
De Jong, Louis. *The Collapse of a Colonial Society: The Dutch in Indonesia During the Second World War*. Published under the auspices of the Netherlands Institute for War Documentation (NIOD) and the Royal Netherlands Institute of Southeast Asian and Caribbean Studies (KITLV), KITLV Press: Leiden, 2002. The title cited is volume 11B of Louis de Jong's twenty-seven volume comprehensive history of the Dutch in WWII, commissioned by the Dutch Ministry of Education and Science. In his introduction to this volume (pp. 1–46), Dr. Jeroen Kemperman, NIOD, states that "De Jong's Magnum Opus Has Become the Standard Work," read both by historians and a broad public. "The Average Print Run for Each Volume Was 75,000 Copies."
Feliz, Jack M. *The Saga of Sailor Jack*. Lincoln, Nebraska: IUniverse, 2001.
Grady, Frank J. and Rebecca Dickson, *Surviving the Day: An American POW in Japan*. Annapolis: Naval Institute Press, 1997.

Bibliography

Hofstadter, Douglas R. *Gödel, Escher, Bach: An Eternal Golden Braid*. New York: Vintage Books, 1980.
Hornfischer, James D. *Ship of Ghosts: The Story of the U.S.S. Houston, F.D.R.'s Lost Cruiser, and the Epic Saga of Her Survivors*, Bantam Books, New York: 2006.
La Capra, Dominick. *Writing History, Writing Trauma*. Baltimore: Johns Hopkins University Press, 2001.
MacDonell, George S. *One Soldier's Story, 1939-1945: From the Fall of Hong Kong to the Defeat of Japan*. Toronto: The Dundurn Group, 2002.
Michno, Gregory F. *Death on the Hellships: Prisoners at Sea in the Pacific War*. Annapolis: Naval Institute Press, 2001.
Raben, Remco, Ed. *Representing the Japanese Occupation of Indonesia*. Zwolle: Waanders Publishers and Amsterdam: Netherlands Institute for War Documentation, 1999.
Remmelink, Willem, ed. *The Invasion of the Dutch East Indies: Compiled by the War History Office of the National Defense College of Japan*. Leiden: The Corts Foundation/ Leiden University Press, 2015.
Scalia, Joseph Mark. *Germany's Last Mission to Japan: The Failed Voyage of U-234*, Naval Institute Press, 2000.
Schattschneider, Doris. *M.C. Escher: Visions of Symmetry*. New York: Harry N. Abrams Inc., 2004.

Pamphlets

Groen, Petra. *Patience and Bluff: De Bevrijding Van De Nederlandse Burgergeïnterneerden Op Midden-Java (augustus-december 1945)*. Mededelingen Van De Sectie Militaire Geschiedenis Van De Landmachtstaf Ns 8 (1985): 91–154. In English, the title and bibliographical information are *Patience and Bluff, the Liberation of the Dutch Civilian Internees in Central Java (August- December 1945), Notices Military History Section VII (1985)*.

Articles

Dower, J.W. "Science, Society, and the Japanese Atomic-Bomb Project During World War Two," *Bulletin of Concerned Asian Scholars* vol. 10, no. 2, 1978, pp. 41–54.
Siong, Han Bing. "The Secret of Major Kido: The Battle of Semarang, 15–19 October 1945." *Bijdragen Tot De Taal_____, Land- En Volkenkunde* vol. 152, no. 3, 1996, pp. 382–428. Leiden: KITLV Press.

Documentary Film

Gutzeit, Andreas. *Hitler's Last U-Boat*, International Historical Films Inc. 2001.

Internet Sites

Dialogue Netherlands-Japan-Indonesia. https://www.dialoognji.org/en/our-organization/. Also see https://www.facebook.com/StichtingDialoogNJI.
Mansell, Roger. Center for Research, Allied POWs under the Japanese, www.mansell.com.
Netherlands Institute for War, Holocaust, and Genocide Studies, *Indisch Kamparchieven* (East Indies Camp Archives), http://www.indischekamparchieven.nl.
Planton, Frank. The memoirs of a Japanese prisoner of the Second World War 1942–1945. http://hyaku-san-juu-ni.blogspot.com.

Index

Abe Kōbō 5
Akihito, Emperor 2
Alderman, Harmon Price, USN RM 54
Aleutian Islands 91, 96
Allan, Samuel, RAF Cpl. 47, 49, 50
Allies 8, 10, 19, 20, 22, 25, 44, 56, 100, 148, 149, 162, 165, 167; advances by 72, 102; air power 98; atomic bombs dropped by 144, 191; B-29 flyovers of Japan by 123, 127, 131; counteroffensive 72, 112; D-Day 4, 123; island hopping 4, 72, 92, 112, 114, 124; Kamaishi bombarded 4, 142, 144, 145; route to the Japanese homeland opened 102; submarine blockade 98; Tokyo bombed 4, 127, 136; *see also* Ohashi Camp; Ohashi Camp Allied POWs
Ambarawa 172, 176, 177
Ambarawa Camp 8 172
the Ambonese 31, 33
"Amicitia vitam ornat" 44, 122, 129, 130, 160
Asahi Shimbun 180
atomic bomb: dropping of 144, 191; Japanese interviews of Lindeijer about 100–103; Japanese scientists vs. military debate about 103; *see also* Dower, John; Kamaishi student play

B-29s 123, 127, 131, 153, 156, 158
Bandung (Bandoeng) 13, 15, 17, 19–21, 23–24, 26–42, 163, 171
Bandung Lyceum 16, 19, 27, 29, 40, 80, 90, 104, 105
Bandung Milk Center, BMC 33–36, 62
Banjobiru Camp 10 172
Barends, Daan, KNIL Sdt. 27, 32, 90
Batavia (Jakarta) 14, 24, 41, 43–44, 56, 65, 72, 163–166
Battle of Ambarawa 176–177
Battle of Kalijati 20, 22, 56, 168, 181
Battle of the Java Sea 20, 47
Bauxite 19, 46, 49
Bei Glodak Prison 43
beriberi 70, 71, 72, 73, 93
Bertsch, Cornelis, KNIL Cpl. 78, 80, 159
Bess, Michael 1

"Bird Legs" 125, 137
black market 77, 80, 113, 128
Blackburn, Arthur, Aust. Brig. Gen. 47
Bogor (Buitenzorg) 20, 56
Bolt, Clarence L., USN SM 1/c 105
Borneo 161, 162, 164
bubonic plague 139
Buitenzorg *see* Bogor
Bunch, Jerry Judson, Jr., USN RM A/C 124; radioman for Hirohito surrender speech 144; risk taken 129, 151; secret radio and 122, 143, 151
Bunyard, Basil C. USN EM/C 213*n*40
Burki, Charles, KNIL Sdt. 29, 30, 37, 38
Burma Railroad 110
Buruma, Ian 2

Camerik, Johan E. W., KNIL Sdt. 1kl 153
Campbell, Edward, AEF Capt. 61, 87
Central Java 15, 32, 35, 64, 163, 167, 169, 171
Changi 44, 117
China 1, 2, 5, 48, 87, 91, 123
Chinese POW camp 140
Chinese POWs 131, 156
Ciater Pass 23
Cihapit internment camp 14, 170, 171, 172, 175, 178
Cimahi 20, 23, 41, 46, 56
Cimahi POW Camp 31, 32, 41, 46, 65
Coffield, Rollin L., USN Ph.M. 1cl 112, 151
colitis 60, 61, 93, 95
"comfort women" 1, 2, 192
Cook, Haruko 2
Cook, Theodore 2
Cooper, Percy George, RAF AC2 151
Corregidor 114
Coughtry, Alfred, RAF AC1 75, 76, 77, 79, 81, 82, 173
Curtis, Franklin Erving, US Army Cpl. 95

D-Day 4, 123
Dago Road 16, 23, 5, 75, 96, 118, 171, 188
dating conventions 14
Delft 168, 179, 187
the "Denki" 116, 118, 125, 127, 128, 131,

223

133, 134, 136, 137, 139, 140, 151, 181, 185; as sanctuary 123, 129, 130; working conditions 116, 126; *see also* Iwashita Hiroe

Depot Battalion 32, 33, 34

de Vogel, Hugo Mathieu H., KNIL Sgt. 105

Dialogue conferences: Netherlands-Japan 189, 190, 191; Netherlands-Japan-Indonesia 193

diarrhea 47, 53, 54, 56, 57, 60, 67, 70, 71, 75, 82, 87, 140,

Dias Dullois, N.A. Petes, KNIL Cpl. 116, 151

diphtheria 53, 54, 61, 62, 64

discrimination 71, 117, 137; *see also* Indonesian Dutch; Iwashita Hiroe; Ohashi Camp Allied POWs

Dockweiler, Edward V., USN Cmdr. 156, 157

Dower, John 1, 208n20

Drabble, Ross, RAAF LAC 94

Dutch East Indies: capitulation 24; Dutch colonial oppression 6, 102, 193; Japanese invasion 20–25; *see also* Indonesia; the Netherlands

dysentery 15, 27, 31, 33, 41, 44, 48, 50, 52, 54, 55, 60, 61, 67, 89, 90

Edmonds, W. Keith, RAAF LAC 127, 146

EKNJ ("Ex-Prisoners of the Japanese and Next of Kin") 179, 180, 181, 182, 184

electrical workshop *see* the "Denki"

Elvy, Stanley, RAF Pvt. 98

Emoto, Ltn. Col. 114, 118

Eppley, James E., USN Jr. Lt. MC 95, 99, 100, 112, 114, 118, 145, 151

Escher, M.C. 168, 177, 183; *Ascending and Descending* 178; *Metamorphose III* 182; perceptual error concerns by 177–178; *The Regular Division of the Plane* 161; *Three Worlds* 162, 177; war trauma of 177

family photograph 10, 13, 16, 27, 35, 42, 59, 66, 75, 80, 81, 84, 102, 138, 154, 161, 173, 181, 188, 190, 192; in Japanese media 188, 189s; smuggling 27, 90; *see also* Kamaishi student play; Lindeijer-van der Baan, Adriana; Lindeijer-Verhulst, Petronella Johanna

Fanghor, Gene, USN Pvt. 61

Feenstra, Klaas, KNIL Pvt. 100, 123

Feliz, Jack Martin, USN MM 1/c 73, 88, 89, 96, 156–157, 159; Bunch, Jerry Judson and 122, 129; Iwashita Hiroe and 92, 121, 124, 128; Japanese language and 71; mistreatment 70, 94; parachute drops and 150, 153, 154; POW leadership 68; Reynolds, James E. and 96–97, 106; secret radio and 122, 100

Foppen, Elisabeth, Dame 13

Formosa (Taiwan) 49, 51, 52, 53, 56, 126

Fujii Sancha 136, 137

Fyvie, Douglas, RAF LAC 124, 125, 137

Garbutt, James, RAF AC2 "Jimmy" 48, 60, 83, 139

Geneva Convention 59, 88

Germany 6, 8, 19, 101, 104, 125, 126, 127, 135, 136, 137, 139

Gilbert Islands 112

Gilkey, Langdon 5

Godfrey, Millard E., US Army Cpl. 111

Gordon, Ernest 7

Grady, Frank, USN Capt. 145, 146

Grant, Larry Sherman, USN PO 3/cl 107, 116, 118, 124

Gribnau, Ir. Wilhelmus George "Wim" 43, 47, 53, 55, 57, 60, 65, 67, 68, 69, 70, 72, 75, 76, 77, 78, 80, 83, 84, 87, 90, 91, 92, 93, 101, 105, 108, 112, 113, 115, 117, 122; family 48; as medic 44, 48; as orderly 37, 59–64, 79, 86, 95, 96, 100, 151; translation for the Japanese by 117, 118; written answers for the Japanese Army 107–108; written dialogue with Iwashita 109–111; *see also* Lindeijer, Evert Willem, Sr.

Groen, Petra 176, 215n2

Groeneveld, J.M., KNIL 1st Lt. 62, 64 68, 72, 78, 99

Guadalcanal 72

Guam 96

Gumbel Pass (Goempel Pass) 176

Gutenberg, W.J. Otto, KNIL Sgt. 159

The Hague (*Den Haag*) 38, 88, 127, 175, 182

Hakatayama, Col. 68, 112, 114

Hakodate 68, 88, 90, 91 93, 99, 106, 111, 114, 115, 122, 145

"Hakodate boys" 90, 91, 95

Hamburg 100, 102

Hatta, Mohammad 161, 152

Hielkema, A., KNIL GNR 26

Hijmans, Vananrody R., KNIL Pvt. 61

Hilling, Jacobus H. KNIL Pvt. 106

Hirohito, Emperor 2, 4, 6, 27, 144, 150, 158, 176

Hiroshima 54, 144, 181, 182

"Hitler" (epithet) 149, 150

Hitler, Adolf 125

Hong Kong 138; Ohashi Camp Canadian POWs and 137–138

"the Honorable Men" (epithet) 94, 106, 113, 125, 126, 136

Honshu 99, 146, 129

Horne, Kenneth E., RAF LAC 127, 148, 149, 150, 154, 155, 157

Hosokawa Morihiro 2

Houston 52, 54, 61, 68, 72, 93, 96, 111, 122, 127, 139; Battle of the Java Sea and 47; Burma Railroad and crewmembers 110; crew given up for lost 74

Hovis, Howard C., US Army Cpl. 72, 75, 76, 79, 80, 90

Humble, Maxwell, US Army Lt. 111, 118, 122, 126, 157, 159

the "Hunger Winter" 137

Index

Ienaga Saburō 2
Inaki Makoto, Sub-Lt. 115, 118, 124, 132, 145–146
Indigenous Javans 96, 196ch1n2
Indo Europeans *see* Indonesian Dutch
Indonesia: declaration of independence 161; Dutch delayed recognition of 6; Dutch postwar violence against 6–7, 193; Pemuda "freedom fighters" 172; war for independence 6–7; *see also* Dialogue Netherlands-Japan-Indonesia; Dutch East Indies; the Netherlands
Indonesian Dutch 31, 32, 46, 47, 59, 65, 68, 74, 76, 78, 80, 87, 90, 98, 100, 102, 116, 124, 151, 157, 159; discrimination against 111, 112; 117, 118, 122; status in Dutch society 65, 80, 102, 111; status in the KNIL 196ch1n2;
internment camps (Java) 158; *see also* Ambarawa Camp 8; Banjobiru Camp 10; Cihapit internment camp; Muntilan internment camp; Solo internment camp; island-hopping *see* Allies
Italy 80, 95, 102, 125
Iwashita Camp Notebook 11, 154, 159
Iwashita Hiroe 7, 14, 75, 76, 77, 80, 96, 99, 100, 102, 107, 112. 120, 128, 131, 136, 144, 152, 154, 156, 159, 160, 174, 177, 180, 182, 184, 187, 191, 193; benign influence of 92, 135; bribes resisted 133; camp photography 84, 85, 92, 116, 131, 154, 159, 180; discrimination concerns 111; fascination with POWs 110, 134, 135; independent thought 103, 110, 118, 124, 129, 132, 159, 184; Kawabe row 132; liaison duties 82; loyalty to country 92, 109–110; novelist aspirations 76, 77, 118, 132; POW repatriation assistance 151; POW support 79, 124, 128; POW visits 77, 110, 116, 124, 129, 133, 156, 159, 160, 174, 177, 180, 182, 184, 187, 191, 193; reprimand and transfer 135; as "Smitty the Spy" 77, 125; *see also* Gribnau, Ir. Wilhelmus George; Iwashita Camp Notebook; Lindeijer, Evert Willem, Jr.; Lindeijer, Evert Willem, Sr.
Iwate Prefecture 58, 189
Iwo Jima 136

Jackson, Harry, RAF LAC 95
Japan: capitulation 144, 145, 158; changing fortunes 3, 4, 15, 94, 98, 99, 112, 123, 132, 136, 140, 142, 144; defeats 72, 102, 114, 124, 127: Dutch East Indies invasion 16, 20–25, 56; Dutch East Indies occupation 30, 34, 41; Southeast Asian aggression 1, 2, 3, 26; surrender 156
Japanese Army: 66, 72, 79, 82, 88, 93, 105, 125, 137, 148, 151, 154, 158; arbitrariness 70; German education of high-level officers 100–101, 102, 107
Japanese language 5, 35, 49, 55, 60, 62, 65, 71, 79, 109, 124, 134, 159
Java: capitulation 24; defense 9, 14, 20–25, 56; *see also* Battle of the Java Sea; internment camps
Juliana *see* Princess Juliana

Kahoku Shinpo 189
Kalijati: airfield 20, 21; Battle of 21–22, 56; *see also* Lindeijer, Evert Willem, Sr.
Kalinowski, Robert John, USN F 1/c 68
Kamaishi Camp 101, 103; bombardments 142, 144; burn victims 145, 149; date established 145; deaths 103, 104, 105, 145, 149; jurisdictions 145; Lindeijer, Evert Willem, Sr. and 101, 103–105, 112; *see also* Ohashi Camp Allied POWs
Kamaishi City: blast furnaces 59, 99, 101; U.S. bombardments 142, 144, 159; *see also* Kamaishi student play; Lindeijer, Evert Willem, Jr.; Lindeijer-van der Baan, Adriana
Kamaishi student play: the family photograph 191; Lindeijer, Evert Willem, Jr. 190–192; Lindeijer, Evert Willem, Sr. 190–191; Lindeijer-Verhulst, Petronella Johanna 191–192; Stenfert, Jürien H. 191
Karssen, H., NL Navy SM 26
Kato Naoko 187, 189–190, Kamaishi International Exchange Association and 218n12
Kato Noriko 217ch15n2
Kawabe Osayasu, Sub-Lt. 126, 132, 135, 159; *see also* Iwashita Hiroe
Kawakatsu, Capt. 28, 35
Kelley, Ben K., US Army Sgt. 106
the *kempeitai* 143, 149
Khyber Pass 167, 169
Kido Shinichirō, Maj. 176, 177
KNIL 20, 23, 116, 162
KNIL 15th Battalion Japanese POW Camp 26–40; atrocity 26; POW educational efforts 28
KNIL 15th Infantry Battalion 20–24
Koreans 59, 83
Kurokawa Chiai 180, 217ch14n5
Kurokawa Hiroshi 179, 180
Kurokawa Shoji 180, 181, 217ch14n5
Kyoto 187, 189
Kyushu 123, 179

Leiden 28, 45, 53, 60, 75, 125, 126, 151, 168
Leiden University 19, 101, 187
Lembang 21. 23, 24, 30, 56
Lens, Hugo, KNIL Sgt. 159
Leuwiliang 24
lice 82, 131, 166
Limpach, Remy 6, 193
Lindeijer, Evert Willem, Jr. "Wim" 16–17, 84–86, 166; breakdown 167; Dialogue conferences and 189; Escher's impact 177–178, 182–184; internment camps 9, 171–172, 175–176; Iwashita Hiroe impact 173, 174, 184, 187; Kamaishi visits 8, 180–181,

185; liberation from internment 169–170; Lindeijer diary impact 168–169, 170, 171, 173–174, 180–181, 182, 184, 187; Lindeijer diary Japanese publication role 187; Kido Shinichirō, Maj., impact 177, 183; marriage and career 167, 173; Mizumaki visit 18, 180, 181–184; mother's influence 7, 8, 172, 177, 185–186; reconciliation efforts 184, 185, 189–190; working through trauma 10, 167–178; *see also* Kamaishi student play

Lindeijer, Evert Willem, Sr. "Wim": camp labor performed by 116, 117; camp teaching 28–32, 40, 41, 72, 79, 90, 94; camp technical work 89, 95, 101, 112, 114, 115, 118, 123, ; credo 86; family concerns 27, 34, 39, 43, 62, 92, 93, 95, 98, 140; Gribnau, Ir. Wilhelmus George and 44, 47–48, 53, 55, 58, 60, 61, 62, 63, 64, 68, 69, 70, 72, 75, 76, 77, 78, 79, 82, 83, 86, 87, 91, 92, 96, 100, 105, 107, 112, 117; illness in captivity 53, 62–63, 70, 71, 75, 82, 87, 140; influence on POW colleagues 93, 117, 127, 132; Iwashita Hiroe and 7, 75, 77, 84, 92, 99, 100, 109, 110, 118, 124, 128, 132, 133, 152, 159; Japanese language and 35, 49, 55, 60, 62, 65; as "Lindy" 1, 6, 7, 13, 17, 19; as medic 9, 20, 21, 24, 41, 44, 48, 50–53, 55, 57, 59, 60–62, 64, 65, 66, 69, 71, 72, 75, 76, 77, 81; mistreatment 56–57, 96, 143; as orderly 83, 84, 86, 87, 90, 93, 95, 96, 100, 103, 104, 105, 106, 110, 114; postwar 167; prewar 19; report on the defense of Java by 20–25; report on the overseas transport by 56–57; Reynolds, James E. and 61, 72, 73, 94, 95, 107, 116, 119, 132; secret radio knowledge 72, 100, 102, 119, 122, 156, 213n35; self-recognition 120, 141; Stenfert, Jürien Hendrick and 44, 47–48, 53, 55, 59, 60, 61–62; van der Baan, Adriana and 162–164, 165–166; working through trauma by 44, 80, 170; *see also* atomic bomb; Kamaishi student play

Lindeijer, Evert Willem, Jr.; Muraoka Takamitsu Lindeijer, Evert-Wim (nephew) 23, 197n15

Lindeijer, Frits "Freddy" 16, 163, 166, 170, 171

Lindeijer, Jan, Dutch Nav. Ch. 16

Lindeijer, Johanna "Joke" 16, 33, 36, 37, 86, 117, 161, 163, 166, 168, 170, 171

Lindeijer, Toon, KNIL SDT 32, 33, 34, 35, 171

Lindeijer diary 3, 9, 13, 139; camp hiding places 59, 119, 125; missing pages 100–103; Japanese media response to 189; Japanese publication 9, 187–188, 189; Kamaishi student play and 10, 190–191; translation into Japanese 187; *see also* Lindeijer-van der Baan, Adriana

Lindeijer-van der Baan, Adriana 184; Delft International Neighbors Group and 187; Dialogue conferences role 189; family photograph and 16, 188; Farewell Letter of Petronella Johanna Lindeijer-Verhulst and 17, 18, 165; internment assistance to Nel 16, 163, 171; Kamaishi visit 183, 187, 190; letters 162–164; Lindeijer diary Japanese publication role 187; marriage to Lindeijer, Evert Willem, Sr. 165–166; Mother Adrie 166, 168; war orphan care by 163; Wim Jr. support by 168, 185

Lindeijer-Verhulst, Petronella Johanna 3, 15, 19, 27, 28, 33, 34, 36, 38–39, 48, 74, 118, 161, 162–163, 170–171; family photo arranged 16; farewell letter 10, 14, 16–18, 165, 187–188; marriage thoughts 120; Mother Nel 166; posthumous impact 188, 189, 192; promises to children 166, 172; remonstrance against hate 7, 8, 172, 177; teeth problems 27, 29; working through trauma 16; *see also* Kamaishi student play

Lindeyer, Herman 13, 16, 29, 32, 33, 34, 36, 41, 42, 48, 58, 62, 67, 93, 95, 104, 110, 133, 163, 165, 166, 170, 171; family documents translated 13

Lohrig, Charles W.W., USN F 1/c 139

London 19, 91, 100

Lutter, Lt, KNIL MC 47, 48, 59

MacArthur, US Gen. Douglas 4, 157
MacDonnell, George S., Can Army WO 138
Manadonese 31, 33
Manchukuo 70
Manila 114, 155
Mariana Islands 112, 127
Marijnen, Mrs. 15, 16, 17, 164, 172, 175, 176
Marinen, Tieneke 15, 172
Marshall Islands 112
Martherus, Rudolph, KNIL Pvt. 64
Meijer, H.F., KNIL Sdt 90
Merapi volcano *see* Mount Merapi
Mercus, J.W., KNIL GNR 26
Merralls, Leslie, RAF L/Cpl. 93
Meys, P.C.F., Dutch Nav Capt. 49, 55, 65
Midway Island 72, 150
Misuzu Shobo 9, 188
Mizumaki 179; Junior High School peace event 182; Monument ceremony 180; *see also* Lindeijer, Evert Willem, Jr.
Moji 54, 59, 61, 123
Morimoto Shinya 190
Morioka 55, 137, 151, 156
Motoshima Hitoshi 2
Mount Merapi 15, 168, 175
Mulder, Alexavith, KNIL SDT 1kl 79, 80
Muntilan internment camp 15, 162, 168, 172, 175, 178
Muraoka, Takamitsu 217ch15n3; Lindeijer diary and 187; *see also* Dialogue conferences
Murayama Tomiichi 2

Naganuma Masaki, Lt. 61, 69, 70, 88, 89, 91, 92, 94, 115, 159
Nagasaki 2, 53, 144

Index

naming conventions 14
Neko Zenzo, Sgt. Maj. MD 62, 79–80, 94, 140
the Netherlands: declaration of war on Japan 19; defense of Java 20–25; Dutch East Indies colonial oppression 6, 102, 193; fall to Germany 19; German food blockade 127; the "Hunger Winter" 137; Indonesia delayed recognition 6; liberation 137; postwar violence against Indonesia 6–7, 193; steps toward acknowledgment of postwar violence 7, 193; *see also* Dutch East Indies; Indonesia
New Georgia 92, 98, 102
New Guinea 72
Nieraeth, Jan N., KNIL SDT 2kl 80
Nippon Kokan Yokohama Shipyard 138
Noble, Austin Black, RAF Pvt. 61

Ogilvie, Rudolph A., KNIL Pvt. 61
Ohashi Camp 82–83, 84; Allied POW officers 59, 64, 87, 111; commandants 61, 115, 126, 137; initial temporary location 58; jurisdictions 115, 137; layout 83; medical staff 55, 59, 60, 61, 62; mine 59, 85; POW accommodations 83; workshops 83; *see also* Ohashi Camp Allied POWs
Ohashi Camp Allied POWs 59, 81, 90, 134; air raid alarms 95, 123, 141, 142; black market activity 77, 113; Christmas observances 63, 104, 106, 130, 131; clothing 54, 56, 62, 69, 82, 108; deaths 60, 61, 62, 93, 95, 106, 108; discrimination 71, 111, 117, 118, 122, 137; diseases 60, 61, 62, 64, 70, 72, 73, 93, 108; educational efforts 72, 73, 79, 89–90, 94; fights 67, 78, 80, 111, 156; "good" camp personnel 71, 91, 92, 106, 113, 115, 125, 159; hardships 62, 68, 69, 81, 82, 87, 88, 98, 142; inspections 55, 59, 68, 71, 93, 114, 124–125, 130, 132, 139, 143; Iwashita Hiroe and 77, 79, 92, 97, 110, 111, 116, 118, 124, 128, 129, 131, 133, 135; Kamaishi POW burn victims treated 145, 146, 149; labor performed 68, 83; mail 109, 130; medical care 60–61, 71, 79–80, 95, 114, 140; minework hazards 83, 87, 88, 93, 119; mistreatment 70, 88, 89, 91, 94, 95, 105, 134, 136, 142, 143; parachute drops 152–153, 154, 155, 156; rations 76; relationships among 87, 116, 131, 137, 151; rumor mill 66, 70, 80, 86, 91, 100, 104, 112, 150; sick parade 71, 73, 78, 79, 89; telegrams 96, 113, 147; transfers 106, 111, 112, 138, 145; *see also* secret radio
Ohashi Camp Japanese personnel: changing attitudes 123, 136, 148–149; impact of war 112–113, 132, 140, 142, 143–144
Ohashi Village 58
Okinawa 136, 140, 153
121 Dago Road 21, 67, 86; *see also* Dago Road
131st Field Artillery, Texas National Guard 24

overseas transport: Allied POW nationalities included 44; conditions 56–57; deaths 51, 57; diseases 54; itinerary 51; Japanese oversight 54; sick care 48, 51, 56; *see also* Lindeijer, Evert Willem, Sr.; *Tofuku Maru*

Padalarang 20
Pakistan 167
parachute drops 149, 152, 158; dangers 153, 156; *see also* Ohashi Camp Allied POWs
Parker, A.F., Aust. Navy L/Wireman 213n47
Pearl Harbor 19, 114
Peck, Richard Edgar Francis, RAF A.C.2 151, 159
Pemuda 172
Perth 47, 74, 110 *see also* Battle of the Java Sea
Pfaff, Gustauf Adolff, KNIL Pvt. 61
the Philippines 4, 114, 124, 127, 143
Pijma, Dr. 104, 105, 142, 145
Planton, Frank Desmond, RAF LAC 113, 139, 148, 149, 150
Plas, Cathrientje 41
pneumonia 53, 54, 56, 60, 61, 62, 64, 103, 104, 108, 189
Pollak, Edward George, USN ENS 151, 157
Poulus, H., KNIL Lt. Col. 26, 28, 32, 35
POW Camp Sendai 4-B *see* Ohashi Camp
POW Camp Sendai 5-B *see* Kamaishi Camp
Price, Fred D., USN SM 1/c 93
Princess Juliana 87, 136
prisoner transfers 32, 33, 91, 106, 111, 112, 138, 145
Prussia 125
Purwakarta 21, 30

Queen Beatrix 6
Queen Wilhelmina 38, 98, 155

racism *see* discrimination
radio workshop (broadband) 124, 129, 132, 140
The Railway Man 3, 5, 195n10
reconciliation 5, 6, 7, 8, 146, 181, 191–193; *see also* Lindeijer, Evert Willem, Jr.; *The Railway Man*; *Unbroken*
Red Cross 4, 13, 23, 41, 44, 62, 64, 75, 95, 113, 115, 116, 117, 125, 126, 132, 161, 162; American Red Cross 90, 112, 113, 130; Red Cross packages 90, 112, 115, 130, 131, 133, 134, 137, 138, 139, 140, 145; Swedish Red Cross 96, 98
Rees, Thomas H., RAF Pvt. 61
Reynolds, James E., USN SM 1/c, "Red": camp illness 72, 93; diary 94, 119; empathy for Japanese 113, 132, 137, 141; Feliz, Jack Martin and 96, 97, 106; Indonesian Dutch friendships 87, 116; report for the Japanese 107, 109; war crimes 94; *see also* Lindeijer, Evert Willem, Sr.
Rich, John E., US Army Pvt. 1cl 80, 111

Index

Riedé, N. Ludwig, KNIL Sgt. 79, 80
Rijnders, Hendrik, KNIL Sdt. 75, 80, 157
Rockett, Wilbur W., US Army Sgt. 151
Rothin, Norman, RAF AC2 214n20
Rotterdam 167
Royal Netherlands East Indies Army (*Koninklijk Netherlands-Indisch Leger* "KNIL") *see* KNIL
Russia 70, 125, 129, 138, 144

Saigon 46, 48, 55
Saipan 124
Samuels, Emile, KNIL Sdt. 2kl 159
Sasaki, Isamu, civ. employee 119, 137
secret radio 72; Bunch, Jerry Judson and 122, 129, 143, 151; distribution of news from 122; Feliz, Jack Martin and 10, 129; hiding place 119, 122, 125, 143; *kempeitai* search 143; Stanbrough, Jess and 122, 143; war information from 4, 72, 92, 98, 100, 102, 110, 141, 144, 150; war's end disclosure 150, 156
Seidel, Alfred Glenn USN Pvt. 61
Semarang 30, 163, 165, 169, 176
Shimonoseki 54, 61
Sicily 94, 98
Silver Cross 13, 41, 116
Singapore: defense 22; fall 20, 22, 47; overseas transport and 44–46, 52, 54, 56, 75, 110, 123
Sinterklaas (feast day) 54, 58, 60, 66, 90, 158, 171
Slotemaker-de Bruine, Christien 16, 17, 165
Solo *see* Surakarta
Solo internment camp 15, 16, 171
Solomon Islands 72, 92
Sparks (US POW) 68
Spitfires 91, 169, 170
Stanbrough, Jesse Hedrick, Jr., US Army T/Sgt.: Bunch, Jerry Judson and 122, 143; Iwashita Hiroe and 92, 124, 128, 151, 156, 159; radio shop and 129; risk taken by 151; secret radio and 122, 143
Stenfert, Jürien H., KNIL Pvt.: death 62, 180; family 48; illness 59, 61; as medic 44, 48; as orderly 60; *see also* Kamaishi student play; Lindeijer, Evert Willem, Sr.
Stewart, William J., USN SM 1 70, 71, 124, 125, 153
Stoddard, George, USN SM 1 100
Stranks, Leslie R., RAF LAC 91
Sukarno 6, 161, 162
Sunda Strait 47, 74
Surabaya 30, 193
Surakarta 15
Swaan, Wim 89

Takahashi Choichiro, Sgt. "the Tiger" 134, 138, 143, 144
Takao 51–52
Tamura, Minoru 192, 193

Tandjong Priok (Tanjung Priok) 44, 51
Tarawa 112
Thurner, Johan, KNIL Sdt. 1kl 80
Tiong Hoa Hwe Koan School 41, 42, 43, 44
Tofuku Maru 43, 44, 50, *Tofuku Maru* ship case summary 210n44, 202n51
Tōjō Hideki, Prime Minister 2, 92, 113, 125
Tokyo: American bombing 127, 134; firebombing 136, 140; Iwashita Hiroe and 77, 79, 84, 128, 152
Toorop, C.G., KNIL Col. 21
trauma 11; Escher and 177–178; Kamaishi Camp and 146; Kamaishi City and 159, 191; Lindeijer, Evert William, Jr., and 167–170, 175, 177–178, Lindeijer, Evert Willem, Sr., and 26, 43, 56–57, 62–63; Lindeijer-Verhulst, Petronella Johanna and 15–16;
Truk Island 114
tuberculosis 93
Tucker, Edwin W., US Army 1st Lt. MC 114, 118, 145, 151, 159
Tullner, Jan 171

Unbroken 3, 5, 7, 195n10
US Air Force 74, 149

van der Baan, Adriana "Adrie" *see* Adriana Lindeijer-van der Baan
van der Baan, Riek 16, 17, 18, 162, 163, 164, 165, 166, 171
van der Veen, R. Theodoor, KNIL Cpl. 79
van Eldick, G.A., Dutch Navy MTRS 159
Van Heutz 169, 170
van Leent, Frederick Johan, KNIL Lt. 66, 69, 75, 77, 78, 79, 82, 93, 95, 96, 99, 111
van Rooij, Dr. 169
van Slooten, KNIL Lt. MC 48, 59
van Wel Groeneveld, J.M. *see* Groeneveld, J.M., KNIL Lt.
van West de Veer, J.F., KNIL Sdt. 26
Verhulst, Petronella Johanna "Nel" *see* Petronella Johanna Lindeijer-Verhulst
Vernon, Amos, Brit. Army GNR 139
Vogel, KNIL Sdt. 28, 29, 30, 32

Wake Island 124
war crimes 2, 7, 94, 123, 149, 179, *Tofuku Maru* Ship Case Summary 210n44, 202n51
war memory: Dialogue N-J-I 193; Germany 1; Indonesia 193; Japan 1–3, 192–193; the Netherlands 6–8, 193; US 8, 10
Warsaw 125
Wetters, August Valeriaan H., KNIL Pvt. 60, 61
"Wingy" (epithet) 106, 114, 125
Winkler, Dolf 179, 180, 192; *see also* EKNJ

Yasukuni Shrine 2, 193
Yogya *see* Yogyakarta
Yogyakarta 35, 37, 40, 41, 66

Index

Yogyanese 37, 40
Yokohama 13, 138, 145, 160
Yomiuri Shimbun/Kyoto Edition 187, 189
Yoshida Zenkichi, Lt. 137, 140, 142, 151

Zeigler, Lundy Leroy, US Army Capt. 59, 61, 91, 94, 111, 113, 117, 118, 122, 129, 132, 133, 137, 140, 150, 156, 157, 159
Zerbis, George J., US Army Pvt. 1/c 75, 90

www.ingramcontent.com/pod-product-compliance
Lightning Source LLC
Chambersburg PA
CBHW052059300426
44117CB00013B/2200